"GOOD TIME COMING?"

CONTRIBUTIONS IN AFRO-AMERICAN AND AFRICAN STUDIES

The Oratory of Negro Leaders: 1900-1968
Marcus Hanna Boulware

Black Labor in America
Milton Cantor, editor

The Black Teacher and the Dramatic Arts: A Dialogue, Bibliography, and Anthology
William R. Reardon and *Thomas D. Pawley*, editors

Refugees South of the Sahara: An African Dilemma
Hugh C. Brooks and *Yassin El-Ayouty*, editors

Bittersweet Encounter: The Afro-American and the American Jew
Robert G. Weisbord and *Arthur Stein*

The Black Infantry in the West, 1869-1891
Arlen L. Fowler

The Decline and Abolition of Negro Slavery in Venezuela, 1820-1854
John V. Lombardi

A Bio-Bibliography of Countee P. Cullen, 1903-1946
Margaret Perry

The Abbé Grégoire, 1787-1831: The Odyssey of an Egalitarian
Ruth F. Necheles

Political Philosophy of Martin Luther King, Jr.
Hanes Walton

The American Slave. Series 1, Vols. 1-7; Series 2, Vols. 8-19
George P. Rawick

Nigeria, Dilemma of Nationhood
Joseph Okpaku, editor

Private Black Colleges at the Crossroads
Daniel Thompson

Ebony Kinship: Africa, Africans, and the Afro-American
Robert G. Weisbord

Slavery and Race Relations in Latin America
Robert Brent Toplin, editor

"GOOD TIME COMING?"

Black Nevadans in the Nineteenth Century

ELMER R. RUSCO

Foreword by Kenneth W. Porter

•

Contributions in Afro-American and African Studies,
Number 15

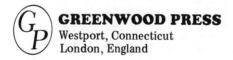

GREENWOOD PRESS
Westport, Connecticut
London, England

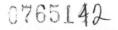

Library of Congress Cataloging in Publication Data

Rusco, Elmer R
    Good time coming?

    (Contributions in Afro-American and African
studies ; no. 15)
    Bibliography: p.
    Includes index.
    1. Afro-Americans—Nevada—History. 2. Nevada
—History. I. Title. II. Series.
E185.93.N52R87   979.3'004'96073   75-16969
ISBN 0-8371-8286-7

Library of Congress Catalog Card Number: 75-16969
ISBN: 0-8371-8286-7

First published in 1975

Greenwood Press, a division of Williamhouse-Regency Inc.
51 Riverside Avenue, Westport, Connecticut 06880

Printed in the United States of America

Contents

v

List of Tables

Foreword

"Although much research on a national and regional scale has been done in black history," comments James A. Fisher, an authority on the legal status of the Negro in California, ". . . little significant study has been achieved in the area of Western black history."[1]

This situation is understandable, however unfortunate. Historians concerned with black history have tended to emphasize the Negro's past in those regions in which, because of slavery and the subsequent "shadow of the plantation," the black population has been most numerous and its condition most fraught with constitutional problems. For the more recent period, the emphasis has been on those northern urban centers in which, because of the need for industrial labor which began about the time of World War I, large Negro populations have come to be concentrated in so-called black ghettoes. Even in the Midwest, where the Negro population has been considerably larger than in most states of the West, statewide histories have been exceedingly rare. One of these—Emma Lou Thornbrough,*The Negro in Indiana before 1900*, Indiana Historical Bureau, 1957—might serve as a model for what such a history should be, save for some regrets that the study was not carried into the twentieth century.

In the West, however, which for my purpose means the region lying
beyond the first tier of trans-Mississippi states, slavery, except for the
Black Belt of East Texas and among the Civilized Tribes of the Indian
Territory (now Oklahoma), was either nonexistent or of minimal importance. Consequently, the Negro population was small—even tiny. Even
in Texas and the Indian Territory, the Negro percentage was smaller
than in regions to the east. Historians, believing that such small black
populations did not merit historical consideration or that source materials
on the subject were virtually nonexistent, have tended not to give substantial attention to the western Negro. Until now, not a single western
state has possessed an adequate study of its Negro population, even for
the nineteenth century.

This lack of adequate attention has extended even to those western
regions in which Negroes were and remain most numerically important,
although it would seem that the one-time existence of slavery in these regions
would have resulted in the same type of studies of the Negro under slavery
and during Reconstruction that were produced for more eastern states.

Negroes in Texas went through much the same experiences as their
racial kinsmen in other Confederate states. Nevertheless, a comprehensive
history of the Texas Negro population, and even of the Texas Negro under
slavery, is still lacking. All that we have are several books and extended
articles dealing with narrow, though important, aspects and periods of
Texas Negro history.[2]

Next to Texas, the western state with the largest percentage of Negroes
is Oklahoma. Although a useful documentary collection, intended for
public school use, has recently been published,[3] and there are a number
of articles, Negroes in Oklahoma still lack anything approaching adequate
historical treatment.

The states and territories in which slavery was virtually nonexistent are
not only those for which Negro history is generally most deficient but
also those for which historical studies of their Negro populations might
be most illuminating.

The comparatively few Negroes who, during the latter half of the
nineteenth century, migrated to territories and states other than Texas
and Oklahoma found themselves in a region in which the normal status
of Negroes had never been that of slavery. Nevertheless, the dominant
white population had, to greater or lesser degrees, been influenced by
views of black inferiority associated with the institution of slavery.
Negroes in this region, although personally free, had to cope with varying
degrees of legal and social discrimination; for its part the white population

had to learn to live with a free black population, the adult male members
of which by 1870 were also constitutionally recognized as citizens and
voters. In other words, Negroes in the postbellum West confronted a
situation very similar to that which a large proportion of the race began
to encounter during the past generation; Negroes, although legally free
and legally citizens, were nevertheless effectively disfranchised throughout
many states and subjected to various types of discrimination and segregation, legal and extralegal, throughout most of the others.

How both races, in various regions and states of the American West,
reacted during the latter half of the nineteenth century and the earliest
decades of the twentieth century to the changing racial situation is a
problem presenting opportunities for a series of case studies. Such studies
should for the most part be of specific states, rather than of larger western
regions, for preliminary and general consideration of the Negro in the West
indicates that variations among states were often substantial. Particularly
hopeful—and disturbing—are the tentative evidences of remarkable postbellum trends, even apart from federal pressure, toward easier and more
relaxed interracial relations. Sooner or later, however, these trends were
thwarted and sometimes reversed, leading to the racial situation so un-
happily familiar to most westerners acquainted with racial conditions in
that region from at least as early as the twentieth century to the 1940s,
and even later. The factors which made possible these more hopeful interracial relations, and those which dashed those early hopes, are worthy of
close examination, both for their historical significance and for what
bearing they may have on current racial problems.

The first nonslaveholding western state to receive a substantial Negro
population was California. Migration to this state took place during a
decade of nationwide controversy over the extension of slavery which
vitally affected the black population. Partly for this reason, the California
Negro has probably received more historical attention than the Negro in
any other western "free" state or territory. The only attempt at a *comprehensive* history, however, is Delilah L. Beasley's *The Negro Trail
Blazers of California* which, although suggestive and, indeed, at this
point, indispensable, is too amateurish to fulfill minimal historical needs.

Kansas Negroes, more numerous proportionately than those in any
other nonslaveholding western state or territory, have recently received
a great deal of solid scholarly attention in historical articles. Still, a comprehensive history is lacking.

Negroes in a few other western states and regions, particularly
Colorado and the Pacific Northwest, have received notice in publications

of various types—newspaper feature stories, semifictitious biographies, articles in historical publications, a couple of "state histories" digested from M.A. theses. In other western states they have either been ignored completely or have been treated in only an article or two.

A promising sign, but so far no more than promising, has been the evidence of increasing interest in the general topic indicated by bibliographical studies of the Negro in the Northwest.[4]

Against this background, Professor Elmer R. Rusco's decision to write a history of the Negro in Nevada during the nineteenth century stands out in particularly bold relief. The undertaking encountered even more difficulties than existed for a study of the Negro in other parts of the Far West. Nevada's Negro population numbered only forty-five in 1860 and at its peak was never as large as 500. In 1890 its Negro population constituted only one-half of one percent of the total and was numerically smaller than that of any other western state or territory except Idaho. At no time during the nineteenth century, so far as he was originally aware, did it include such outstanding colored citizens—business or professional men, officeholders, or community leaders—as had emerged in California, Colorado, Washington, and even Wyoming. Moreover, no Negro-owned newspaper, even of the most ephemeral kind, was published in Nevada. On the other hand, such publications had appeared before the end of the nineteenth century in at least ten other western states and territories, including California, Washington, Utah, and Colorado.

Nevertheless, his research disclosed that the small black population in Nevada was able to maintain an active and self-conscious social, religious, and cultural identity, was aggressive in asserting its rights to legal and educational equality, and included a number of able and reasonably prosperous community leaders.

A number of sources of information proved to be available. The basic source was the original United States census reports through 1880. After this year the reports were either missing (1890) or, at the time of research and writing, not yet available to scholars (1900). He also discovered that although Nevada never had a Negro newspaper, two San Francisco papers—the *Pacific Appeal* and the *Elevator*—were published until nearly the end of the nineteenth century. These papers had news coverage extending far beyond the Bay Area or even California, through volunteer correspondents in other western states, including Nevada. Indeed, Nevada at that time was a sort of extension of its western neighbor. In addition, "white" Nevada newspapers occasionally published news about the state's colored communities.

Utilizing these and other less important sources, Professor Rusco has produced a historical case study, on a statewide basis, of a small colored community in the Far West during one of the most crucial periods in Afro-American history. The work is not only interesting and valuable in itself but also, as a pioneering work, is immensely suggestive and stimulating for further historical study. If one student could accomplish so much for a community of below-average size and completely lacking in a local press, others should be able to achieve approximately as much for far western communities with merely those sources available for the Nevada study, and even more for states fortunate enough to have had a colored press. A recent brief study of the Negro press in Montana, a state which until very recently was hardly recognized as possessing a Negro population except for colored soldiers, has displayed how immensely valuable even short-lived Negro newspapers can be for an understanding of the colored communities which they served.[5] The argument that histories of the Negro in other western states cannot be written because material is unavailable has been invalidated by this study.

Historians who may be encouraged by the rising interest in the history of Negroes in the West will find the Nevada study of greater value than merely as an indicator of possible sources of information. The study in depth of a particular western state has confirmed for that state tentative impressions and conclusions which I have arrived at through a much more superficial general survey of the Negro in the West. Among these impressions was the extent to which the history of the Negro in the West, as well as in the South and most of the rest of the country, was that of a rise from an originally nearly rightless position, at about 1860, to a comparatively high legal and social status in the 1870s and 1880s, and then a gradual or in some cases precipitate decline to what Professor Rayford W. Logan styles its nadir in the 1890s and early 1900s. What is surprising to an observer looking back from the perspective of, say, the 1920s, is not the low antebellum and early twentieth century status but the relatively elevated intervening plateau. Another feature is the extent to which the colored community in the West, long before the NAACP (organized in 1909), received support in its aspirations for legal and social justice. This support came not merely from Republican politicians seeking votes or dutifully carrying out national party policy, but also from obscure and sometimes nameless whites—school teachers, for example—at considerable risk of retaliation from the frequently bigoted white establishment. A minor but highly interesting point is the position of the colored barber, who was normally high in the ranks of community leaders and, indeed, sometimes *was* the community leader.

One would not expect to find in other states and territories exactly the patterns that existed in Nevada, but these patterns should nevertheless be looked for and their presence or absence noted. Among the factors demanding state, and even sometimes community, studies is the extent to which each state, each community, sometimes each establishment and individual in the West was literally a law unto itself (or himself) where racial practices were concerned. Only after grassroots studies of the Negro in all regions and states are available can any valid generalizations as to racial policies and practices become possible.

Kenneth Wiggins Porter
Professor Emeritus of History
University of Oregon
Author: *The Negro on the
American Frontier* (1971)

NOTES

1. "The Political Development of the Black Community in California, 1850-1950," *California Historical Quarterly*, Vol. L, No. 3 (September 1971), p. 264.

2. E. g., Harold Schoen, "The Free Negro in the Republic of Texas," *Southwestern Historical Quarterly*, 39-41 (April 1936-July 1937); J. Mason Brewer, *Negro Legislators of Texas and Their Descendants* (1935); Lawrence D. Rice, *The Negro in Texas 1874-1900* (1971).

3. Kaye M. Teall, editor, *Black History in Oklahoma* (1971).

4. Hazel E. Mills and Nancy Prior, *The Negro in the State of Washington, 1788-1969* (rev. ed., 1970); Lucille Thompson and Alma Smith Jacobs, *The Negro in Montana 1800-1945* (1970); Lenwood G. Davis, "Sources for History of Blacks in Oregon," *Oregon Historical Quarterly* (September 1972), and *Blacks in the State of Oregon, 1788-1971* (Monticello, Ill., 1974).

5. Rex C. Myers, "Montana's Negro Newspapers, 1894-1911," *Montana Journalism Review* (1973).

Preface

In 1870, when the ratification of the Fifteenth Amendment opened the vote to blacks, many of the members of Nevada's small but vigorous black community looked ahead with hope.[1] As one of the founders of the Lincoln Union Club in Virginia City put it, "The object of our club is . . . united political action . . . in view of the good time coming." The extent to which the good time really did come is treated in this history of a group that shared with many others the exciting life of nineteenth-century Nevada but whose story has not previously been told.

The histories of the territory and state of Nevada have not treated adequately the life and activities of any nonwhite groups, but the absence of writings about blacks is particularly striking. The standard Nevada bibliography contains no entries under "black," "colored," or "Negro," and there has been only one article in an academic journal on any aspect of black life in the state.[2] Russell R. Elliott's *History of Nevada*,[3] which will undoubtedly remain the outstanding history of the state for some time to come, contains a section on racial minorities and makes occasional references to blacks, but the absence of significant prior research into black history limited what could be said about the subject.[4] The neglect of black history is general and not confined to one state, of course. There are only two books about black history in the West as a whole, and neither deals with Nevada.[5]

It seems to me that the neglect of the history of various nonwhite groups in the United States is part of a general pattern of white racism, which needs to be recognized and then rejected. Until relatively recently, there was deliberate neglect of the achievements or even existence of nonwhites,[6] but for a number of years now their continued neglect has been an aspect chiefly of institutional racism. Once a pattern of subordination becomes well established, it can perpetuate itself without conscious adherence to the values that originally led to its establishment.[7] Current Nevada historians and social scientists are personally nonracist, yet most of the gap remains. I hope this study will make a substantial beginning toward the writing of more accurate and complete Nevada history.

Good Time Coming? is not intended merely to document the existence of a previously ignored group, however. I have tried to note some of the ways in which blacks have been important to white society. Much of the first part of the book, in fact, goes into detail about the constitutions and laws that launched white Nevada and about the attitudes toward blacks and other nonwhites that the white founders brought with them and developed. It is my conviction that racial patterns and attitudes have played a great role in American history and continue to be more important than most people admit. While much more needs to be done merely to describe the importance of race in one state, this work is a beginning of that task.

While the book deals with only one state, it points toward conclusions of much wider significance. While writing this book, I have learned that black Nevadans were linked with black people in other western states and that they shared many of the experiences of other black westerners. Indeed, if the economic rise and fall that occurred in one state turns out to have been duplicated throughout the North, as I believe it was, the present economic position of black Americans will be much easier to understand. The last chapter elaborates some of the implications that can be explored further by similar studies of other states. Fortunately, such studies are now going forward, and in the next few years it should be possible to make sounder generalizations than we can now.

Finally, some readers may wish to know why this history does not continue into the twentieth century, particularly since one of my major conclusions is that black Nevadans suffered a decline in status after the nineteenth century. There are several answers to this. One is that there

proved to be so much material on the nineteenth century that had not
been brought to anyone's attention before that I thought it worthwhile
to do a book on this subject alone. Second, I discovered that there was
much less material on black life in Nevada during the first half of the
twentieth century than there was for the last century; most of what I
found for the period before 1950 is included in the book. Part of the
reason for this is that some sources (such as census data and black newspapers with a strong interest in the state) are unavailable. But also, I
believe that there are fewer items in Nevada's white press, and that this
is because at least some Nevada newspapers deliberately discouraged
news about the black community. The long-time editor of one of the
most important newspapers in Las Vegas, the *Review-Journal*, has stated
that he followed a policy of refusing to print news of "unrest" in the
black Westside of Las Vegas because he felt that reporting it tended to
encourage it.[8] A reporter for the same newspaper for many years has
told me privately that the ban on news of the Westside extended to most
kinds of events until the late 1950s. Finally, a substantial black population
has developed in Las Vegas in the last twenty years; to study the history
of this community requires different research techniques than the ones
necessary where there are no survivors to interview or observe. Further,
in my view this kind of research is best done by black scholars, or at least
in collaboration with them. Fortunately, a black scholar at the University
of Nevada, Las Vegas, is now studying Las Vegas black history, and he
may be able to fill much of the gap which still exists in twentieth-
century black history in this state.

The assistance I have received in doing the research and writing for
this book is one testimony to the fact that interest in black history is
growing. I owe debts to a number of people and institutions. The staffs
of several libraries have been very helpful, especially those of Special
Collections and Government Documents at the University of Nevada,
Reno; Bancroft Library; the Nevada Historical Society; the Nevada State
Museum; the Nevada State Library; the Library of the California Historical
Society; and the California State Library.

A number of individuals have given advice or provided information
that I would otherwise have missed. Mary Ellen Glass, director of the
Oral History Project, University of Nevada, Reno, James Abajian, and
Dennis Thompson have been most helpful. I am grateful also to Kenneth
W. Porter, William N. Hanchett, Rudolph M. Lapp, Jack D. Forbes, Anthony
Amaral, Philip I. Earl, John M. Townley, L. James Higgins, Jr., Donald
Tuohy, Pamela Crowell, Robert D. Armstrong, Elizabeth M. Roberts,

Ellen Guerricagoitia, Marian Goldman, Marjorie Lee Mortenson, Edna Patterson, Richard H. Lane, Russell R. Elliott, William A. Douglass, and Joan R. Sherman.

Several people have read the manuscript at various stages and made helpful comments. Kenneth W. Porter devoted a great deal of time to helping me with it, and Russell R. Elliott, Wilbur R. Shepperson, and Michael Coray gave useful advice. Bruce and Pat Miller and their family were very helpful in a number of ways, and I am much in their debt. My gratitude also goes to Sheryl Clerico, who helped prepare the index. Kenna Boyer typed the manuscript twice with skill and patience, and I very much appreciate her work.

Errors of fact or interpretation remain, of course, my responsibility.

NOTES

1. For the sake of consistency, the words "black" and "blacks" are used throughout this book except in quotations. While these terms are most often preferred today, especially by black scholars, there was little consistency in the nineteenth century; "black," "colored," and "Negro" were all fairly widely used.

2. See Russell R. Elliott and Helen J. Poulton, *Writings on Nevada* (Reno: University of Nevada Press, 1963), and William Hanchett, "Yankee Law and the Negro in Nevada, 1861-1869," *Western Humanities Review* 10 (Summer 1956): 241-249.

3. Russell R. Elliott, *History of Nevada* (Lincoln, Nebraska: University of Nebraska Press, 1973).

4. A few place names testify to black presence in the state, often in a derogatory fashion. There are two Nigger creeks in White Pine County, a Negro Creek and Negro Creek Ranch northwest of Gerlach in Washoe County, and a Nigger Ravine north of Silver City in the Comstock area. See Nevada Highway Department, *Directory of Geographic Names* (1971), and the 1950 U. S. Geological Survey topographic map of Virginia City. Curiously, the recently published *Nevada Place Names* by Helen S. Carlson (Reno: University of Nevada Press, 1974), mentions none of these locations. The many geographic features with names containing "black" probably owe nothing to racial categories, but the several names containing the word "coon" are more problematic.

5. Kenneth W. Porter, *The Negro on the American Frontier* (New York: Arno Press and the New York Times, 1971), and William L. Katz, *The Black West* (Garden City, New York: Doubleday and Co., 1971).

A recent review article summarizes the present status of western black history. See Lawrence B. de Graaf, "Recognition, Racism, and Reflections on the Writing of Western Black History," *Pacific Historical Review* 44 (February 1975), 22-51. A comprehensive bibliography recently published will make future research much easier. See James Abajian, *Blacks and Their Contribution to the American West* (Boston: G. K. Hall, 1974).

6. Two excellent histories of white racism to World War I are Winthrop Jordan, *White over Black* (Baltimore, Maryland: Penguin Books, 1969), and George M. Fredrickson, *The Black Image in the White Mind* (New York: Harper and Row, 1971).

7. The later writings of Martin Luther King, Jr., and the report of the Kerner Commission seem to me to make the point about institutional racism very clearly; black people still get less of "what there is to get" in American society in a number of ways, and this fact is a result of white racism, in a number of ways.

8. John F. Cahlan, "Reminiscences of a Reno and Las Vegas, Nevada Newspaperman, University Regent, and Public-Spirited Citizen" (Reno, Nevada: Oral History Project, University of Nevada, 1970), pp. 78-80.

"GOOD TIME COMING?"

—1—

Pathfinders and Pioneers

Black people were part of the earliest American parties that explored what became the state of Nevada, crossed it on the way to California, or established settlements in what had been the exclusive home of the peoples we call today Northern and Southern Paiutes, Shoshones, or Washos. The area that became Nevada had been claimed by Spain and Mexico before the United States acquired it by the Treaty of Guadelupe Hidalgo in 1848, but the Spanish and Mexicans made no effort to settle the area and did not explore it to any substantial extent. The Old Spanish Trail crossed what is now the southern tip of Nevada, and a number of parties used this trail at various times; whether any of these parties included blacks is not yet known. It is known, however, that blacks were members of some of the most famous groups of explorers who entered the area from the United States from the 1820s into the 1840s.

MOUNTAIN MEN AND EXPLORERS

Jedediah Strong Smith, a mountain man-fur trapper remembered for prodigious feats of exploration in the West, led parties that contained blacks through Nevada on two different occasions in the 1820s. In 1826

a party of fur trappers he commanded traveled south from Great Salt
Lake to the Colorado River, passing through Nevada along either the
Muddy or the Virgin River. A member of this party was John Peter
Ranne, a "colored" man.[1] Ranne was a member of the party as it traveled
through Nevada, crossed the Colorado, journeyed west to San Gabriel
Mission, and then turned north to the Stanislaus River. At this point
Smith and two of his men, Silas Gobel and Robert Evans, left the party
to cross the Sierra Nevada and traverse Nevada from west to east across
the center of the state on their way back to the Great Salt Lake area.
Ranne stayed with the others on the Stanislaus River until Smith and a
new party joined them the next year.[2]

In 1827 Smith again led a party of trappers south from Great Salt Lake
to the Colorado River, traversing essentially the same route through what
became eastern Nevada (although he changed his route through Utah). A
member of this expedition was Polette (or Polite) Labross, a mulatto,[3]
who was one of the men killed by Mohave Indians as the Smith party
was crossing the Colorado River.[4] The survivors of this attack, led by
Smith, went west to San Gabriel Mission, then north to rejoin the party,
including Ranne, which had been camped on the Stanislaus River since
the previous year. The combined parties, after a delay caused by the
Spanish authorities, headed north on December 30, 1827. They trapped
for a while in northern California and made a difficult march through the
mountains of northern California and along the California and Oregon
coast, reaching a camping site along the Umpqua River in southern Oregon.
There, an Indian attack killed most of the party, including Ranne. Only
Smith and three other men escaped.[5]

John Charles Frémont led several famous exploring expeditions during
the 1840s, and two of them crossed Nevada. On the best known of these
explorations, when he and his men became the first non-Indians to see
Pyramid Lake (so named by Frémont), a black man, Jacob Dodson, was
a member of the party. Dodson probably crossed Nevada on another
expedition with Frémont, too.

Frémont saw and named Pyramid Lake on his 1843-1844 expedition.
In reporting the members of this expedition, he listed "Jacob Dodson, a
free young colored man of Washington city, who volunteered to accompany
the expedition, and performed his duty manfully throughout the voyage."[6]
Dodson was eighteen and, according to Allan Nevins, "devoted to the
Benton family."[7] Frémont was the son-in-law of Missouri Senator Thomas
Hart Benton, and it is probable that Dodson had been a servant in the
Benton family before he joined Frémont. In describing the writing of the
report of this expedition at home in Washington, D.C., Frémont reported

that "Jacob kept up the camp habit and very early brought me coffee."[8] However, Dodson was not just a personal servant; he participated fully in the work of the expedition. According to Frémont, he was chosen from the main party for various side trips, such as the canoe trip from the Dalles on the Columbia River to Vancouver and back. During the difficult winter crossing of the Sierra Nevada range, Dodson rescued a member of the party who had become delirious.[9]

Frémont did not mention Jacob Dodson in describing his return to the United States on the second expedition and did not give a list of the members of the third expedition (in 1846) when he and his men participated in the conquest of California; however, Dodson probably was with Frémont on these trips. If not, he must have stayed in California after the first trip because he was one of the two men who rode with Frémont on a daring ride from Los Angeles to Monterey and back in 1847; the three men managed to ride more than eight hundred miles in a little more than eight days. Western historian Hubert Howe Bancroft justly speaks of Dodson as a "skillful vaquero."[10]

Evidently a number of blacks must have come with Frémont on one or more of his four trips to California. Kenneth G. Goode names Saunders Jackson as one of these, and Delilah Beasley says James Duff, who settled in Mariposa County, and a "bodyguard or servant" named Ben were "with Captain Frémont on his trip to California."[11] Tamas Towns, born in Texas, was one of these; his son became the chief cook for the Central Pacific when it was constructed through Nevada.

Another black man said to have accompanied Frémont on one of his trips to California was very helpful to later white emigrants, although his name is not known. The accounts of at least three white emigrant parties going to southern California by way of Utah in 1849 mention a black man at Cucamonga Rancho, the first stopping place after the crossing of Cajon Pass. Jacob Y. Stover says Cucamonga Rancho was called "Negro Ranch" and that "the owner was a negro." Addison Pratt, chronicler for the Jefferson Hunt wagon train, says that "the Steward of the ranch was a negro from the United States . . . [who had been] a waiting man in the army for some of the U.S. officers." Peter Derr, a member of the first white emigrant train to go this route in 1849, tells how six of the men from the party nearly died of starvation while trying to get food for the wagon train. When the six reached Cucamonga Rancho, "they found a negro who had been with Fremont and knew how to treat them, giving them but a little at a time, thus saving their lives."[12] Since Cucamonga Rancho was owned at that time by Victor Prudhomme and his wife, the black man referred to was probably a foreman or steward.[13]

James P. Beckwourth, a mountain man whose autobiography has been widely reprinted and read, in spite of doubts about its accuracy and credibility, was partly black although in his autobiography he does not refer to himself as black. His father was a white planter who moved from Virginia to St. Louis, Missouri, where Beckwourth grew up. The identity of his mother is not clear, but she was probably a slave. In fact, Beckwourth may have been born a slave and have been freed by his father. Whatever his ancestry, most of the people who knew him assumed he was black, and his photograph (see page 116) makes it evident that he would be classified as black in this society, where evidence of any black ancestry is sufficient to place one in that category.[14]

After many years of exploration and hunting in the West, when he lived with Crow Indians (who treated him as a war leader, by his account), Beckwourth went to California. In 1850-1851, he discovered the pass later named for him just northwest of present-day Reno, Nevada, and guided several emigrant parties through it into California. For several years in the 1850s he maintained a ranch in Sierra Valley, close to Beckwourth Pass, which offered accommodations to travelers. Although he says little about explorations in Nevada, he was familiar with Pyramid Lake and Mary's River, now called the Humboldt River.[15]

"MEN IN A BLAZING FIRE"

Beginning in the 1840s, many emigrants to California journeyed across Nevada along several routes, although the best traveled was the Humboldt River Trail. Many blacks must have crossed Nevada on one or another of these routes. One of these was Alvin Aaron Coffey who came by way of the Humboldt River in 1849. Coffey, a successful farmer in Tehama County, California, in later years and "the only Black Pioneer enrolled as a member of the Society of California Pioneers,"[16] told about the trip in his *Reminiscences*. His party used the Lassen Trail after leaving the Humboldt route. Coffey gives a vivid account of the Black Rock Desert and Black Rock Springs.[17] Daniel Rodgers and Biddy Mason, two other blacks who were early arrivals in California, came overland and thus probably through Nevada.[18] Sarah Winnemucca, daughter of Northern Paiute leader Old Winnemucca, reported in her well-known book in 1883 on the response of some Northern Paiutes to the first black people they had seen, before Frémont's expedition in 1844. In an emigrant train moving along the Humboldt River, the Indians saw "something among them that was burning all in a blaze . . . it looked like a man; it had legs and hands and a head, but the head had quit burning, and it was left quite black." The "men in a blazing fire" turned out to be "two Negroes wearing red shirts!" Somewhat later, probably before 1860, she reports that a party of Northern Paiutes refused to continue traveling with a white party because "the captain of the train was whipping negroes who were driving his team."[19]

"WE PETITIONED FOR SIMPLE JUSTICE"

Remarkable blacks arrived in California in the 1850s, and many of them subsequently moved to Nevada or other western states. Some came as slaves and were not necessarily freed merely because they had moved into a state in which slavery was not legally recognized. Indeed, in the famous case of Archy Lee, the California Supreme Court ruled that a runaway slave had to be returned to his master.[20] In addition to the official toleration of slavery, the early black arrivals in California had to contend with severely racist laws: they could not vote, serve on juries, or testify against whites in either civil or criminal cases, for example.[21] Finally, there is little question that most whites regarded and treated them as inferiors, regardless of laws. In this situation, the small number of blacks in California organized state conventions, petitioned the state legislature and Congress, published a newspaper, built schools and churches, and, with the assistance of some whites, undertook to free the remaining slaves in California. Participants in this remarkable and brave burst of activity became leaders of the black community in a number of western states, including Nevada.[22] (After the Civil War, California blacks continued to show a remarkable vigor and to provide leadership and means of communication for blacks throughout the West, but only the activity of the 1850s will be sketched at this point.)

In 1855, 1856, 1857, and 1858 California blacks held conventions to plan ways and means of securing their rights.[23] Out of these conventions came executive committees, which petitioned the California legislature chiefly to repeal the laws forbidding testimony of blacks but also to work for the right to access to the public schools without discrimination. A newspaper, the *Mirror of the Times*, was begun, and the 1856 convention established it as the executive committee organ. Unfortunately, the petitions to the legislature met with no success at that time, and the newspaper could not be sustained for long. After 1858, no more conventions were held until the end of the Civil War, and there is evidence that many, if not most, of the black leaders of the West had virtually given up attempts to be accepted as equals by white Americans. Howard Holman Bell has shown that the black leaders of the national convention movement suffered a similar disillusionment in the late 1850s and early 1860s, with many of them advocating and/or attempting emigration to escape the injustice of American racism.[24] In 1862, a group of 220 California blacks petitioned Congress for financial aid to enable those free blacks who wished to do so to emigrate to Africa or tropical America. This memorial stated that

> in view of the many disadvantages which the colored population of the United States labor under—their being deprived of many of the most important privileges of citizenship, and denied the rights and franchises freely extended to all other native-born citizens, and also to every other class of aliens; their being marked out, not only by law, but also by public sentiment, which is stronger or more effective than law, as an inferior and degraded caste, prevented by the force of circumstances from engaging in honorable or lucrative employments, thus being in a great measure prevented from leading a life either honorable to themselves or useful to their country—a strong and rapidly increasing feeling has grown up among a large portion of the free colored population (probably already a majority of the whole) in favor of emigration to those countries where color is not considered a badge of degradation, and has ceased to act as a barrier to honorable advancement.[25]

Although Congress did not respond to the appeal and there is little reason to believe that many blacks left California for Africa or Latin America, a number did leave for Canada and for other western states. It seems highly likely that many of the black leaders of Nevada in the 1860s and 1870s were in the state partly because of the disillusionment resulting from the failure to make any headway against racism in California.

The early career of Thomas Detter, a remarkable writer and black leader who lived in Nevada from at least 1869 through 1880 and who deserves far more attention than he has received, may illustrate the points made above. Detter was born between 1827 and 1831 in Maryland or the District of Columbia. (The 1870 census gives his age as forty-three while the 1880 census says he was forty-nine, and the 1870 census gives his birthplace as Maryland while in 1880 it is given as Washington. The 1870 census also says his father was of foreign birth, although the country is not given, while the 1880 census lists Maryland as the place of birth of both parents.) His father was probably Thomas Detro or Dettrow, who was listed in a city directory for the District of Columbia in 1830 as a stonemason and on District of Columbia tax rolls as owner of a lot in 1830 and 1835. The last will and testament of Thomas Detro, dated May 13, 1840, left a house and other unspecified property to his wife Eleanor, son Thomas, and daughter Martha. The will also indicates that his son Thomas was to be apprenticed to a shoemaker until he reached the age of twenty-one.[26] What is probably of greatest importance for his later life is the fact that, as Detter wrote, "I was raised in the District of Columbia, where the education of colored persons was very limited."[27] While it is true that education for blacks was limited in Washington, it was practically nonexistent elsewhere in the country. In most of the southern states, it was illegal to teach slaves to read and write, and blacks were almost as universally excluded from the public schools in the North. In the District of Columbia, by contrast, there were no laws forbidding the education of blacks. In spite of some white opposition to educating them and in spite of the fact that white violence closed the black schools for a year or two in the 1830s, there were a number of schools for blacks in the District of Columbia from 1807 up to the Civil War.[28] Detter may have acquired his literary abilities through formal education. In any case, he was not just literate but also highly articulate when he arrived in the West, and this fact contributed to his ability to be a leader of the black community.[29]

In 1870 Detter wrote that he had arrived in San Francisco by ship in 1852. "Eighteen years ago I landed in San Francisco, and long before the gallant steamer John L. Stephens weighed anchor, as she ploughed the treacherous deep, we beheld the 'City of Hills' far in the distance." He said that he and his friends who also arrived at this time "looked only to the sunny side of life and for glittering gold." He recalled "what an exciting picture California presented. . . . All was tumult and bustle." There was much gambling, no security for life and property, no respect for the Sabbath, and "crime was bold and defiant." Noting that "when I arrived in California we had no schools," he told of the establishment of the first day school in the basement of a new church building built by blacks in San Francisco.[30]

The excitement of the new and vigorous city did not long obscure the fact, however, that blacks were forced into the position of an "inferior and degraded caste," as the 1862 memorial put it. Detter wrote in 1870: "Little did many of us contemplate the reverses and misfortunes California had in reserve for us." He described the colored convention movement, which had attempted to change the racist laws: "We often petitioned for simple justice. The Democracy, then in power, stopped their ears to our supplications and closed their eyes to our sufferings."[31] In 1864 the editor of the *Pacific Appeal*, one of the important black newspapers published in San Francisco for several decades in the late nineteenth century, commented:

> Mr. Detter was one of the old "wheel-horses" among us in this State, and helped to do much in common with many others in petitioning the Legislature through our convention and otherwise, for the repeal of laws, enacted by the slave power, which prevented colored persons from testifying, as at present, in the courts of Justice in this State.[32]

Detter was a member of three of the colored conventions of the 1850s. While the proceedings do not indicate that he played an important role in 1855, he was a delegate from Sacramento County and at the end of the convention was chosen a member of the ten-man executive committee, which was to act for the convention until the next one could be convened. In 1856 he was once again a delegate from Sacramento County, and he played a prominent role. Although he was not an officer of the convention, he was a member of the business committee, made many motions, spoke often in debate, and was again chosen a member of the executive committee, which was enlarged to fifteen members. While the records of the 1857 convention have not yet been discovered, apparently he was a member of the executive committee but left the state later that year.[33] He was probably not in the state during the 1858 convention.

There is no precise evidence regarding Detter's departure from California, but in the fall of 1857 he left the state, evidently spending the next ten years at various places, including Idaho and Washington territories.[34] In 1869 he moved to Elko and thus began his stay in Nevada. Detter's years in California fit a common pattern for black leaders in the state at that time. He probably left California at least partly because of discouragement at the failure of efforts to win equality. As a participant in three colored conventions, he must have been disappointed at the lack of success of these efforts, and in 1862 he was a signer of the memorial to Congress asking for aid in leaving the United States.

Other blacks who played prominent roles in California in the 1850s and then later lived in Nevada at various times include Isaac Morton, a delegate to the 1855 convention, and Joseph J. Underwood, who was evidently not present but who was appointed to circulate petitions. Delegates to the 1856 convention who moved to Nevada include William H. Hall, Charles

H. Wilson, F. W. B. Grinage, and Charles Satchell. Hall, who became a
mine owner at Treasure Hill, was elected president of this convention, and
Wilson played a prominent role in its deliberations. Petition circulators
included William M. Bird, Isaac Morton, and J. J. Underwood. Detter,
Hall, and Underwood were elected to the executive committee, which was
to act until the 1857 convention. Later, in 1865, Hall played a major role
at another colored convention. Signers of the 1862 memorial to Congress
who later lived in Nevada include James M. Whitfield, a poet who had
received recognition in the East before his move to California, William
Bird, at one time a candidate for mayor of Virginia City, Samuel Cuney,
and Samuel Wagner.

"SHOOTING WAS THE ORDER OF THE DAY"

There are only scattered references to blacks in the 1850s in what became
Nevada, but they were present. Furthermore, the surviving items about
them indicate that they shared with whites the dangers and excitement of
a frontier area without effective government; western Nevada was tech-
nically part of the Territory of Utah and therefore governed from Salt Lake
City, nearly five hundred miles away, but in practice there was little law
and order.

The first criminal case tried before Probate Judge Orson Hyde of Carson
County, Utah Territory, on November 2, 1855, involved a black man named
Robert Thacker. Thacker was accused of using threatening language, specifically of saying "'that he had spite enough in his heart against A. J.
Wyckoff to kill him,' and 'that he could cut the heart out of Mrs. Jacob
Rose and roast it on the coals.'" Judge Hyde ordered Thacker's arrest,
found that he had made the utterances he was alleged to have made, fined
him fifty dollars "for costs of suit," and advised him "'for his own safety,'
to go over the mountains to his master, in California." "The Court records
the remark that 'A man may have malice enough at heart to kill another,
and judgment and discretion to prevent him from committing the deed; he
may have the ability to cut a lady's heart out and roast it upon the coals
and at the same time he may have good sense enough not to do it.'"[35]
Nothing is said in the available accounts of this incident about the controversy that led to these remarks, and nothing is said about Thacker,
although the judge's remark about his master implies that the judge thought
Thacker was a slave.

We do not know whether any of the blacks present in the 1850s were
slaves. There were slaves in Utah (of which Nevada was nominally a part)

at that time, and the Utah territorial government sanctioned slavery. A
law passed in Utah in 1851 gave slave owners the right to compel their
slaves to give obedience to them, and a bill of sale for a slave sold in Salt
Lake County in 1859 has been found. An official of the Mormon church
(Orson Hyde, who later became Probate Judge of Carson County) said
in 1851 that Mormon teachings neither authorized nor prohibited slavery.[36]
The 1850 census enumerated twenty-six slaves in Utah Territory, and
twenty-nine were counted in 1860. All of the blacks in portions which
later became Nevada were free in 1860, but some of the Mormon settlers
in present northwestern and southeastern Nevada may have brought slaves
with them at some time during the 1850s. By the 1860s there was a small
group of black farmers at Genoa, the main Mormon farming settlement in
northwestern Nevada, and it is possible that some of these had come with
the Mormons as slaves.

J. Ross Browne, in recounting a trip to the Comstock lode in 1860,
relates that he rode with a black man for part of the way as he was leaving
Nevada. He says that "an ox-wagon was going to Woodford's for lumber,
and I contracted with the driver, a good-humoured negro, to give me a lift
there for the sum of fifty cents."[37] Browne includes a sketch of himself
in the wagon and the black driving the oxen (see page 120).

A former slave who escaped to freedom was known as John Thomas
Evans while a slave but changed his name to James Williams after he became
free. Williams published the story of his life in Sacramento in 1874.
Although he was not in Nevada long, he visited Virginia City and Carson
City several times between 1859 and the mid-1860s at the very beginning
of the rapid growth of this area following the discovery of the Comstock
lode. Williams describes how he escaped from slavery in Maryland. He
lived in Pennsylvania and New York for several years, helping other slaves
escape on the Underground Railroad, but he constantly feared capture
and return to slavery. For this reason he went to California, arriving in
1851. During the 1850s he moved around a great deal, living in various
cities in California and also for brief periods in Mexico and Canada. In 1859,
"when the Washo excitement broke out," he was driving an express wagon
in Sacramento. He says: "I caught the fever also, and sold out" in order to
go to Virginia City. He tells of camping in the snow at Strawberry Valley
and crossing the mountains while they were snow covered, thus "proving
by demonstration that a man cannot tell what he can endure until he puts
his might into his will." He had prudently brought three hundred pounds of
flour with him and sold it in Virginia City for three hundred dollars.
Williams says that he thought about buying land in Virginia City, "but

after inquiry, I found the customs did not suit me, as I learned that shooting was the order of the day." Instead, he returned to Sacramento for more "produce" to sell at the high prices prevailing on the Comstock. Although he lost all of his supplies in a storm while crossing the Sierra Nevada, Williams nevertheless continued on to Carson City where he "sold one horse, and bought six lots, and then went to work by hand." Apparently he worked in Carson City for only two months in 1860 (which accounts for the fact that he was not enumerated there by census takers in 1860). But he says, somewhat unclearly, that, "receiving nothing, the customs being such, I returned to California." In 1863 he went back to Carson City and sold his lots. "I then went to Virginia City, and bought six lots, and went back in '65 and sold two lots, realizing $2,500 for them." He once more returned to California and said nothing further about visits to Nevada until 1873 when he visited the Comstock mines.[38] If this account is correct, Williams must have made some money on his various trips to Nevada but did not care to settle there.[39]

A newspaper article written from Virginia City by Frank Soule on May 24, 1860, gives an interesting report about an unnamed black. Soule wrote that after Indians defeated white volunteers at Pyramid Lake (in what is now known as the first battle of the Pyramid Lake "war"), A. J. Bailey of Napa, California, who was camping with fifteen to twenty men at a point along the Carson River some miles from Carson City, made an interesting discovery. Bailey and his men, who presumably were there as volunteers because of the conflict with the Indians, "detected at or near Carson, a negro and a Mormon in possession of powder, and forty or fifty bowie knives, and, I understand, of other warlike stores, which they were about to convey to the Indians. The negro is reported to have been doing this sort of business for a year past. He has an Indian squaw and lives with them." Bailey and his men reportedly confiscated the "munitions of war." What happened to the Mormon is not reported, but "the negro made his escape."[40]

Soule also reported another story involving an unnamed black man in 1860. He wrote that the incident, if true, was a "piece of cruelty which ... should consign the actors to eternal infamy, and banish them from civilization." As he heard the story, a man named Houston, said to be a relative of General Sam Houston, was suffering from "congestion of the lungs" at a tavern in Gold Hill. "This morning, about daylight, the landlord—I do not know his name—took him, by force, from his bed, and aided by one or two more persons, forced him out of the house, cursing him, and telling him to walk, an exertion of which he was incapable. They then dragged him into the street, and left him there, with his head resting upon a stone!" Some people who heard Houston's heavy breathing "went out and found him already in charge of a colored man and a white person, who had wrapped him in blankets, having taken him from the public road where they had found him. He soon died."[41]

An unnamed black man was reported by Dan De Quille to be in charge of a crossing of the Carson River near Chinatown (later Dayton) in 1860.[42]

THE CENSUS OF POPULATION OF 1860

There were forty-four blacks enumerated by the 1860 census of population in areas that later became Nevada;[43] they all lived in Carson County, the western part of the territory centering around the Virginia City-Gold Hill area, where 98 percent of the whites enumerated in what was to be Nevada also lived. There were thirteen blacks in Carson City, ten in Carson Valley, eight each in Genoa and Virginia City, two in China Town (later Dayton), and one each at Fort Churchill, Jacks Valley, and Silver City.

Nevada's white population in 1860 was almost exclusively male (89 percent), and the black population was only somewhat more evenly balanced; ten of the forty-four were females, for a male proportion of 77 percent. Most of the blacks, like most of the whites, were mature adults, with children and old people scarce; there were no children under five, only four under fifteen, and only one person more than fifty.

Some of the single black men who were identified were: Peter Simmons, a thirty-seven-year-old cook born in Ohio who was evidently living by himself; Mr. Gibbon, a thirty-eight-year-old barber from Ohio, who lived with I. L. Chapman, a forty-four-year-old black miner from Louisiana, and a thirty-year-old white teamster born in France. A good many of the single white men lived in hotels or rooming houses, and some of the black men were to be found in these places as well. For example, Jacques Malbourne,[44] a forty-one-year-old black cook from Delaware, lived in a hotel in Carson City, which listed twelve single white males ranging in age from twenty-one to thirty-six, most of whom were miners, carpenters, or teamsters. Some black men lived with white families; for example, John Williams, a twenty-four-year-old mulatto laborer from Virginia, lived in the household of Mr. and Mrs. Charles Burke and their four-year-old daughter. Burke, a white man, was twenty-five and a shoemaker from New York.

One of the ten females lived alone; all of the others were in one of five households. Isaac and Amanda Davis, neither listed as having an occupation,

shared a household with a white male farm hand. William and Louisa
Bird, thirty-eight and twenty-six, respectively, shared a household with
two single mulatto men. Mr. Bird and the other men were barbers. One
of these men, J. J. Underwood, thirty-seven, born in Ohio, figured in a
significant shooting later, and Bird was a prominent member of the
Nevada black community for many years. Anna Dunn, forty-two, with
an occupation given as "washing," was listed with Henry F. Jackson, a
forty-year-old mulatto cook from Virginia. A curious household consisted
of six blacks named Anderson. The oldest, Louis, was twenty-eight
and a laborer; the next oldest, Gilbert, was twenty-four and also a laborer;
two girls, eighteen and sixteen, were servants; and a boy of nine and a girl
of fourteen completed the household.

All but one of the forty-four blacks were born in the United States;
the exception was William Wilson, a thirty-two-year-old miner from Santo
Domingo. Just over half came from the South; twelve were from the Deep
South and eleven from border states. (In this and subsequent tabulations,
the Deep South is defined as the eleven states that formed the Confederacy—
Alabama, Arkansas, Florida, Georgia, Louisiana, Mississippi, North and
South Carolina, Tennessee, Texas, and Virginia—while the border states
are considered to be Delaware, Kentucky, Maryland, Missouri, Oklahoma,
West Virginia, and the District of Columbia. Collectively, these two groups
of states form the South.) Six, the largest number from any one state, were
from Missouri. Among the half not from the South, the place of birth
of five could not be determined, five were from Ohio, two each were
from New York and Pennsylvania, and one each were from Indiana,
Kansas, Maine, and Montana.

The occupations given for persons over fifteen were as follows:

barber	9
laborer	6
cook	5
miner	3
servant	3
wash woman or washing	2
baker	1
barkeeper	1
gardener	1
restaurant	1
housewife	4
undetermined	2

The occupational pattern revealed by these data is similar to that for
the next couple of decades, and therefore the significance of it will be
commented on later; however, two things need to be mentioned here
because they represent deviations to some degree from the later pattern.
First, there were three black miners listed in 1860, and two of these were
on the Comstock: I. L. Chapman lived in Virginia City and William
Wilson lived in Silver City. (The third miner, David Overton, thirty-seven
and born in South Carolina, was enumerated in Carson Valley.) After 1860
there is no evidence that there were black miners on the Comstock (with
the exception of one in 1870), although there were blacks in the Treasure
Hill area who were prospecting and mining. The second matter worthy
of comment is that a minority of blacks in 1860 were listed with unskilled
occupations. While there was a significant group of skilled black workers
and black businessmen later, the bulk of blacks later were unskilled workers;
evidently this was not true of the tiny group of early settlers.

Although the number of blacks in Nevada before the 1860s was quite
small, they were present at every stage after white Americans began to
come into the area. Blacks accompanied Jedediah Smith and John C.
Frémont on their explorations of the Great Basin, were present among
the few non-Indian settlers before the Comstock lode was discovered,
and arrived on the lode in the first few frantic months of exploration and
staking out of claims.

NOTES

1. Or Rannee, Raney, Ranna, or Ransa, as the name is variously
spelled by Smith or his clerk, Harrison G. Rogers.
2. Smith's first expedition is described in the following: Dale L.
Morgan, *Jedediah Smith and the Opening of the West* (Lincoln, Nebraska:
University of Nebraska Press, 1953), pp. 193-215; Harrison C. Dale, *The
Ashley-Smith Explorations and the Discovery of a Central Route to the
Pacific, 1822-1829* (Glendale, California: The Arthur H. Clarke Co.,
1941), pp. 179-190; John G. Neihardt, *The Splendid Wayfaring* (New
York: The Macmillan Company, 1927), pp. 233-256; Maurice S. Sullivan,
The Travels of Jedediah Smith (Santa Ana, California: The Fine Arts
Press, 1934), pp. 14-26. The presence of Ranne in the company is estab-
lished by the journal of Harrison G. Rogers and various writings of Smith.
See Maurice S. Sullivan, *Jedediah Smith, Trader and Trail Breaker* (New
York: Press of the Pioneers, 1936), pp. 68-113.

3. Morgan, *Jedediah Smith*, p. 236, Dale, *Ashley-Smith Explorations*, p. 227, and Neihardt, *Splendid Wayfaring*, p. 258, list "Polite" as a member of the party. Labross is identified simply as "Polite" in a list of persons killed on various expeditions financed by William Ashley and the firm of Smith, Jackson and Sublette; the list was compiled by Jedediah Smith, apparently in 1830. See Morgan, *Jedediah Smith*, p. 344. A letter from Smith to General William Clark written in 1829 lists "Potette Labross (mulatto)" among those killed along the Colorado River. Morgan, *Jedediah Smith*, p. 341.

4. Morgan, *Jedediah Smith*, pp. 239-241; Dale, *Ashley-Smith Explorations*, pp. 228-229; Neihardt, *Splendid Wayfaring*, pp. 258-259.

5. Smith's second expedition to California is described in Morgan, *Jedediah Smith*, pp. 236-279; Dale, *Ashley-Smith Explorations*, pp. 226-285; Neihardt, *Splendid Wayfaring*, pp. 257-273; Sullivan, *Jedediah Smith*, pp. 114-192, and *Travels of Jedediah Smith*, pp. 26-109. Smith comments once about Ranne. See Sullivan, *Travels of Jedediah Smith*, pp. 96-97. Ranne appears in Rogers' journal several times. See Dale, *Ashley-Smith Explorations*, pp. 219, 246, 256, 274. However, these few entries say nothing significant about the man.

6. John Charles Frémont, *Report of the Exploring Expedition to the Rocky Mountains* (Ann Arbor: University Microfilms, 1966), p. 106. This is a facsimile of a congressional document printed in 1845.

7. Allan Nevins, *Frémont, Pathmarker of the West* (New York: Frederick Ungar, 1961), I:129.

8. John Charles Frémont, *Memoirs of My Life* (Chicago and New York: Belford, Clarke and Co., 1887), p. 414.

9. Frémont, *Report of the Exploring Expedition*, pp. 121, 152, 188-195, 235, 238-239, 240, and *Memoirs*, pp. 188, 229, 275, 334, 337.

10. Nevins, *Frémont*, p. 320; Hubert Howe Bancroft, *History of California*, vol. 5, *1846-1848* (San Francisco: The History Company, 1886), p. 443.

For further references to Dodson, see Kenneth W. Porter, *The Negro on the American Frontier* (New York: Arno Press and the New York Times, 1971), p. 137.

11. Delilah Beasley, *The Negro Trail Blazers of California* (Los Angeles: Times-Mirror Printing and Binding House, 1919), p. 33. Kenneth G. Goode, *California's Black Pioneers* (Santa Barbara: McNally & Loftin, 1974), p. 24.

12. See Leroy R. and Ann W. Hafen, *Journals of Forty-Niners* (Glendale, California: Arthur H. Clarke Co., 1954). For the Stover train, see pp. 273-291; for the Hunt party, see pp. 66-112; for the Gruwell-Derr train, see pp. 51-55. See also George William Beattie and Helen Pruitt Beattie, *Heritage of the Valley, San Bernardino's First Century* (Oakland, California: Biobooks, 1951), p. 330.

13. Beattie and Beattie, *Heritage*, pp. 138-153.

14. See Elinor Wilson, *James P. Beckwourth* (Norman, Oklahoma: University of Oklahoma Press, 1972), pp. 11-19; T. D. Bonner, ed., *The Life and Adventures of James P. Beckwourth* (New York: Alfred A. Knopf, 1931), introduction by Bernard DeVoto, p. xxxi; and Nolie Mumey, *James Pierson Beckwourth, 1856-1866* (Denver, Colorado: Old West Publishing Co., 1957), pp. 29, 145, 165, 168-169.

15. Wilson, *Beckwourth*, pp. 128-137, 147-152, 158-160, and Bonner, *Life and Adventures*, pp. 353, 355-364.

16. Phil Montesano, "A Black Pioneer's Trip to California," *The Pacific Historian* 13 (Winter 1969):62.

17. Ibid., 60-61.

18. Sue Bailey Thurman, *Pioneers of Negro Origin in California* (San Francisco: Acme Publishing Co., 1952), pp. 4, 11-12, 17.

19. Sarah Winnemucca Hopkins, *Life Among the Piutes* (1883; reprint ed., Bishop, California: Chalfant Press, Inc., 1969), pp. 9, 23.

20. See Rudolph M. Lapp, *Archy Lee* (San Francisco: The Book Club of California, 1969).

21. The full extent of legal white racism toward Indians and Chinese as well as Negroes has been documented recently in Robert F. Heizer and Alan F. Almquist, *The Other Californians* (Berkeley: University of California Press, 1971). See also Goode, *California's Black Pioneers*, pp. 59-66, 73-87.

22. There is still no definitive treatment of the black community of California in the 1850s. Sources used in this book are listed in the bibliography.

23. A facsimile of the proceedings of the 1855 and 1856 conventions, plus one held in 1865, has been published. See *Proceedings of the First State Convention of the Colored Citizens of the State of California, 1855, 1856, 1865* [*sic*] (San Francisco: R. and E. Associates, 1969). A brief report of the 1858 convention was published in *Address of the State Executive Committee, to the Colored People of the State of California* (Sacramento: Printed for the Committee, 1859). Only two copies of the *Mirror of the Times* have survived, and they are in the California State Library, Sacramento, with reproductions in the library of the California Historical Society, San Francisco.

24. See Howard Holman Bell, *A Survey of the Negro Convention Movement 1830-1861* (New York: Arno Press, 1969), pp. 206-265, 271-273.

25. U.S., Congress, House, *Memorial of Leonard Dugged, George A. Bailey, et. al.,* 37th Cong., 2d sess., Misc. Doc. 31, 1862.

26. Information on Thomas Detro or Dettrow in 1830 and 1835 was secured from Letitia Woods Brown, *Free Negroes in the District of Columbia, 1790-1846* (New York: Oxford University Press, 1972), pp. 148, 156, and letter from Barbara Hanley, Washingtoniana Division, Martin Luther King Memorial Library, District of Columbia Public Library, dated October 5, 1973. The will is in the National Archives.

27. Preface to *Nellie Brown* (San Francisco: Cuddy and Hughes, 1871), p. 1.

28. See Kenneth M. Stampp, *The Peculiar Institution* (New York: Random House, 1956), p. 208; Leon L. Litwack, *North of Slavery* (Chicago: University of Chicago Press, 1961), pp. 113-149. For the District of Columbia, see George W. Williams, *History of the Negro Race in America from 1619 to 1880* (New York: G. P. Putnam's Sons, 1883): II: 181-213.

29. However, some of the black leaders of the 1850s learned to read and write less formally or taught themselves. In a discussion of education during the 1863 annual convention of the AME church in San Francisco, J. T. Jenifer, later a minister in Virginia City, said: "Born in a slave State, he had had no school privileges; but he had felt an innate thirst for knowledge. As a boy he remembered how he had, by stealth, mastered the contents of a Primer. With a book in his bosom, the wharf, the deck of the steamboat, behind the bale of cotton, in the open air or in the chamber hidden, had been his school." Peter Green, also later a minister in Virginia City, stated during this discussion that "a little girl in a slave State had been his teacher in the rudiments of the language. As a boy I learned to read by asking help of every willing boy or girl I was acquainted with. Children are generally willing to give instruction. After I came to California I learned to write." *Journal of Proceedings of the Third Annual Convention of the Ministers and Lay Delegates of the African Methodist Episcopal Church* (San Francisco: B. F. Sterett, Printer, 1863), p. 9.

30. *Pacific Appeal*, November 26, 1870.

31. Ibid.

32. Ibid., January 30, 1864.

33. An article about the 1857 convention written several years later reported him as a delegate to the convention but not a member of the executive committee. I am assuming he was not listed on the committee because he left soon after the convention. See *Pacific Appeal*, May 3, 1862.

34. At the time of a visit Detter made to San Francisco in December 1865, the editor of the *Elevator* remarked that he had left California and had traveled in Washington and Idaho territories for six or seven years; he went on to say that "Mr. Detter is a pioneer and an old worker in California; is well known for his warm interest in everything which appertains to our welfare on this coast." *Elevator*, December 15, 1865. It is assumed he left California between August and December; the issue of the *Mirror of the Times* for August 22, 1857, listed him as a member of the state executive committee (and also one of two treasurers), but he was not so listed in the December 12, 1857, issue.

35. The quotations are from Myron Angel, *History of Nevada, 1881* (Berkeley, California: Howell-North, 1958), p. 333. Hubert Howe Bancroft, *Works*, vol. 25, *History of Nevada, Colorado and Wyoming, 1540-1888* (San Francisco: The History Company, 1890), pp. 76-77, has a similar account. Chester W. Cheel, "Historic Development of Western Utah,

Between 118 and 120 Degrees West Longitude, 1827-1861" (Masters thesis, University of Nevada, 1939), pp. 48-49, quotes Bancroft but also reproduces a document concerning the case from the Nevada territorial records then in the possession of the secretary of state in Carson City.
36. Dennis L. Lythgoe, "Negro Slavery in Utah," *Utah Historical Quarterly* 39'(Winter 1971): 40-54, and Jack Beller, "Negro Slaves in Utah," *Utah Historical Quarterly* 2 (October 1929): 122-126.
37. J. Ross Browne, *A Peep at Washoe and Washoe Revisited* (Balboa Island, California: Paisano Press, 1959), pp. 108-110.
38. James Williams, *Life and Adventures of James Williams, A Fugitive Slave,* 3d ed. (1874; reprint ed., San Francisco, R & E Associates, 1969), pp. 35-37.
39. Williams quotes several newspaper articles commenting on his book, including some items from the *Virginia City Chronicle* and the *Gold Hill News.* The *Chronicle,* he says, commented: "We hope that the citizens will patronize and aid him in selling his book." Williams, *Life and Adventures,* p. 107. At the end of his book, Williams includes various short pieces that probably were written by other people, but there seems no reason to doubt that he wrote the bulk of his book.
40. Newspaper article, datelined May 24, 1860, Early Washoe History and Correspondence, Bancroft Library, University of California, Berkeley. The date of publication cannot be determined with certainty.
41. Newspaper article datelined May 25, 1860, Early Washoe History and Correspondence.
42. Dan De Quille, *The Big Bonanza* (New York: Alfred A. Knopf, 1947), p. 409.
43. The published returns for Carson County give forty-five as the number, but one of these was a person born in "S. Sea Islands"; I concluded that he was unlikely to be an American-born black.
44. Where original census returns are used, it is sometimes difficult to be sure of the spelling of a name; where this is the case, I have indicated it by a question mark.

—2—

"To Legislate for White Men": White Racism, 1861-1865

The fact that black people were present when Nevada came into being does not mean that they were allowed to participate on an equal basis with whites. Nevada was racist during the territorial and early statehood period. Its constitutions and laws clearly placed blacks, along with other nonwhites, in an inferior position; they were not entitled to participate in any way in the political system, but they were nevertheless required to obey the laws white men made. That this was the situation even though Nevada came into the Union during the Civil War, partly because of its opposition to slavery, may surprise some people, but the facts are clear. There were occasional dissents from the general pattern of overt white racism, but these dissents were not regarded as serious enough to require recognition of them, and some people who had taken antiracist actions in other states found themselves in trouble for doing so in Nevada.

Nevada Territory was split off from Utah Territory in 1861 during the first year of the Civil War. Partly because of the timing of its birth, Nevada was dominated by members of the Union party from its inception through the 1860s. In the early years, opposition was almost completely lacking; the Union ticket won every election overwhelmingly. The president of the council in the first territorial legislature, J. L. Van Bokkelen, stated

on the first day of the session that "we meet here, each and every one of
us, elected on what is known as the Union ticket . . . pledged to preserve
our own nationality."[1] All the delegates to the 1863 constitutional
convention were Union men, and so were all but one of the delegates
to the 1864 convention.[2] The Union forces were united in opposing
slavery, but they were also virtually unanimous in approving laws founded
on the premise that "they had met to legislate for white men," as a member of the house put it in 1862.[3]

THE 1861 AND 1862 LEGISLATURES

The 1861 legislative assembly passed the basic laws for Nevada
Territory at its beginning. Although Nevada had been part of Utah
Territory, the delegates did not wish to continue in force the Utah laws;
instead they wrote new ones, modeling them to a substantial extent on
those of the neighboring state of California, from which most of the
white residents of the new territory had come.[4] The debates of the 1861
and 1862 legislative sessions have recently been published, and it is
possible to say something about the attitudes of legislative leaders in this
formative period.

The 1861 legislative assembly passed a law forbidding slavery in
Nevada and also adopted a similar statute that probably was directed
against a form of de facto slavery for Indians which had existed in
California in the 1850s.[5] Slavery, however, received little attention in
this session; Governor James W. Nye did not mention the subject in his
address to the legislature, and the reporter who kept a record of debates
did not mention any discussion of slavery.[6] A resolution supporting the
efforts of President Lincoln to suppress the rebellion of the southern states
did not touch on slavery.[7]

In 1862 Governor Nye did discuss the question in his legislative address,
chiefly because the war had begun to destroy the institution. Among other
things, the governor said:

> Only the persistent obstinacy of their self-imposed leaders, in madly
> prolonging their doomed struggle . . . has impelled the President, after
> long and anxious deliberation, to resort to the last measure of legitimate
> warfare within his power, as Commander-in-Chief of the Army—the
> liberation of the Slaves in the disloyal States. . . . As an engine of war
> its formidability is a powerful warrant of early peace, and [as] a measure
> of humanity the enlightened world receives it with acclamations of
> unbounded joy.[8]

While resolutions endorsing the preliminary emancipation proclamation and strongly supporting the Union were extensively debated during the 1862 session, no resolution on any aspect of the war was finally adopted.[9] The reasons for this failure of the territorial legislature to express itself on either question are not clear, but no one openly defended slavery.[10] The 1861 and 1862 legislatures were as openly racist as they were antislavery. The congressional statute creating Nevada Territory had restricted voting and office holding initially to "free white male" citizens over twenty-one but allowed the legislative assembly to set voter qualifications after the first election.[11] The 1861 session of the assembly continued the restriction of voting to "white male" citizens over twenty-one. It passed another statute providing substantial criminal penalties (imprisonment from six months to two years and a fine of one hundred to one thousand dollars) for any election judge convicted of allowing any person to vote if "such person has a distinct and visible admixture of African blood."[12] There are no reports of debates on the suffrage question, but the action of the 1861 session on other matters and the statements legislators made in discussing these measures make it clear that just about everyone believed that blacks (and other nonwhites) were inferior.

Being qualified to vote was a requirement for office holding and for jury service; hence, nonwhites were automatically excluded from these privileges of citizenship by the suffrage restriction.[13] In addition, the 1861 legislative assembly enacted the following racist laws:

1. Attorneys had to be "white male" citizens in addition to meeting other qualifications.[14] No debates on this question were reported.

2. Militia duty was restricted to "free, able-bodied, white male" inhabitants. This law was copied, with little change, from California's militia law; if the legislators debated the racial restriction, it has not been recorded.[15]

3. A law prohibiting intermarriage and cohabitation of whites with nonwhites was given considerable attention by the legislature. The statute did not prohibit the intermarriage of nonwhites with other nonwhites but provided that "if any white man or woman intermarry with any black person, mulatto, Indian, or Chinese, the parties to such marriage shall be deemed guilty of a misdemeanor."[16] In considering the measure, the house passed a version of the bill that applied only to Indians and Chinese, but the council insisted on including "black" and "mulatto" persons as well, and it eventually prevailed. The reasons for this difference of opinion between the two houses do not appear clearly from the report of the dispute.[17]

4. Nonwhites were forbidden to testify against whites in both criminal and civil cases. The Crimes and Punishments Act, the basic criminal statute,

provided that "no black, or mulatto person, or Indian, or Chinese, shall be permitted to give evidence in favor of, or against, any white person." This law defined a mulatto as "every person who shall have one eighth part, or more, of negro blood."[18] (Inconsistently, the same law defined an Indian as "every person who shall have one half of Indian blood.") The basic statute governing civil actions, the Civil Practice Act, provided that "the following persons shall not be witnesses: . . . Third. Indians, or persons having one half or more of Indian blood and negroes or persons having one half or more of negro blood, in an action or proceeding to which a white person is a party."[19]

When the crimes and punishments bill came up for consideration in the house, Representative Samuel Youngs of Aurora "called attention" to the section banning nonwhite testimony. Apparently he objected to the inconsistency in the definitions of mulattoes and Indians, but "as it was apparent the House would disagree with him, he would not offer an amendment." It is not clear what amendment he would have offered if there had been a better prospect of success, and no further significant debate on the question seems to have occurred.[20] At the end of the session, however, Governor Nye sent a special message to the council objecting to the criminal testimony provision. Stating that he had signed the Crimes and Punishments Act despite his doubts about some sections, he specifically asked the council to amend the section prohibiting testimony of nonwhites. Part of his objection was to the inconsistency of defining mulattoes as persons one-half or more Negro in the Civil Practice Act but as persons one-eighth or more Negro in the Crimes and Punishments Act; as he put it, "a person of one-eighth black blood is not a mulatto in truth nor in fact." But he also objected to the testimony provision in general terms, stating that "the sentiment conveyed is behind the spirit of the age, which is progressive and calculated to enlarge in every proper way the privilege of testifying, the object of testimony being to open wide the door for the admission of evidence, and leaving questions relating thereto to be settled by the Court and jury, upon the ground of credibility rather than competency."[21]

The legislative assembly made no effort to amend the law in 1861 in response to the governor's message and similarly ignored the same request in 1862. The legislature, in banning testimony by blacks, was not following typical northern practice but was copying California practice. The Crimes and Punishments Act was essentially no different from California's criminal law statute, and that state was one of five northern ones that had banned testimony by blacks before the Civil War.[22]

In contrast with the denial of rights to nonwhites, the 1861 legislature imposed obligations without regard to race. Although there was no specific statement that the criminal law applied to Indians too, undoubtedly some legislators thought it did. The antimiscegenation law applied to Indians, and some Indians were convicted of crimes in the 1860s.[23] In any case, there is no doubt that the criminal laws applied to blacks from the beginning of the territory, although they were denied any part in making the laws. It is also clear that taxation laws were applied to all nonwhites, although the state could not tax Indian reservations.[24]

The 1861 legislative session had adopted the basic laws for the territory, and the 1862 session made few changes; however, the legislative assembly had an opportunity to amend the law banning testimony of nonwhites in criminal cases. In his opening address to the legislature, Governor Nye asked for repeal of the law. His reasons for this action and the response to them throw some light on white views of nonwhites at this time. First, as in 1861, he objected to the varying definitions of what constituted a mulatto in the criminal and civil laws. Pointing out that "there is a discrimination made in behalf of colored persons testifying in civil proceedings," he said: "This I regard as wrong. If any discrimination is to be made at all it should be in behalf of persons accused of crime. In the one case property only is involved, in the other, reputation, liberty, life." He urged outright repeal of both sections.

A careful examination of the matter, under the experience and observation of nearly a quarter of a century of professional life, persuades me that all persons of all races that are held amenable to law, who share in its protection and are subject to its power, who are visited by its penalties and taxed for its maintenance, should be allowed to testify in Court.

The governor offered several reasons for this stand. First, he argued that treating blacks equally would not make them equals of whites.

It is urged by many that in permitting persons of color to testify we elevate them in the scale of humanity, and make them nearer the equals of the white man. Admitting such an assumption to be true, it furnishes no argument against its propriety. I do not believe that if the entire energies of the superior race were directed to the elevation of the colored races, it would place them higher in the scale of being than the Creator designed them to occupy.

He asserted that allowing nonwhites to testify was of value "for the white race chiefly" because such a policy would allow testimony that might be important in cases involving whites.

Justice in her administration demands the shedding of all light possible upon questions under adjudication; and she will be satisfied with nothing less. She seeks for truth, come it from what source it may; and she stops not to inquire what the color of the party giving utterance to it may be.

Finally, he suggested that testimony should be given weight according to the individual characteristics of the person giving testimony and his circumstances and not according to his race: "The surroundings of the witness, his position in society, his general intelligence, the opportunity he may have had of ascertaining somewhat concerning the subject on which he is testifying; his general truthfulness; his demeanor in life; and the whole man, are proper subjects of inquiry for Courts and Juries."[25]

The governor's request for change in the law was not honored; in fact, there were no floor votes on the issue in either house. The governor's message prompted a report from the judiciary committee of the house, which vigorously supported the ban on testimony of nonwhites with some strong expressions of white racism. It clearly identified all "colored races" as inferior; Indians, Chinese, and blacks were attacked as "subordinate race [sic] whose dark skins are but an evidence of their inferiority." Speaking specifically of blacks, the report said that "his Excellency concedes the inferiority of the black race and argues in favor of their testimony as a circumstance. Your Committee yield to to [sic] the proposition of their inferiority, and demand their exclusion because of their inferiority." Expanding on the nature of the "inferiority" of blacks, the report said:

And who is the Negro? A wretched creature borne to the earth by generations of serfdom in our land. His native land surrounded for four thousand years with the appliance of Ancient and Modern Civilization has ever been in the lowest stage of human degredation [sic]. Surrounded and in immediate contact with the Egyptians, Phoenicians and Romans, the nations of Africa without a solitary exception continue to this day immersed in the grossest barbarism. Africa has not produced one great man—no Hercules—or Theseus or Confucius. There is not an Alphabet in the Ethiopian language. For four thousand years to which our information extends the Negro tribes are either ferocious savages or grossly sensual and ignorant. From the remotest antiquity they have been the Slaves of their enterprising neighbours. No Section of their Country has emitted one spark of intellectual light. Caffies, Bushmen and Bushanees are equally involved in intellectual darkness. Souls as dark as their bodies. The African is humanity in its dawn. He is the brute race in progress to man race. Praxatelles conceived the faun, half animal and half human. But the faun was distinguished for beauty of proportion and expression and with a pallid face. The African is yet a deformity. His immediate hope is amalgamation. The Quadroon Dumas had brains. It will take many ages to lift up the African to the level with the white.

Strike the fetters to day from every African in the land, he would still be a social slave, a helot from imbecility. His employer would hold his body and his Soul. Truth is the brightest jewel in the tiara of an intellectual freeman. There is no truth in Servitude. Your Committee believe that the black man's oath should never be arrayed against a free white man's. The Negro, serf or manumitted will ever be under the heel of the white man.[26]

That some representatives felt embarrassment at the strong language of the judiciary committee's report is suggested by the fact that a motion to print five hundred copies was withdrawn after a brief discussion on the floor of the house; however, a motion to table the report during the same discussion was defeated by a vote of seven to fourteen.[27] Subsequently, the report was kept with the manuscript records of the session but not printed in the proceedings of the house.[28]

Governor Nye's views on this question also resulted in a "bitter parody" delivered before the third house, an institution for poking fun at the legislature. A speaker satirizing one of the governor's messages during this period declared:

I most earnestly recommend the passage of a law permitting Niggers to swear in all cases, civil or criminal, in the Courts of Justice of this Territory, wherein white men or women are parties, whether the Nigger has any knowledge of the facts or not; and also that Niggers, both male and female, be guaranteed by law the exclusive exercise of the elective franchise, and to hold and administer the various offices of this Territory, and to represent the people in the legislative halls

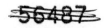

and other deliberative assemblies, and that any and all persons failing to give a hearty and cordial support to the law, shall by common consent be adjudged guilty of a felony and hung like a dog.[29]

Andrew Marsh, the reporter of the 1862 session, suggested that the governor may have been aware that repeal of the testimony laws was unlikely. He said that the governor's address had met with "universal commendation of citizens and legislators, except that portion wherein the Governor recommends that negroes, etc. shall no longer be exempt from testifying in Courts of Justice."

In explaining this reaction, Marsh stated:

> Several of the law-makers appear to have an idea that it would exalt an African to force him to tell the truth under oath, and others say the thing is impracticable in a country like this, abounding in degraded and diabolical Pah-Utes and Shoshones, with a smart sprinkling of Chinamen, negroes, and halfbreeds of various sorts and hues. They say Governor Nye has only done his duty to his party in making the recommendation, but cannot expect the Legislature to carry it out. We shall see.[30]

It seems likely that Nye was sincere in his request; in December 1861, he wrote Secretary of State William H. Seward, his superior, expressing the opinion that restriction of testimony by blacks was "behind the Spirit of the Age."[31]

THE 1863 CONVENTION

In 1863 a constitutional convention produced a document that might have become the constitution of the state of Nevada if it had been approved by the voters of the territory and if Congress had accepted it; however, the voters of the territory rejected it, and so it was never submitted to Congress. The debates and proceedings of this convention have recently been published, and they shed light on the racial attitudes of officeholders in early Nevada.

All the members of this convention were elected as Union candidates.[32] Perhaps because of this fact, an antislavery provision was adopted by the convention without debate on the fourth day. The only other reference to slavery was a speech by James Stark of Esmeralda County attacking the southern "traitors" in which he also asserted that the southern social system was "an oligarchy, whose foundation is slavery, that remnant of barbarism (soon, thank God, to be banished into the realms of eternal night)."[33] In spite of this agreement on slavery, however, the convention was unwilling to extend rights to blacks or other nonwhites. The constitutional provision on suffrage qualifications came from committee with membership in the "white" race as a qualification for voting. Delegate William G. Alban of Storey County wanted an explicit provision to prohibit the voting of a "negro, mulatto, or Chinaman"; however, when J. Neely Johnson of Ormsby County reminded him that the word "white" had already accomplished this purpose, Alban dropped his proposal.[34] On the fourth day, John W. North of Washoe County, who had been elected president of the convention, while participating in an extended discussion of the disfranchisement of "rebels," remarked that "it was not just and fair to disfranchise the loyal negroes of the South while at the same time they allowed their masters to vote."[35] However, neither North nor anyone else proposed eliminating the restriction of voting to whites (although another delegate did make such a proposal in the 1864 convention). North's biographer suggests that "if he had been on the floor of the convention, he would again have championed negro suffrage."[36] He also says that North led the convention in many ways and was specifically responsible for several constitutional provisions, including the section attacking the theory of secession and stating the supremacy of the national government; it seems more likely that North recognized the overwhelming sentiment against a position he supported and prudently refrained from raising it.

Discussion of the poll tax brought forth the statement from a delegate that the tax should be collected from all males who were protected by government, regardless of whether they could vote;[37] this point of view also reigned in the 1864 convention.

The militia clause stated that "white male citizens" would be subject to militia duty. This was adopted without debate on the twenty-second day, but later was changed to charge the legislature with providing for a militia, without constitutional specification of those eligible for such duty.[38]

The education clause produced the most disagreement about racial questions. The 1861 legislature adopted school laws essentially the same as those in California,[39] but it did not incorporate the provision of California law forbidding education of nonwhites except in separate schools; hence, the school laws of Nevada Territory did not discriminate on a racial basis. The reasons for failing to adopt the racist aspect of California's school law are unclear; apparently the education law was not extensively debated in 1861. When the issue came up in the 1863 convention, how-

ever, the delegates first decided to provide compulsory education for
whites only and then to omit the compulsory education provision altogether because it raised the issue of educating nonwhites.
The education section of the constitution as first presented to the
convention made education compulsory. In debate on this provision,
C. M. Brosnan of Storey County "suggested that, as the section now stood,
it compelled the education of negroes and Chinese along with white
children." Delegate C. N. Noteware of Douglas County asked that the
compulsory education provision be amended "so as not to compel men
to send their children to the same schools with the children of negroes,
Chinamen and Indians." When James H. Ralston of Lander County sought
to accomplish this end by inserting the word "white" in the compulsory
education provision, the amendment was opposed and narrowly defeated.
John W. North, president of the convention, objected to denying education to nonwhites "because any man having a negro or Indian child under
his charge ought to be compelled to educate such child." Delegate Samuel
A. Chapin of Storey County agreed with North, stating that "he would
sooner exclude these races from the State altogether than prevent their
being educated while here." The amendment was defeated by a vote of
eleven to thirteen.[40]
The next day, however, Noteware again brought up the objection to
having nonwhites educated with whites, and this time the word "white"
was written into the proposed constitution after a debate in which it
developed that some delegates favored exclusion of blacks from the state,
others favored segregated education, and most preferred exclusion of
blacks from the schools to allowing them to be educated with whites.
Even John W. North urged segregation of blacks, because he saw it as an
alternative to their exclusion altogether:

> Mr. North opposed the amendment strenuously, as oppressive in its
> tendency upon a weak and degraded race. He did not think this com-
> pulsory clause was understood, and contended that the Legislature
> could regulate the matter so as not to require whi[te and] black
> children to go to the same school. He appealed to the magnanimity,
> manliness and humanity of the Convention to vote down this
> proposition.

Delegates Samuel Youngs of Esmeralda County and Noteware, who
had made the motion under debate, both agreed that they were "ready
to prohibit the immigration of Negroes," as Noteware put it, but Youngs
opposed the amendment on this ground while Noteware favored it for

this reason because, no matter how it was done, "he did not want to allow them to go to school with white children." Marcus D. Larrowe of Lander County voiced the sentiments of those delegates who favored segregated schools:

> The blacks were naturally inferior to the whites, and black ignorance was therefore worse than white ignorance, and consequently the blacks needed education fully as much as the whites. Yet he was unalterably opposed to allowing white and black children to sit upon the same bench, and therefore objected to granting the Legislature power to compel the white children to go to the same school with the blacks. He preferred the establishment of separate schools for the blacks.

After substantial debate on the matter, during which Brosnan "warned the Convention that if they refused to pass it, they would thereby endanger the adoption of the Constitution by the people," the amendment was approved by a vote of nineteen to nine. Miles N. Mitchell of Storey County had said during the debate that he would offer an amendment later providing for "separate schools for other than white children," but he did not do so, and the school section providing compulsory education for white children but not for nonwhites was approved by a vote of twenty-one to seven on the same day.[41] On the final consideration of the education section several days later, however, the compulsory education section was deleted altogether, and with it any specific reference to race in this portion of the constitution.[42] It is clear that a majority of delegates favored the approach adopted later by the first state legislature, which was to exclude nonwhites from the schools altogether rather than to allow them to attend schools for white children.

In the section of the constitution dealing with a state university, a racist provision was adopted by the convention. In debating a provision authorizing the establishment of a mining school, Noteware had moved an amendment "so as to admit only 'white' pupils to the University." Characteristically North opposed this motion, saying that "he thought that matter could be left to the discretion of the Legislature. He hoped Mr. Noteware would not insist on his peculiar views being incorporated here." Noteware's proposal was defeated at this point, apparently with little discussion, but three days later William B. Hickok of Lyon County made a motion to provide free tuition for "white male pupils" between fourteen and twenty-one which was approved by a vote of thirteen to ten after being amended to allow free tuition for white females as well as males. The constitution presented to the voters contained this provision.[43]

John W. North was a firmly committed abolitionist and radical Republican who had fought for black suffrage in the Minnesota Constitutional Convention of 1857, even though he could not carry a majority of his own party for the proposal at that time. He had come to Nevada in 1861 with an appointment from President Lincoln as surveyor-general of the territory, and the next year Lincoln appointed him to the most important territorial judgeship. He was a man of high character, "a gentleman on whose character the breath of scandal has never cast a taint," as the *Virginia City Union* stated at the time of his judicial appointment;[44] he was proposed unanimously for the judgeship by the Nevada bar and legislature. For two years he served as superintendent of schools for Washoe County,[45] was elected president of the 1863 constitutional convention, and seemed destined for election to one of the most important offices in the soon-to-be state of Nevada.

William M. Stewart, the principal attorney for the major mining companies on the Comstock and soon to be a United States senator from Nevada (although he had joined in proposing North for appointment as a judge), in 1864 began an attack on him, which contributed to North's departure from Nevada without attaining any important elective office. North had led the successful forces in the 1863 convention that favored taxing mines on the same basis as other property, while Stewart had led the opposing forces; defeated in the convention, Stewart had vigorously opposed adoption of the document and had helped to secure its rejection by the voters. Stewart also opposed many of North's judicial decisions in mining cases, in part because North refused to accept the theory that the Comstock lode was a single body of ore and in part because he was a rival of North for major state office. For a variety of reasons, then, Stewart led a bitter assault on North. He began with a charge of bribery, which North forced him to retract in the newspapers.

Stewart's next step was to arrange a public meeting at Maguire's Opera House in January 1864 at which he accused North of "extravagance" in supporting high salaries for state officers during the 1863 convention and of having "radical" views on the taxation of mines; his law partner repeated the discredited charges of bribery. Although there were these other charges, contemporary accounts indicate that Stewart's main attack was centered on North's views on racial issues. The *Territorial Enterprise* stated that, "as the greatest objection," Stewart "adduced Judge North's opinions on the equality of the white and black races. In illustrating this position, he read from the reports of the Minnesota Constitutional Convention, of which Judge North was a member, a speech of that gentleman contending for the right of negro suffrage, in which he declared that they were as much entitled to that privilege as foreigners." The *Virginia Daily Union* reported of this meeting that the "sum total" of Stewart's charges was that "during the year 1858 [*sic*] Judge North was a member of the Constitutional Convention of Minnesota, in which Convention he made a speech in favor of allowing all the male inhabitants of the State to vote."[46] The newspapers and Judge North felt that he had had the best of this debate, but it is significant for understanding white attitudes on race at the time to note that Stewart assumed that a charge of this kind would be highly damaging to North.

Later Stewart blocked North's nomination as the Union candidate for governor of Nevada and continued to try to force him off the bench: North did resign in the summer of 1864 and left Nevada for Tennessee as Nevada became a state, but his resignation was partly a consequence of ill health. In 1865 referees appointed to decide the merits of a slander suit brought by North against Stewart completely vindicated North by finding "the conduct and motions of . . . Wm. M. Stewart . . . wrong and unjustifiable."[47]

THE 1864 CONVENTION AND LEGISLATURE

After the voters defeated the proposed constitution, a new constitutional convention, this time authorized by Congress, proposed the constitution that became the fundamental law of the new state of Nevada and is still in force. As was the case with the territorial legislatures in 1861 and 1862, and the 1863 convention, the Union-dominated convention opposed slavery without dissent but also passed racist laws and openly said that nonwhites were inferior to whites.[48]

The Enabling Act—by which Congress agreed to admit Nevada as a state—contained a provision that the constitution of the new state was to "provide, by an ordinance irrevocable without the consent of the United States" and the people of Nevada, that slavery was not to exist,[49] and of course the constitutional convention did frame a document barring slavery, without debate on the merits of the question.[50] But the debates of the convention indicate that no direction by Congress was necessary to produce this ban on slavery; the members were strongly opposed to the institution. B. S. Mason of Esmeralda County drew applause when he praised John Brown and attacked slavery as "the great blight of the United States of America—the blackest blot upon humanity"; Mason and James A. Banks of Humboldt County expressed shame and regret that they had once supported slavery, Banks saying that he had been "monstrously wrong" in his former position; George A. Nourse of Washoe County referred to a decision of the United States Supreme Court upholding the fugitive slave law as "a most flagrant

and gross abuse of power" and stated that he had once been threatened
with indictment for treason because "he would not acknowledge the
Dred Scott decision"; and C. E. DeLong of Storey County asserted that
another delegate from the same county, John A. Collins, had been hostile
to the California Supreme Court "ever since the time when that Court
gave, as the saying was, 'the law to the North, and the nigger to the
South,' in the decision involving the right to hold the slave Archie."[51] The
decision referred to had ordered a fugitive slave returned to his owner in
spite of an antislavery provision of the state constitution. Later, the fugitive
was allowed to stay in California as a free man.[52]

In spite of their opposition to slavery, the delegates to the 1864 convention were explicit about their belief that nonwhites were inferior to
whites. For example, delegate E. F. Dunne of Humboldt County, in arguing
against the disfranchisement of persons who had supported the Confederacy during the Civil War, predicted that the southern rebels would
probably be loyal men at some future date and that he did not want
them to be able to say, "You attempted to sink us down to the level of
the negroes and Chinamen and the aboriginal inhabitants of the country."
Charles E. DeLong of Storey County used a similar argument, stating that
the disfranchisement of rebels would enable them "to feel that we have
put them down among the negroes and Chinamen, and refused to give them
a chance to be good citizens again." George A. Nourse, who had indicated
his long-standing opposition to slavery, was explicit about the status of
blacks when he discussed the meaning of the clause of the constitution,
already agreed upon, which declared that "all men are by nature free
and equal." He said of this sentence that "we do not mean equal politically or socially, of course . . . we have said that blacks are not equal
to whites."[53]

The delegates acted consistently with these views. In several areas they
explicitly denied privileges or rights to nonwhites while subjecting them
to the same obligations as whites.

The 1864 constitution continued the earlier practice of restricting
voting, and therefore also office holding and jury service, to whites. At
one point, Nourse made a motion to strike the word "white" from the
voting qualifications section.[54] The motion died without a second, however, and Nourse was aware that it would not be adopted. He said:

> I wish to make one motion here, which I suppose, will be voted down,
> but I will not occupy much time with it. I move to simply strike out
> the word "white." . . . I think it is pandering to an old and disgraceful
> prejudice—and none the less disgraceful, I will say, because I myself

have partaken of it—against that race which is certainly doing grand
work for the Union now. I suppose that here this is not in reality a
practical question, and while I would not be in favor of the proposition
in a population where there would be a great many of those ignorant
people to turn loose at the polls, still I think here it is a mere theoretical
matter. I offer the amendment, therefore, although I presume it will
be voted down, simply because I think it my duty to do so.[55]

William Hanchett, who has studied white attitudes toward race in
Nevada during this period, has said that "the convention's attitude towards
Negro enfranchisement was perhaps better reflected by the member from
New York [Nelson E. Murdock of Churchill County] who asked, 'Why
should we condescend to make any of the inferior races our equals?'"[56]

It is clear that delegates thought their constituents were strongly
opposed to allowing nonwhites to vote. E. F. Dunne complained that a
prominent opponent of the constitution was attempting to convince
people to vote against it by stating publicly that the members of the
convention "were bound by their solemn oaths to incorporate a clause
in the Constitution allowing Negroes to vote." Dunne obviously thought
the charge was unfair.[57]

Nevada was following typical northern practice in restricting voting to
whites. After the admission of Maine in 1819, no state was admitted to the
Union with a constitution permitting nonwhites to vote until the end of
the Civil War; in 1860 only five states, containing about 6 percent of the
black population of the country, permitted blacks to vote.[58]

The education provisions of the 1864 constitution did not contain any
racial restrictions, although this was partly because the issue was left to
the legislature. The committee on education proposed a section dealing
with the state university that was similar to the 1863 provision and
extended free tuition to whites. No one opposed the section because of
its racial discrimination, but there was debate over other aspects of the
section; ultimately it was amended to allow the legislature and the board
of regents to set admission qualifications.[59]

In debating the public education article, E. F. Dunne offered a motion
to provide for compulsory attendance of "all white children." There was
some discussion of the racial aspects of this amendment, with J. H. Warwick
of Lander County asking Dunne if he wanted to give more "liberty" to
blacks than whites because "it seems that white people are to be compelled to send their children to school, while the negroes are not." Dunne's
amendment was defeated, and it was agreed to allow the legislature to
decide whether there was to be any compulsory education.[60]

As in the previous year, the 1864 convention provided that obligations were to be shared by all races, although nonwhites were not allowed to participate in making the laws. Delegate J. Neely Johnson of Ormsby County was explicit that everyone had to pay the poll tax. He said:

It is not property alone, but the man himself who is also protected, in all his various relations and interests, by the Government; and it is provided in this section that all male citizens of the age of twenty-one years or over, be they white or black, yellow or copper-colored, shall pay an annual poll-tax in addition to any tax that may be assessed upon their property, for the protection which the Government affords to their persons. I want this clause extended so as to reach every class of individuals.

George A. Nourse made a similar statement.[61] Later the clause was amended to exclude "uncivilized American Indians" from payment of the tax, and John A. Collins of Storey County noted that the provision "requires Negroes, Chinese and every class of men to pay the poll tax, except uncivilized American Indians."[62]

The 1864 legislative assembly adopted a strong resolution condemning slavery. It labeled "treason" the views of northerners who "have said let the nation perish rather than Slavery suffer in the contest."[63] In 1866 the *Territorial Enterprise*, in an editorial, stated that there had been an informal attempt to repeal the testimony laws in the 1864 legislature but that the effort was abandoned when it was apparent that there was insufficient support for it.[64] No change in the racist laws was made by this session of the legislature, the last of Nevada's territorial days.

THE 1865 LEGISLATURE

The first legislature under the new state constitution, in 1865, continued with the racist provisions of previous laws, with two exceptions. Only two Democrats were elected to this legislature, one in each house. In the field of education, the 1865 lawmakers enacted the provision of the California school law that forbade educating nonwhites in white schools and allowed (but not required) them to attend separate schools. The 1867 legislature simplified the wording of this law; as it read after 1867 until it was declared unconstitutional in 1872 the school law provided that "Negroes, Mongolians, and Indians, shall not be admitted into the Public Schools, but the Board of Trustees may establish a separate school for their education, and use the Public School Funds for the support of the same."[65]

The 1865 legislature also changed the Crimes and Punishments Act to permit blacks to testify in criminal trials, though on a discriminatory basis. The new law read:

> No Indian or Chinese shall be permitted to give evidence in favor or against any white person. . . . In no case shall the Act of which this is amendatory be construed to exclude as witnesses any negro, black or mulatto person, but the credibility of such negro, black or mulatto persons shall be left entirely with the jury.[66]

The 1865 legislative session ratified the Thirteenth Amendment early in its session and also took the unusual step of authorizing the governor to telegraph the resolution of ratification to President Lincoln. A resolution commending President Lincoln and his administration stated that the amendment to abolish slavery marked "the dawn of a new political era, and [we] pray that its principles may be ever enforced until regenerated America shall forget the name of slave." By the next year, the need to prevent the introduction of slavery into Mexico was being given as a reason for opposing the regime of Maximilian. The legislature urged overthrow of his government, by war if necessary, and stated that "the recent promulgation of an edict by Maximilian, having in view the establishment of slavery upon the soil of Mexico, is in derogation of the recently adopted policy of this Government."[67]

At the 1865 convention of the Union party, which in effect chose Nevada's first congressman, two of the three aspirants for the nomination expressed antiblack sentiments. Charles H. Sumner "said he was opposed to negro suffrage" while D. R. Ashley, who was nominated and subsequently elected to Congress, stated that "he did not wish to degrade and debase the people of the South by putting them on a level with their former slaves. He believed that for the present the negro had his full reward in his freedom; though when properly cultivated and elevated in the scale of humanity, he *might* become entitled to greater privileges."[68]

The governments of Nevada Territory and the state of Nevada were being established between 1861 and 1865. Legislative sessions and constitutional conventions during this period were dominated overwhelmingly by the Union party, whose members, though against slavery, by and large were also racist. Governor James W. Nye objected twice, though unsuccessfully, to laws forbidding the testimony in criminal or civil cases of blacks and other nonwhites, and convention delegates George A. Nourse and John W. North made some objections to racist constitutional provisions and laws; North later was attacked publicly for his racial views.

During the territorial period, blacks (along with other nonwhites) could
not vote, hold office, serve on juries, testify in civil or criminal cases,
be attorneys, serve in the militia, or marry whites. When Nevada became
a state, almost all of these discriminations were continued. Although the
first state legislature modified the criminal testimony law to allow blacks
to testify, but not on a basis of complete equality with whites, this action
was more than counterbalanced by a new law excluding them from public
schools unless separate schools were established for them. Finally, it was
clear that early white Nevada legislators thought blacks, as well as other
nonwhites, were inferior.

NOTES

1. Andrew J. Marsh, *Letters from Nevada Territory, 1861-1862*
(Carson City, Nevada: Legislative Counsel Bureau, 1972), p. 8.
2. This strongly pro-Union situation was partly a result of the fact
that Nevada's white settlers came chiefly from the North. In 1860 only
14 percent of the non-Indian population had come from states in which
slavery was legal, and in 1870 only 6 percent had come from states in
which slavery had been legal. See William Hanchett, "Yankee Law and the
Negro in Nevada, 1861-1869," *Western Humanities Review* 10 (Summer
1956): 242.
3. Marsh, *Letters*, p. 553.
4. Ibid., pp. 23-24, 86, 109.
5. See Robert F. Heizer and Alan F. Almquist, *The Other Californians*
(Berkeley: University of California Press, 1971), pp. 39-58.
6. Marsh, *Letters*, pp. 17-26.
7. Nevada, *Statutes*, 1861, resolution V, p. 616.
8. Marsh, *Letters*, p. 429.
9. Ibid., pp. 511-512, 552-553, 609-612, 640-642, 645-646, 656-658.
10. Andrew J. Marsh, the reporter of the session, said that "the truth
is, that a great majority of the members of the House are passably loyal,
at least so far as test oaths go, but like most politicians, they are time-servers.
They are looking forward to some reaction in public sentiment, and do
not wish to be 'nailed' so as not to be able to jump down on either side of
the fence." Ibid., pp. 611-612.
11. "Act of Congress Organizing the Territory of Nevada," sec. 5, in
Nevada, *Statutes*, 1861, p. xl.
12. Nevada, *Statutes*, 1861, chap. 48, sec. 4.
13. The 1864 constitution required officeholders to be "qualified electors"
and excluded nonvoters from jury duty. Art. XV, sec. 3, and Art. III, sec. 27.

14. Nevada, *Statutes*, 1861, chap. 6, sec. 2, 5.
15. Ibid., chap. 39, sec. 11; Marsh, *Letters*, p. 315.
16. Nevada, *Statutes*, 1861, chap. 32.
17. Marsh, *Letters*, pp. 107, 167-168, 206, 230, 247, 270-271, 305, 311, 322, 326, 329-330, 339, 343, 347, 357, 373.
18. Nevada, *Statutes*, 1861, chap. 28.
19. Ibid., chap. 103.
20. Marsh, *Letters*, p. 187.
21. Ibid., p. 356.
22. Ibid., p. 86; Leon L. Litwack, *North of Slavery* (Chicago: University of Chicago Press, 1961), p. 93.
23. At least ten Indians were inmates of the Nevada state prison from 1865 through 1884, the period before criminal law was specifically applied to them. See *Reports* of the Warden.
24. Another indication of the racial attitudes of the delegates is the use of the word "nigger" in debate. Councilman Isaac Roop of Honey Lake, in discussing the controversy over the miscegenation statute, "stated that some of the members of the House were willing to strike out 'niggers and Hong Kongs,' but wanted Indians to remain." Similar derogatory terms for Indians and Chinese were used freely by delegates.
25. Marsh, *Letters*, pp. 441-442.
26. Nevada, Assembly, *Journal* (1862), pp. 87-91. (This report is not published in Marsh, *Letters*, but is available in a microfilm copy of the manuscript *Journal* at Special Collections, Getchell Library, University of Nevada, Reno.)
27. Marsh, *Letters*, p. 495.
28. Several representatives used a phrase derogatory to blacks to suggest that proposals were designed to accomplish unrevealed purposes. Two members, opposing a franchise bill because its author had earlier opposed all franchise bills, said that "there must necessarily be 'a nigger in the fence.'" Ibid., p. 507. A bill to incorporate Virginia City was opposed by Representative Williams, who intimated "the presence of an individual of the African persuasion in the fence." Ibid., p. 547. Representative Davenport voted against a bill to legalize tax assessments in Washoe County, "for fear of that 'gentleman from Africa' in the fence." Ibid., p. 569.
29. Quoted in Hanchett, "Yankee Law and the Negro in Nevada," pp. 243-244.
30. Marsh, *Letters*, p. 423.
31. Quoted in Hanchett, "Yankee Law and the Negro in Nevada," p. 243.
32. Andrew Marsh, *Reports of the 1863 Constitutional Convention* (Carson City, Nevada: Legislative Counsel Bureau, 1972), p. 52.
33. Ibid., p. 104.
34. Ibid., p. 48.
35. Ibid., p. 53.

36. Merlin Stonehouse, *John Wesley North and the Reform Frontier* (Minneapolis: University of Minnesota Press, 1965), p. 156.

37. Marsh, *Reports of the Convention*, p. 267.

38. Ibid., pp. 288, 308, 330-331.

39. Harold N. Brown, "A History of the Public Elementary School System of Nevada, 1861-1934" (Ph.D. diss., University of California, Berkeley, 1935), p. 23.

40. Marsh, *Reports of the 1863 Convention*, pp. 235-236.

41. Ibid., pp. 260-261.

42. Ibid., p. 330.

43. Ibid., pp. 236, 291, 293.

44. Newspaper clipping, datelined September 12, 1863, quoting the *Union*, in Bancroft Scraps, vol. 95-2, p. 284, in Bancroft Library, University of California, Berkeley.

45. Myron Angel, ed., *History of Nevada, 1881* (Berkeley, California: Howell-North, 1958), pp. 335-336, 630.

46. Newspaper clippings from *Territorial Enterprise*, January 15, 1864, and Virginia *Union*, n.d., in Bancroft Scraps, vol. 95-1, pp. 105-106.

47. The chief source on the Stewart attack on North is Stonehouse, *John Wesley North*, pp. 150-177, 253. See also Russell R. Elliott, *History of Nevada* (Lincoln: University of Nebraska Press, 1973), pp. 79-82.

48. Only one member of the convention, Charles M. Proctor of Nye County, was not elected as a Union candidate; he was a Democrat. Historians have concluded that the 1863 constitution was rejected for a number of reasons, including the controversy over taxation of mine property and conflicts over nominations for public offices within the Union party. See Elliott, *History of Nevada*, pp. 79-83.

49. "Enabling Act, passed by Congress," sec. 4, in Nevada, *Statutes*, 1865, pp. 33-38.

50. Andrew J. Marsh, *Nevada Constitutional Debates and Proceedings* (San Francisco: Frank Eastman, 1866), pp. 50-51, 66-67, 193, 780.

51. Ibid., pp. 21, 97, 256. This is not to say that the Democratic party, then overwhelmingly unpopular in the territory, was also opposed to slavery. In February 1863 the Democratic central committee of Storey County adopted a statement defending slavery as beneficial to the "negro." Orion Clemens Scrapbooks, 1861-1864, Bancroft Library, University of California, Berkeley.

52. See Rudolph M. Lapp, *Archy Lee* (San Francisco: Book Club of California, 1969).

53. March, *Nevada Constitutional Debates*, pp. 91-92, 261. As noted above, DeLong used the word "nigger" in discussing the Archy case. Ibid., p. 21. Albert T. Hawley of Douglas County referred to mining as "the 'nigger' of this coast." Ibid., p. 225. Nourse talked about his reluctance to "catch runaway darkeys" before the Civil War. Ibid., p. 69.

54. Nourse had been a Republican ally of North in Minnesota and had followed him to Nevada; he became the state's first attorney general. See Stonehouse, *John Wesley North*, pp. 92, 118, 162.

55. Marsh, *Nevada Constitutional Debates*, p. 73.

56. Hanchett, "Yankee Law and the Negro in Nevada," pp. 241-249.

57. Marsh, *Nevada Constitutional Debates*, p. 317.

58. Litwack, *North of Slavery*, p. 91.

59. Marsh, *Nevada Constitutional Debates*, pp. 580-582, 585-587.

60. Ibid., pp. 566-568, 569-574.

61. Ibid., p. 113.

62. Ibid., pp. 114, 120, 145-146, 787.

63. Nevada, *Statutes*, 1864, pp. 163-164.

64. *Territorial Enterprise*, May 22, 1866.

65. Nevada, *Statutes*, 1865, chap. 145, *Statutes*, 1867, chap. 52.

66. Ibid., 1865, chap. 136.

67. Ibid., Resolution 11, pp. 459-460; *Statutes*, 1866, Resolution 4, pp. 262-263.

68. Newspaper article, October 18, 1865, Bancroft Scraps, vol. 95-1, p. 131.

—3—

"A Revolution of Opinion": Changing White Attitudes

White racism was overt and strong in the early 1860s; but by the end of that decade and during the 1870s, there was a gradual erosion of racism, at least toward blacks. While the major impetus for this was the congeries of national and southern events set off by the Civil War that we now call Reconstruction, the effect was an apparently major shift in white attitudes toward blacks. As the *Territorial Enterprise* put it in 1866, "The revolution of force having been suppressed, a revolution of opinion has set in."[1] This "revolution of opinion" resulted, by 1882, in the repeal of all but one of Nevada's racist laws, although it did not produce any antiracist legislation to parallel that enacted on the national level and although the legal changes were slower in Nevada than they were nationally and were invariably behind the demands of the black community.

REPUBLICAN DOMINANCE OF NEVADA POLITICS AND PRESS

Although the lopsided dominance of the Union-Republican party in Nevada politics lasted only through the 1860s, the Republicans remained the most important party throughout the nineteenth century. From 1865 to 1900, the Democrats elected one United States senator (James G. Fair in 1881), three congressmen (Charles W. Kendall in 1870 and 1872, George W. Cassidy in 1880 and 1882 and Francis G. Newlands from 1892 through the end of the century, when he ran as a candidate of the Silver party as well), and two governors (Lewis R. Bradley in 1870 and 1874 and Jewett W. Adams in 1882). Republicans served for 111 years in these offices during the nineteenth century while Democrats served for twenty-nine years. Republican control was even more complete in the legislature. The first state legislature had only two Democrats to fifty-one Republicans and the Democrats never had as many as one fifth of the members of the legislature at any time in the 1860s. The party contest for legislative control was a little more even in the 1870s, but the Democrats did not have their first majority in either house until they won control of the assembly in the election of 1880, permitting the election of the only Democratic senator to serve Nevada in the nineteenth century. Thereafter for the rest of the century, Republican control of the legislature was customary.[2]

Furthermore, throughout this period the leading newspapers of western Nevada, the major population center of the state, were Union-Republican in their politics. In an age when newspapers were openly partisan, this was an important fact. Often the editors or publishers of these newspapers were Republican politicians. An example is the *Carson City Appeal* and Henry R. Mighels. Under variations of the name *Appeal*, Mighels edited the paper from its establishment in 1865 to 1870 and from 1872 to his death in 1879; during his editorship, the *Appeal* was vigorously Republican. Mighels was elected to the state assembly in 1876 and served as speaker during the 1877 session. In 1878 he was an unsuccessful Republican candidate for lieutenant-governor. Myron Angel referred to him as one "whose pen for years had been a wand of fire in the State, wielded in the interests of Republicanism."[3]

The *Territorial Enterprise*, the most famous Nevada newspaper of the last century, was a partisan Republican journal from its move to Virginia City (from Carson City) in 1860 until its demise in 1893. For a decade and a half, Joseph T. Goodman, a devoted Republican, was a publisher of the paper; from 1863 to 1874 he was sole publisher. Goodman sold the *Enterprise* in 1874 to Rollin M. Daggett, who received financial aid from Republican Senator William Sharon. Daggett was a Republican politician, who had been elected to the council of the territorial legislature in 1863 and to the post of superintendent of schools in Storey County in 1865 and who was subsequently elected congressman from Nevada for

one term from 1879 through 1880. When Daggett retired in 1875, Judge
Charles C. Goodwin, another Republican politician, became editor of
the *Enterprise;* except for Daggett's return for a few months in 1877-
1878, Goodwin remained editor until 1880. He had been elected a district
judge in the district consisting of Washoe and Roop counties in 1864 and
was a Republican candidate for Congress in 1870, although he was not
elected.[4]

The *Gold Hill Daily News,* which has been described as "the leading
political and mining journal of the State" during the period when the
Comstock lode was most productive, was a Union-Republican paper from
1863 to its demise in 1882. From May 1865 to November 1867 its editor
was Charles A. Sumner, a Republican state senator from Storey County
(from 1865 through 1868). Sumner was also a reporter for the *Territorial
Enterprise* at one time. Its most famous editor, however, was Alf Doten,
who was associate editor or editor from 1867 to 1881. Although Doten
did not become a candidate for office himself, the *News* under his leadership
was an outstanding Republican paper.[5]

In short, a Republican leadership group (calling itself Union in the
early years), which was partly allied with and partly combined with the
editors and publishers of the leading newspapers in the part of Nevada
where most of the white population lived, was of major importance in
determining Nevada government's actions toward blacks and other nonwhites, particularly in the 1860s and 1870s. Congress was also dominated
by the Republican party during these years; it was a Republican-domi-
nated national government that brought an end to slavery and undertook
a series of measures to extend rights to the freed slaves in the period from
the Civil War to 1876, when blacks were abandoned to the mercies of
"redemption" white governments in the South. The dominant Nevada
group was much more likely to agree with these national actions and to
respond to racial questions in ways similar to those of the national
government because they were largely of the same party and saw their
interests in the same way. At the same time, the failure of Nevada
government to do more than was absolutely essential to respond to
national leadership is a measure of the degree to which racist attitudes
persisted in the state.

REACTIONS TO NATIONAL CHANGES

The Civil War had brought the end of slavery, although that had not
been the intent of President Lincoln or of Congress when the war began.
In a similar manner, the war and the necessities of reconstruction led

Congress, against even the opposition of President Johnson, to extend more and more legal rights to the freed slaves. Allowing blacks to vote and adopting constitutional amendments and laws designed to extend to them most rights already possessed by white Americans were steps Congress took gradually in the 1860s and 1870s. Many of the changes in the thinking of Nevada's political leaders can be traced to these national changes.

"We Of The North Can Do Little"

It was quite common for Nevada politicians or newspapers to applaud national actions without advocating action to deal with similar racist laws or practices in Nevada. Part of the reason for this attitude was probably simple hypocrisy, but it also seems that racial practices of the South were more visible to Nevada leaders than racial practices at home. It was a common assumption that racism was confined to the South. In November 1865, for example, the *Carson Daily Appeal* indicated approvingly that "friends of equal rights" were "moving slowly, but surely" toward the implementation of the promise of equality contained in the Declaration of Independence; however, this was seen primarily as a southern development and problem.

> We of the North can do little else than contend for the application of the principle of equality before the law; it remains mainly within the hands of sound thinkers of the South to apply that principle in its broadest sense. And such men are at work, faithfully and courageously in the Southern States.[6]

As a particularly striking illustration of the failure to apply attitudes toward the South to the Nevada scene, this same newspaper contained another editorial attacking "relics of barbarism" in the South. Basing its argument on an extract from a Nashville newspaper, the *Appeal* asserted that "one of the most barbarous and dangerous of the slave code prohibitions is being so vigorously and persistently assailed that its repeal in favor of an act of justice toward the freedman is a result which we may hope to see done at no very distant day."[7] The subject of this attack was the prohibition of testimony by blacks in court. At this time, Nevada law forbade the testimony of blacks in civil cases and put such testimony on a discriminatory basis in criminal cases. Whether the writer of this editorial, who was probably Henry Mighels, knew these facts and was being hypocritical or simply was ignorant of Nevada law cannot be established with certainty, but the conflict between condemning a southern law while ignoring the same law in Nevada is patent, whatever its explanation.

"Give The Free Black His Ballot"

Developing white attitudes in Nevada can be traced through reactions to the question of black suffrage. From the middle of 1865, the *Carson Daily Appeal* favored black suffrage on several grounds. One was that black troops had been important in winning the Civil War; another was that the blacks could be counted on to support reconstruction governments in the South. The *Appeal* neatly combined these two arguments in an editorial commending an address delivered in Los Angeles by General Irvin McDowell. According to the *Appeal*, the gist of the general's arguments was that blacks had won the right to vote by supplying two hundred thousand troops to the Union side during the Civil War. The general concluded that the North had "whipped" the rebels with blacks, and "we will outvote them with their negroes, we will regenerate the South with the same element."[8]

A third argument for black suffrage was that it would be to the interest of white southerners to let blacks vote. Pointing out that the South had enjoyed representation in Congress on the basis of counting three-fifths of the slaves before the Civil War, the *Appeal* noted that, in order to restore their number of representatives to the prewar level, they would have to let the freedmen vote; "and when they do that a long stride will be taken in the direction of negro suffrage. Self interest will sooner or later help to give the free black his ballot."[9]

A fourth argument was that there was an "inevitable logic" in the emancipation of the slaves, since "it is a well-established principle of law that the loss or destruction of a thing or system does away with all the regulations of that thing or system." Consequently, the newspaper argued, the South would be forced to extend equality to blacks in the matter of voting, in the right to serve on juries, and in other areas.[10]

In the case of suffrage, the legislature did not repeal the state constitutional provision restricting voting to whites until ten years after it had been invalidated by ratification of the Fifteenth Amendment to the United States Constitution, although action was begun soon after the ratification.

In 1867 "objections were strong and immediate" to a "reconstruction resolution . . . which favored the enfranchisement of all adult males, regardless of race, creed, or color." A number of legislators spoke against it, and it was never brought to a vote.[11]

In 1869, however, Senator William M. Stewart of Nevada, who had strongly opposed black suffrage in 1864 and had attacked Judge North on the issue, was the chief congressional sponsor of the Fifteenth Amend-

ment.[12] Nevada was the first state to ratify it, partly because Senator
Stewart telegraphed the news of congressional passage of the amendment
to the legislature so that it could act before adjournment.[13]

The assembly voted to ratify the amendment by a vote of twenty-three
to sixteen and the senate by a vote of eleven to six. The six dissenting
senators entered a "protest" in the senate *Journal*, which asserted that
the requisite number of United States senators had not voted for the
amendment, that it had not been properly presented to the Nevada legislature, that the Nevada senate was behaving with "haste and undignified
action" in voting on the measure, that the control of the right to vote
was left with the states by the original Constitution and should remain
there, and that the people of the state clearly opposed an amendment
which "gives to the Mongolians full political rights in this Republic."[14]

The 1869 legislature also passed a state constitutional amendment to
remove the word "white" from the suffrage clause. The assembly passed
the proposal twenty-five to fourteen and the senate adopted it without a
record vote.[15]

Nevada legislative constitutional amendments must be passed by two
successive legislatures, as well as submitted to popular vote, and the 1871
legislature took no action on the issue. It was 1877 before the proposal
came up again, and by that time the advocates of repealing the "white"
restriction on voting could not discover why the 1871 legislature had
failed to act. On January 12, 1877, the assembly passed a constitutional
amendment to remove the word "white" from the list of voting qualifications. Its chief sponsor, Speaker Henry R. Mighels of Ormsby County,
merely noted the 1869 action and stated, "I find no record anywhere that
this most righteous amendment ever received the sanction of a succeeding
Legislature."[16]

No governor mentioned removing the racial bar to voting from the state
constitution until 1879, although electoral laws had been frequently discussed in gubernatorial messages earlier. In that year Governor John H.
Kinkead asked the legislature to eliminate the word "white" from the list
of voting qualifications to make the constitution "conform to the amended
Constitution of the United States, which confers upon all native-born
citizens of this Republic, irrespective of color, race, or previous condition
of servitude, a station of full and exact equality."[17] By this time, the
legislature had already proposed such an amendment once, of course; the
amendment was proposed again in 1879 and approved by the voters in
the general election of 1880. In addition to striking the word "white,"
this amendment added a new section stating: "The rights of suffrage and

office-holding shall not be withheld from any male citizen of the United
States by reason of his color or previous condition of servitude." In the
resolution proposing these changes to the voters, the legislature pointed
out that Nevada practice was in conflict with the federal Constitution on
this matter but asserted that "this amendment shall not be construed as
conferring the rights of naturalization, suffrage, and office-holding upon
any native of the Chinese Empire."[18]

"Social Equalities"

The fact that blacks were taking advantage of their new freedom to
found newspapers and seek education was duly noted as a reason to give
them greater freedom. In May 1865 the *Appeal* commented on a newspaper published in New Orleans, *The Black Republican*, and also noted
that the *Elevator*, which was run by blacks, was being published in San
Francisco. These two papers, the paper said, "are beginning to demonstrate
that the black man *is* 'able to take care himself.'"[19]

Later that year the *Appeal* reported that there were three black newspapers in California and stated that the *Appeal* favored letting the editors
of these papers vote, "for one of these days, we may need their ballots to
help us sustain the liberty of the press."[20] A short time earlier the *Appeal*
had commented favorably on a black convention in California and reported
that a speech delivered at the convention by Peter Anderson, editor of the
Pacific Appeal, "will compare favorably with any white man's speech in
point of diction, and . . . in good common sense is infinitely superior
to any 'Democratic' speech or platform which we have read for the past
four years." As the editorial put it, "All that we need fear from the black
are the results of his ignorance. The intelligent and influential among
them seemed determined that their more unfortunate and degraded
brethren shall enjoy the blessing of education as fitting to their new condition of freedom. Give them a chance."[21]

In taking these stands, however, the *Appeal* was advocating suffrage and
legal rights for blacks in the South, *not* in Nevada, and it was careful to
make clear a number of times that it did not favor "social equality" for
blacks even in the South.[22]

The Civil Rights Bill

As the civil rights bill moved through Congress in 1866, the *Carson
Daily Appeal* and the *Territorial Enterprise* indicated strong support for
it, using many of the arguments advanced earlier in favor of black suffrage.
In February 1866 the *Appeal* reported that the bill was sure to pass Con-

gress but might be vetoed by President Johnson. The newspaper was convinced that Nevada's Senator James Nye would vote to override a veto but was unsure about Senator William M. Stewart. This being the case, an "emergency" existed, and it called for the legislature to act:

> Regarding the passage of the bill referred to as a most urgent necessity, we conceive it to be the duty as well as the right policy of the Legislature to pass a joint resolution instructing our Senators and requesting our Representative to sustain the action of Congress as against any contrary policy which may be adopted by the President.[23]

The legislature did not attempt to instruct the congressional delegation, but leading Nevada newspapers continued to advocate passage of the civil rights bill.

The *Appeal* demanded President Johnson's impeachment in February 1866,[24] and in March it attacked his veto of the civil rights bill as "unworthy of the Presidential office" and said of the bill that it "has the grand purpose in view of extending equal and just protection under the laws of the Nation to every person in the Republic."[25] In April the paper denied that the civil rights bill would give blacks the right to vote but asserted that it did and should give citizenship to all blacks and Chinese born in the country. The *Appeal* asserted that

> the great minds which framed the Civil Rights Bill appreciated that all men born or reared in the civilized communities of these United States were justly entitled to the protection of the law, toward the sustainment of which they must pay their proportion of the taxes, and should be entitled to justice and right under laws which are enacted for the public good.[26]

When Congress overrode the President's veto of the civil rights bill, the *Appeal* crowed: "The right is triumphant and the country is safe."[27]

Throughout this period the *Appeal* consistently supported the Freedmen's Bureau and the congressional bill to extend it, also vetoed by President Johnson and also enacted over his veto. It also supported the Fourteenth Amendment, which was moving through Congress at this time.[28]

Again though, as in the early period, the *Appeal* was thinking mainly about the South and about something short of "social equality." In an editorial supporting education for southern blacks, the *Appeal* asserted:

Nor have we heard that they [blacks], because of being educated, have
particular claims to social and marital equality with the whites; nor do
we think they will. But should they, these are not things which can be
forced; and the colored people are greatly in the minority in the United
States, and likely to so continue.[29]

"Social equality" undoubtedly meant "intermarriage" to most whites in
Nevada in the nineteenth century. For example, General Logan, in a speech
reprinted in the *Carson Daily Appeal*, asserted that "social intercourse will
regulate itself." He then went on to comment on the number of racially
mixed children in the South, who "would be almost as universally free as
they are slaves" if their "status" came from their fathers instead of their
mothers.[30] In 1866 the *Carson Daily Appeal*, in one of its criticisms of
President Johnson, referred to his "ridiculous" argument that the civil
rights bill "permitted the intermarriage of whites and blacks."[31]

"The Blacks Vote The Straight Republican Ticket"

The interest of the Republican party, particularly in the South, was
an element in the attitude of the Republican politicians and newspapers
in Nevada. In September 1867 the *Carson Daily Appeal* stated that there
was an "emergency" need to disfranchise "disloyal" southerners and
enfranchise black southerners. Although it admitted that it was desirable
in principle that "intelligence" should be a condition of voting, it said
that the situation in the South required enfranchising blacks before their
"intelligence" could be improved by education. "Intelligent disloyalty
and organized vice must be met and overcome by the best materials at
hand, and those materials are colored voters. Education, progressing with
wonderful strides, will, before many years, better fit the Freedmen for
the exercise of their new privilege."[32] The next day the newspaper put
it even more explicitly: "The free blacks of the South, with ballots in
their hands and protected in the enjoyment of the franchise by the strong
arm of this government, can save this nation from the horrors of rebel
rule."[33]

It is probable that even the small number of black voters in Nevada
were considered important by the Republican leaders, especially as they
were almost unanimously for that party during the nineteenth century.
In 1867 a former Nevada legislator who had moved to Montana, Jack
Simmons, wrote a friend in Nevada reporting that blacks had been
enfranchised there with good results; the Republicans, he thought,
had gained many black votes while losing an insignificant number of

white votes. "The blacks are possessed of sufficient intelligence to vote the straight Republican ticket," he said. Further, "[We don't have to] make him our equal socially, or sleep with him" just to get his vote.[34] The relationship of the black suffrage question to Nevada was discussed in another editorial in 1867. The *Carson Daily Appeal* asserted that enfranchising blacks in the South would result in "compromise" and

that compromise will result in the enfranchisement of disloyal whites at the South and the enfranchisement of loyal colored men at the North. We suspect that when the importance of the black vote at the South comes to be apparent, all parties will try to conciliate it. The "Democracy" cannot then afford to insult colored President makers in Dixie by denying the ballot to the dark skinned men of the North.

The compromise was explicitly advocated for Nevada. The *Appeal* urged large Union majorities in the legislature "if we would not have rebel sympathizers enfranchising what few white disloyalists there are within our limits to the exclusion of such darker skinned friends and supporters of the government as live amongst us."[35]

Before the 1870 general election, Congressman Thomas Fitch told the Nye County Union Republican Convention that "the Fifteenth Amendment has made voters of some 400 colored men in Nevada, of whom 395 will vote the straight Republican ticket."[36]

CIVIL RIGHTS FOR NEVADA?

The tendency of the most important Republican newspapers of Nevada to strongly support national Reconstruction for the South while failing to note the existence of racist laws in Nevada is particularly illustrated by the *Territorial Enterprise* during the late 1860s. In 1866 the *Enterprise* noted that the civil rights bill had made blacks citizens, and it wondered "how we could ever have regarded them in any other light." The newspaper similarly stated that "men blush to think that they were ever betrayed by prejudice into the support of such a measure of injustice . . . as the enormity of ruling persons from the witness-stand because of their color." The same editorial reported, incorrectly, that Nevada law no longer discriminated against blacks in court testimony. The newspaper noted that, despite strong Republican majorities in the territorial assembly of 1864, an attempt "to give the negro the right to testify" had been abandoned because of insufficient support. The editorial then claimed that "both California and Nevada did partial justice to the blacks, however, before the passage of the Civil Rights Law made State enactments in favor of negro testimony unnecessary."[37] The "partial justice" mentioned here no doubt refers to the fact that the 1865 legislature amended the law on testimony in criminal cases to allow a "negro, black or mulatto person" to testify against whites, with "the credibility of such . . . person . . . left entirely with the jury."

The reluctance of the *Enterprise* to apply its doctrines of racial equality to Nevada is also well illustrated by the reaction to an attempt to seat a black juror in a state court trial in 1866 and the failure to support its earlier judgment that laws against black testimony had been invalidated by the Civil Rights Act when the question actually arose in Nevada.

The reaction in Nevada to the 1866 Civil Rights Act illustrates the point that while Nevada's political leaders of this period applauded national action, they were unwilling to take similar action on a state level or to enforce the national law vigorously within the state. The Civil Rights Act granted national citizenship to the freed slaves, made it a crime for anyone acting "under color" of state law to deprive anyone of constitutional rights on racial grounds, and asserted that every citizen, without regard to race, had the same right "to make and enforce contracts, to sue, be parties, and give evidence, to inherit, purchase, lease, sell, hold, and convey real and personal property, and to full and equal benefit of all laws and proceedings for the security of person and property."[38]

In the first legislature after passage of this act, an attempt to repeal state laws in conflict with the Civil Rights Act failed. On the thirty-first day of the 1867 legislature, Assembly Bill 71, which would have repealed "all Acts or parts of Acts so far as they conflict with the provisions of" the Civil Rights Act, was introduced. It was promptly approved by the committee on federal relations and was unanimously passed by the assembly by a vote of twenty-two to zero.[39] When the bill reached the Senate, however, the senate judiciary committee approved it, but opposition arose from Charles A. Sumner of Storey County, who was president pro tem of the senate, and F. M. Proctor of Nye County. Sumner and Proctor filed a minority report recommending against passage of the bill, arguing that it was unnecessary if the Civil Rights Act was constitutional because "all laws, both National and State, which are in conflict with it, cease to be laws, and become inoperative until a repeal of said Act, as though never enacted." They indicated, however, that another complication was that some people, including President Andrew Johnson, thought the Civil Rights Act was unconstitutional. If the Supreme Court declared the act unconstitutional after the passage of Assembly Bill 71, they argued, "we would be placed in the anomalous condition of having abrogated important laws to prevent a supposed conflict with that which proves not to be a law." Sumner and Proctor also argued that the bill was too vague; "the general terms employed leave it in doubt and uncertainty as to which of the laws of the State are repealed, and the result may be that the laws will be by judicial construction declared repealed, which the present Legislature did not design to annul, and for the repeal of which a constitutional vote could not possibly be obtained." They argued further that the bill would

> render persons competent to act as jurors, and to testify in civil cases, who cannot become, under our Constitution, voters; while the undersigned feel confident that bills rendering such persons competent jurors and witnesses in all cases, could not receive the assent of the Legislature, or meet the approbation of the people of the State.[40]

Faced with these objections, the senate agreed to recommit the bill to the judiciary committee. Two days later the chairman of this committee, D. W. Welty of Lander County, reported that the committee "had come to a favorable conclusion on the subject matter thereof; had directed their chairman to report to the Senate a substitute for the same, and to recommend its passage." Five days after this, the substitute bill, Senate Bill 146, was reported. This bill would have specifically repealed the two sections of Nevada law restricting the testimony of blacks in civil and criminal cases. After debate in the committee of the whole, the bill was indefinitely postponed by a vote of nine to eight.[41] Thus, the attempt to annul a number of Nevada's racist laws because they were in conflict with national law was defeated, even after the legislature restricted its application to nothing more than the right to testify in court.

These events also illustrate the hypocrisy of the legislature. The same legislative session that refused to pass even a watered-down bill to apply the Civil Rights Act to Nevada and refused to consider black suffrage also adopted a strongly worded resolution endorsing national Reconstruction which referred to the Civil Rights Act as a "just and righteous measure" and urged

> that it should be rigidly enforced in every State and in the domain of the Federal Government, any statute, resolution, or custom of any State, Territory, or community, to the contrary notwithstanding; and, if necessary, the military, as well as the civil power of the Government, should be exercised therein.[42]

Governor H. G. Blasdel, in his address to the 1867 legislature, had
described the actions of the national government through 1866 in terms
that exaggerated considerably its efforts against racism but also suggested
that he approved of sweeping action against racial discrimination. He
said that "a great and magnanimous Government has . . . repealed all discriminating laws; obliterated all odious distinctions of race or class; made
all born upon the soil American citizens; guaranteed them protection as
such, and lifted a race heretofore oppressed to absolute equality before
the law."[43] The controversy over this bill, however, demonstrated that even
legislators were unclear about the effect of the Civil Rights Act on Nevada law.

Newspaper editors were also uncertain about the effect of the 1866 Civil
Rights Act, although there was probably some hypocrisy in this uncertainty.
In 1866 the *Territorial Enterprise* had stated that "the passage of the Civil
Rights law made State enactments in favor of negro testimony unnecessary."[44]
In early 1867, however, it urged the passage of Assembly Bill 71, asserting
that "the laws proposed to be repealed are those denying negroes the right
to testify in civil cases. This is all the bill asks for."[45] The newspaper did
not suggest that the bill was unnecessary because it had been repealed
already by the Civil Rights Act.

On March 18, 1867, Federal District Judge A. W. Baldwin instructed
the recently convened federal grand jury specifically to look into possible
violations of the Civil Rights Act. Reviewing the Civil War and the fact that
the war had led to the abolition of slavery, Judge Baldwin noted:

> Those Negro Slaves throughout the Struggle were, almost to a man, on
> the side of the Nation. They rendered it signal service. When the Cause
> was won, they were not forgotten, a debt was due to them. . . . To
> complete their enfranchisement it was necessary by amendment of
> the Constitution and by Congressional enactment to place them squarely
> upon the footing of equal citizenship.[46]

Judge Baldwin did not enlighten the grand jurors about the precise meaning
of the act, however. He read them the first two sections of the law and
said that it was

> too plain to be misunderstood, or to need any more explicit construc-
> tion from me than its letter imports. You must find indictments against
> any person who under color of any law of this State, has subjected or
> caused to be subjected, any inhabitant of this State, born in the United
> States, or not subject to any foreign power, to the deprivation of any
> of the rights just enumerated.

Section one of the act enumerated a number of rights that could not be denied on the basis of race or previous condition of servitude, including the right to "give evidence," all of which were to be enjoyed regardless of "any law, statute, ordinance, regulation or custom, to the contrary." It is difficult to see how either of Nevada's laws restricting testimony by blacks could be regarded as consistent with this statute. Judge Baldwin, however, neither noted any problems of this sort nor drew the attention of the grand jurors to the testimony laws. He did imply that some Nevada laws were in conflict with the Civil Rights Act by stating: "While it is a matter of regret that the Statutes of this State have not voluntarily been made harmonious with the Supreme law of the land, the failure to do so cannot affect the enforcement of the latter."

Section two of the act made it a crime for anyone acting "under color of any law, statute, ordinance, regulation, or custom" to deprive any person of "any right secured or protected by this Act, or to different punishment, pains, or penalties, on account of such person having at any time been held in a condition of Slavery or involuntary servitude . . . or by reason of his color or race, than is prescribed for the punishment of white persons." (In the 1940s, when the national government undertook to revitalize the Civil Rights Act, it experienced a great deal of difficulty in determining its meaning; the meaning of the phrase "under color of" state law was particularly obscure.)[47]

On April 29, 1867, the grand jury made its final report and was discharged. Although it had handed down sixty-eight indictments for violation of the revenue laws, it found none for violation of the Civil Rights Act. The jury's report stated:

> The Grand Jury . . . have directed their especial attention to ascertain whether any infractions of the Civil Rights Act occurred in the district. They have had before them one of the most intelligent and respectable colored men in Virginia City, but nothing in his evidence caused the Jury to suspect any party spoken of by him of the least wish or intention to deprive any colored person of his rights under the above mentioned act. The Jury have also made a point of questioning every witness brought before them as to their knowledge regarding the matter, and with great pleasure have the honor to state that a general feeling seems to exist throughout the Country to protect people of color in all their rights under the law.

A challenge to the testimony law by blacks, to be discussed in the next chapter, may have been based on the Civil Rights Act. In 1869 the legislature repealed the section of law forbidding nonwhites to testify in civil cases, although it did not repeal the statute discriminating against blacks testifying in criminal cases until 1881.[48]

In June 1866 the question of whether the Civil Rights Act invalidated the Nevada constitutional provision that excluded blacks from jury service because they were not qualified electors came up in a state court, and the conclusion was that it did not. The county assessor of Storey County had prepared a list of two hundred potential jurymen from the property tax rolls, and one of these was William A. G. Brown, a black citizen. Brown was the proprietor of the Boston Saloon, located at the corner of D and Union streets. His saloon was described in 1866 as "the popular resort for many of the colored population."[49] One of the attorneys for the plaintiff in the suit objected to Brown's presence on the ground that he was not a voter, while an attorney for the defendant supported Brown's right to serve on the ground that the Civil Rights Act had invalidated the constitutional provision. After an animated discussion between the attorneys, District Judge Caleb Burbank was called upon to decide the issue.[50] The judge was reported to have stated that "he would give no arbitrary decision in the matter of the Civil Rights bill, but did not consider that it annulled the provisions of the Constitution of the State of Nevada." This being so, the state constitution clearly prevented Mr. Brown from serving on a jury, and the judge so ruled.[51] Alfred Doten reported that there was a "big crowd in Court, as this was thought a test question."[52]

In an editorial the *Enterprise* charged that Brown's name had deliberately been introduced by the Democratic assessor who had "boasted that he would deal the Union (Congressional) party of the State a staggering blow by showing that the Civil Rights bill . . . conferred upon negroes the right to sit upon grand and trial juries." To the argument that the Civil Rights Act had invalidated the state constitutional provisions used to keep Brown from becoming a juror, the *Enterprise* argued: "The Act makes no such provision." The newspaper intimated that the Civil Rights Act might apply where one of the parties to a trial was black.

> Should it be found impossible to get an impartial white jury in trying a case between a white man and a black, whether in Nevada or South Carolina, would the negro not have a right to demand that a portion of the jury be composed of persons of his color? This is one of the possibilities of the law, but it had nothing to do with the case before the District Court yesterday.[53]

"WE CANNOT RECEIVE COLORED ORPHANS"

Although new racist laws were not being enacted, for the most part, during the late 1860s and 1870s, the legislature was not completely free of racist actions. Until the state supreme court ruled the practice unconstitutional on other grounds in 1881, several legislatures appropriated state funds for the Nevada Orphan Asylum at Virginia City, operated by a Catholic order, the Sisters of Charity, and at least once the legislature knowingly provided funds for it in spite of the fact that it admitted only white children. The orphanage opened October 16, 1864. When a committee of the state senate recommended in 1866 that it be supported by the state, the legislature passed a bill appropriating ten thousand dollars for it for the biennium. Governor H. G. Blasdel vetoed the bill on the grounds that it violated a constitutional prohibition against "sectarian instruction," that care of orphans should be a county function, and that the state could not afford the appropriation.[54] In 1867 an appropriation of five thousand dollars for the 1867-1869 biennium was voted by the legislature and approved by Governor Blasdel. Accompanying this appropriation was a requirement that the institution accept all orphans sent to it by boards of county commissioners, who in turn were empowered to send "any white orphan child or children" to the asylum.[55] In enacting this law, the legislators were accepting the racial restrictions of the Sisters of Charity. During legislative consideration of the bill, Sister M. Frederica of the home wrote a letter, which was quoted in the *Territorial Enterprise*, in which she stated, "We cannot receive colored orphans with the white ones. We can see to them in a separate house."[56] Because of this stand, the *Enterprise* opposed passage of the bill. In a later editorial, the newspaper indicated that it did not oppose segregated orphanages or schools but that it would oppose the exclusion of blacks altogether; "Strike the word 'white' from the bill, and our only objection to it will be removed."[57] The *Gold Hill Daily News* did not agree with the *Enterprise* in this stand. After the session was over, the *News* wrote of

how the Chinaman's organ and smaller but more reputable sheets bitterly denounced the proposition to lend State aid to take care of the parentless little ones of the State, because negroes and Mongolians were not to be admitted to the same board, dormitory and school room with white orphans. It is a great credit to the large majority of the legislators of Nevada, at the last regular session, that they discarded all appeals to prejudice, and gave an endowing endorsement to the Nevada Asylum.[58]

The 1869 legislature again appropriated funds for the orphan asylum, as did two subsequent legislatures, without the statutory restriction to white children; whether black children were in fact admitted during this time is not known.[59] (All 117 of the children reported at the Nevada Orphan Asylum by the census of population of 1880 were white.) In 1880 a constitutional amendment forbidding state support for sectarian institutions became part of the state constitution. When the state controller refused to make payments from the state treasury to the asylum because of this amendment, the state supreme court sustained him and ruled that state support of an institution run by a religious order was unconstitutional.[60] In 1869 the legislature created a state orphans' home, which began operations in 1870. There were never any legal racial restrictions on admission to the home, and in 1873 a black visitor to Nevada reported that a black child at the home was being treated like the other children.[61] According to the census of population of 1880, all of the children in the state orphans' home in that year were white.

BLACKS VOTE IN 1870

In spite of its obvious reluctance to respond to national moves that extended freedom to blacks, Nevada did not oppose the granting of the right to vote to blacks by the ratification of the Fifteenth Amendment, although it took ten years to amend its own constitution.[62] Apparently there was no attempt to keep blacks from voting in 1870, and the amendment also opened up jury service to them. Blacks voted in Hamilton City elections in spring 1870 and in state elections in fall 1870.

In Virginia City a newspaper reported that Dr. Stephenson, "a well known colored citizen of this city," had registered to vote, but it also said that "we understand that a person of lighter skin but darker heart refused to register because he would not place his name under the Doctor's." The newspaper opined that Dr. Stephenson would not have objected to having this man sign before him because "Dr. Stephenson has intelligence enough to see that it would not detract from him to have his name follow that of an inferior."[63]

F. G. Grice, a black barber who had long been active in defending black rights, even thought he detected a new respect for his race from Democrats after the ratification of the Fifteenth Amendment. Reporting on a major Democratic meeting in Elko, he remarked: "The speakers seem to abandon entirely the word 'niggers,' and assert in its place the word 'negroes,' and 'colored fellow citizens.'"[64]

It further appears that the Fifteenth Amendment opened up jury service to blacks. In July 1870 Grice reported from Elko that four blacks had been selected as jurors in a civil case in that county. (The men were J. M. Whitfield, Charles M. Wilson, Thomas Detter, and A. Scott.) Grice stated: "I think this is the first time in the annals of Nevada that colored men have acted as jurors."[65] In Virginia City in 1871, an all-black jury was empaneled to try a black man, Clem Berry, who was accused in justice court of disturbing the peace. Berry had "called for" the all-black jury, which found him guilty after a considerable amount of time spent in "fierce discussion." The *Territorial Enterprise* reported that "it was the first colored jury ever seen in this city and the novelty of the thing attracted quite a crowd of spectators."[66] In 1874 a letter from "Whiskiyou" in Elko reported that an unidentified black man had served on the jury in a murder trial; however, black jury service was still rare enough in Nevada in 1878 to merit a mention in the black press. In that year M. Howard of Virginia City, another black, was appointed a member of a jury to try a police officer, William M. Davis, who was accused of killing a black man.[67]

As late as 1875, the legislature endorsed efforts of the national government to uphold Reconstruction in the South.[68] Louisiana was one of the last two states to be "redeemed" by white supremacists, partly because the national government resisted the illegal suppression of the Reconstruction government. In September 1874 President Grant had used troops to restore to power the Republican government of Louisiana after that government was forced out of office by violence, and at the beginning of 1875 General P. R. de Trobriand, later supported by the President, forcibly halted a seizure of the lower house of the Louisiana Legislature by Democrats.[69] The 1875 legislature passed a resolution supporting the President's actions in Louisiana and specifically stating in reference to the latter incident that while it did not approve of "interference of the military with the civil power," it believed that General de Trobriand "was not guilty of any intentional wrong." The resolution approved "the course of the President of the United States in relation to the recent difficulties in Louisiana."[70]

"A MISCEGENATION SOCIETY
SOMEWHERE IN THE EAST"

The actions and attitudes of Nevada white officeholders have been reviewed at length. A similar pattern of open racism in the early 1860s followed by a gradual change toward greater acceptance of blacks as equals is suggested by scattered evidence of other kinds.

In November and December 1863 a debate over the question whether
Christian doctrine supports slavery was conducted through editorials and
letters to the *Virginia Evening Bulletin,* with the *Bulletin* taking an anti-
slavery position. On November 16 the *Bulletin* announced the arrival in
the city of Reverend M. Evans of the Methodist Episcopal Church South.
Noting that Mr. Evans believed in slavery, the *Bulletin* remarked that, for
this reason, "we could not, without doing violence to our feelings, wish
the new minister God's speed in his work." Mr. Evans replied with a letter
explaining the doctrines of his church on slavery. The editor of the *Bulletin*
stated that there was not "an iota of evidence" to support slavery in the
Bible and that it was "blaspheming" to assert that God favored it. The
same day, a letter to the editor from Reverend C. V. Anthony of the
northern Methodist church took issue with Evans' defense of slavery. Over
the next two weeks, the two ministers argued with each other over the
spiritual support for slavery, with the *Bulletin* itself remaining relatively
silent on the subject but consistently attacking slavery as unchristian when
it expressed an opinion.[71]

The same newspaper in the same year clearly expressed a judgment
that blacks were inferior. An editorial in the *Virginia Evening Bulletin* in
October 1863 began with the question: "What shall we do with the negro—
the poor, unfriended, persecuted, outcast son of Ham?" The editorial
clearly rejected slavery but indicated that "there may be some who will
favor the total exclusion of all those races who cannot become citizens."
While admitting that blacks may be "the unconscious and inert cause . . .
of all our present national calamities," the newspaper went on to deny
that blacks could legitimately be blamed for these calamities. Because
they had originally been brought to and kept in the United States against
their will, blacks could not be held responsible for the difficulties their
presence had caused.

The main issue involving blacks, according to this editorial, was whether
to admit them and Chinese to the state. While Chinese could not be
excluded because of treaties with China, blacks *could* legally be excluded,
and in several northern states they were actually excluded before the
Civil War, the newspaper pointed out. But the *Bulletin* argued against this
position: "We believe it would be the most humane and general policy
to let them come." Furthermore, a government that had to rely on exclusion of "deleterious substances" was displaying weakness. The *Bulletin*
thus was clearly against slavery and against the exclusion of blacks from
Nevada—but it also clearly assumed that blacks were inferior, and it
wanted to maintain this condition.

Then let them come, from all classes, kingdoms and nations, who have a wish to come, and by our laws we should provide rigidly against amalgamation, so as to prevent our own race from degenerating, keep them in their proper sphere and make useful laborers of them. *In the course of many centuries* they may become numerous as a class and then give us some trouble if they should not be admitted to the full privileges of citizenship, but in the same course of time our institutions will have had an opportunity of exerting upon them the salutary influences of religion, morality, and order, nor is it probable that their increase will be anything to compare to that of our own race, who will thus be enabled always to maintain the superiority.[72]

The attitudes of whites toward blacks are illustrated by exclusion of blacks from a Fourth of July parade. In 1865, the Comstock held an elaborate Independence Day celebration, to celebrate the end of the Civil War. Most elements of the community participated in a parade which was a major event of the day; the Mexican Association and a mounted group of Paiutes joined the parade, although the latter were assigned to the last position. The blacks, however, "were not allowed a place in the procession."[73] The reason was clearly opposition from some whites; Alfred Doten, a prominent Comstock journalist, noted in his journal that the blacks "were not invited to participate, therefore the question of dignity among the scrub-stock and snobs was not brought to the test, although they freely expressed the determination 'not to turn out at all if the niggers did.'"[74] The *Territorial Enterprise* was hypocritical enough to criticize the California cities of Placerville and Stockton for withdrawing blacks from their parades when whites protested and to express pleasure that such feelings "did not find expression in Nevada."[75] State Senator Charles A. Sumner apparently saw no conflict between praising the "music of [the] falling shackles" of the slaves "shaking and enrapturing the souls of good willing men all over the earth" and the exclusion of the local blacks from the parade.[76]

Samuel Clemens, who became Mark Twain during his three-year stay in Nevada, was a reporter on the *Territorial Enterprise* from 1862 to 1864. When he left Nevada in May 1864, a story he had written was partly responsible for his departure. The background for the incident was Twain's racial views. Arthur Pettit has shown that he had had strongly racist views as a youth and still held them during his stay in Virginia City. Several of his Nevada newspaper articles discussed "niggers" in derogatory terms, and one of his celebrated hoaxes ridiculed the notion that it was wrong to use "language derogatory of the character of our fellow-citizens of African descent."[77]

In May 1864 a group of women in Carson City held a ball to raise money for the Sanitary Fund, the Civil War equivalent of the Red Cross. Twain admitted later that, while drunk, he had written a story asserting that it had been "stated that the money raised at the Sanitary Fancy Dress Ball, recently held in Carson for the St. Louis Fair, had been diverted from its legitimate course, and was to be sent to aid a Miscegenation Society somewhere in the East." He had intended to publish the story but was talked out of it by Dan De Quille, a more sober or responsible member of the *Enterprise* staff. Twain, however, left the story on a table in the *Enterprise* office, where the composing-room foreman found it and printed it. Although the story appeared with a statement that it was a hoax, the women who had held the ball were furious. They wrote a letter of protest to the *Enterprise*, which that paper did not print, although it was published in the *Virginia Union*. Several days later, Twain wrote an apology, which the *Enterprise* published.[78]

In the meantime, however, he had also started a controversy with the *Union* over the amount of money the *Union* had contributed to the Sanitary Fund, and this controversy had escalated to the point of Twain's issuance of a duelling challenge to the *Union*'s editor, Laird. Not all the husbands of the Carson City women were mollified by his apology to them, either. One, W. K. Cutler, issued a duelling challenge to Twain, and Twain at one point wrote to his brother Orion that he was "a man open to a challenge from three persons, & already awaiting the issue of such a message to another." The identity of the other two challengers (besides Laird and Cutler) is not known. None of these challenges resulted in an actual duel, but Twain abruptly left Nevada on May 28, 1864, with his friend Steve Gillis, who had become embroiled in Twain's controversies.

The exact role played in his flight from Nevada by Twain's unsupported charge that Sanitary Fund contributions were being diverted to a miscegenation society remains unclear, but "probably no issue could have generated more controversy in the 1860s . . . than racial amalgamation."[79] Evidently not many people in western Nevada were willing to treat such a hoax as a joke to be passed off lightly, and the incident therefore says something significant about white racial attitudes.

In 1867, the warden of the state prison, James S. Slingerland, thanked a black for helping save the prison from a disastrous fire. In reporting a fire at the institution on the night of May 1, 1867, in his *Biennial Report*, the warden wrote:

Before it was discovered that the fire was coming up through the floor of the upper story, a colored man employed at the Warm Springs Hotel, by the name of Alphonso Moore, known as "Mose," was despatched to Carson for assistance, which arrived in time to aid materially in preventing the escape of prisoners, and in saving a portion of the building. Much credit is due him for his disinterested act.[80]

In 1869, the senate adopted a resolution to require the board of state prison commissioners to pay two hundred dollars each to two engine companies that had fought the fire and one hundred dollars to "the Negro boy [*sic*] 'Mose.'" The assembly, however, rejected the resolution without a record vote.[81] Alphonso Moore was identified as a thirty-year-old laborer born in Louisiana by the census in 1870; in 1880 he was still living in Carson City and the other information about him was the same, but his age was given as fifty-seven.

"INSUFFICIENT TO SUBSTANTIATE THE CHARGE"

There is some evidence about attitudes of white fraternal organizations toward participation by blacks in these organizations. Two black Prince Hall Masonic lodges existed in Nevada during the nineteenth century; there is no reason to doubt that white Masonic organizations in Nevada joined almost all of their brethren in other states in refusing to recognize them as legitimate Masonic organizations. For example, the white Masonic Grand Lodge in California adopted a resolution "forbidding intercourse with clandestine 'negro Masons'" in 1854; this decision was reaffirmed when it was questioned in 1871, and it was still regarded as being in force in 1931. Because the California Grand Lodge was one of those that objected to the granting of "partial recognition to Prince Hall Masonry" by the white Grand Lodge of Massachusetts in 1947, evidently this attitude was still present at that late date. Blacks were theoretically eligible to become members of white Masonic lodges in California from at least 1871 on,[82] however, and from at least 1873 on black Masons had the same legal rights to visit white lodges as white Masons.[83] In practice, it was probably seldom possible for blacks to become members of white lodges or be accepted by them as visitors, but there were no rules against it.

The contrast between rules and practice, and the fact that practice sometimes was changed because of conflict with the rules, is revealed by an incident involving a Nevada member of a white Odd Fellows lodge in the 1870s. H. M. Nichols, a miner, was a member of Dayton Lodge No. 5 of the International Order of Odd Fellows in Dayton, Nevada. While living in Georgetown, California, he married Laura M. Lucket, on May 16, 1870. Members of the Georgetown lodge of the IOOF wrote the Dayton lodge to say that it was their duty to inform the Nevada lodge "of the unbecoming conduct of one of your members that of Brother H. M. Nickols [sic] in marrying a mulatto woman of this place and is living with her in this vicinity." In April 1871 W. S. McFadden, a member of the Dayton lodge, formally accused Nichols "of violating the rules, regulations, and principals [sic] of our order in this as follows: That on or about the 16th day of May, 1870, in the County of El Dorado, State of California, said Bro. H. M. Nichols, did marry a Mulatto woman and has been living with her in said place."

Nichols was "tried" by a committee of five Odd Fellows from the Georgetown lodge in May 1871. Evidently Nichols and his lodge brothers were not in agreement about the race of his wife. Nichols said that he considered "her to be a Quadroon" but that he did not know the race of her parents. None of the brothers could testify with certainty that Mrs. Nichols was a mulatto. One said that she had some "negro" characteristics, a second said he considered her mother to be a mulatto, and a third said he considered her to be a quadroon but that her grandmother was reputed to be a Delaware Indian.

The results of the hearing were evaluated by a committee of five members of the Dayton lodge (M. C. Hicky, J. H. Jaqua, S. Stoner, M. Johnson, and L. S. Crockett), meeting with W. S. McFadden, who had made the charges against Nichols. This committee unanimously reached several conclusions. They concluded that the testimony presented to them had not been properly "certified" as having come from an Odd Fellows lodge, that there was no proof that the persons testifying were Odd Fellows and had testified under oath, and that the testimony, in any case, was "insufficient to substantiate the charge." The most important conclusion of the committee, however, was "that your Comt^{ee} have been unable to find any legislation in our order upon this subject or that the same is in violation to any printed or established rule or principal [sic] of our order. We therefore recommend that the same be dismissed or ignored."[84]

Although there is a farcical aspect to this incident, several conclusions can be drawn from it. First, an assertion that a brother had married a mulatto was taken seriously; formal charges and a "trial" were held, and the members of two lodges contemplated disciplinary action against a member believed to have married a mulatto. Second, it turned out that there were no IOOF rules or regulations forbidding the conduct complained of, and ultimately the decision was made to dismiss the charges for this reason; in other words, when the racist attitudes of the members came into conflict with nonracist formal rules, the racist attitudes gave way. Third, the Dayton lodge members refused to act against a white brother; it is more difficult to believe that the conflict between their racist views and the rules of the organization would have been resolved in favor of a black applicant for membership.

By 1881, blacks could vote, hold office and serve on juries, testify in both civil and criminal proceedings on the same basis as whites, and attend the public schools, and a number of other minor discriminatory laws had been repealed. However, the antimiscegenation law and two minor discriminatory laws remained on the statute books,[85] and the Nevada legislature did not enact any laws to forbid discrimination on a racial basis until the 1960s. The result, then, was that although there were few racially discriminatory laws applying to blacks by the 1880s, there was no attempt to overcome private discrimination.

NOTES

1. *Territorial Enterprise*, November 27, 1866.
2. See John Koontz and Arthur Palmer, *Political History of Nevada*, 5th ed. (Carson City: State Printing Office, 1965), pp. 109-111, for lists of major state officers. Material on the partisan composition of the legislatures is from Myron Angel, ed., *History of Nevada, 1881* (Berkeley, California: Howell-North, 1958), and Russell R. Elliott, *History of Nevada* (Lincoln: University of Nebraska Press, 1973).
3. Angel, *History of Nevada*, p. 96; Hubert Howe Bancroft, *History of Nevada, Colorado and Wyoming, 1540-1888* (San Francisco: The History Company, 1890), p. 170.
4. See John Gregg Folkes, *Nevada's Newspapers: A Bibliography* (Reno: University of Nevada Press, 1964), pp. 147-149, and Richard E. Lingenfelter, *The Newspapers of Nevada, 1858-1958* (San Francisco: John Howell Books, 1964), pp. 84-85.
5. Folkes, *Nevada's Newspapers*, p. 144, and Lingenfelter, *Newspapers of Nevada*, pp. 52-54.
6. *Carson Daily Appeal*, November 18, 1865.
7. Ibid.
8. Ibid., June 14, 1865.
9. Ibid., July 22, 1865.

10. Ibid., November 10, 1865.

11. William Hanchett, "Yankee Law and the Negro in Nevada, 1861-1869," *Western Humanities Review* 10 (Summer 1956): 247-248.

12. See William Gillette, *The Right to Vote: Politics and the Passage of the Fifteenth Amendment* (Baltimore: Johns Hopkins Press, 1965), p. 54, and George Rothwell Brown, ed., *Reminiscences of Senator William M. Stewart* (New York: Neale Publishing Co., 1908), pp. 231-238. However, Senator Stewart said many years later that he did not believe that the measures would be effective in assuring black suffrage in the South "when the whites of the South undertook, in good faith, to carry on their own governments." Ibid., p. 232.

13. Gillette, *Right to Vote*, p. 84, and Brown, *Reminiscences*, pp. 237-238.

14. Nevada, Assembly, *Journal*, 1869, pp. 243-244; Nevada, Senate, *Journal*, 1869, pp. 249-250; Nevada, *Statutes*, 1869, Senate Resolution 21, p. 302.

15. Assembly, *Journal*, pp. 227, 238; Senate, *Journal*, p. 231.

16. *Carson Daily Appeal*, January 13, 1877.

17. *First Biennial Message* of Gov. John H. Kinkead, January 7, 1879, p. 17.

18. *Statutes*, 1877, Assembly Resolution 6, pp. 213-214; *Statutes*, 1879, Assembly Resolution 7, pp. 149-150.

19. *Carson Daily Appeal*, May 30, 1865.

20. Ibid., November 14, 1865.

21. Ibid., November 4, 1865.

22. Ibid., August 27, September 22, November 14, 18, 1865.

23. Ibid., February 9, 1866. The Nevada constitution provides that "the people shall have the right . . . to instruct their representatives." Art. I, sec. 10.

24. *Carson Daily Appeal*, February 27, 1866.

25. Ibid., March 30, 1866.

26. Ibid., April 4, 1866.

27. Ibid., April 8, 1866.

28. Ibid., September 5, 1865, February 9, March 7, April 5, May 23, 26, September 12, 1866.

29. Ibid., September 7, 1867.

30. Ibid., August 27, 1865.

31. Ibid., May 19, 1866.

32. Ibid., September 17, 1867.

33. Ibid., September 18, 1867.

34. *Elevator*, November 29, 1867, reprinting an article from the *Territorial Enterprise*, n.d.

35. *Carson Daily Appeal*, November 12, 1867.

36. *Territorial Enterprise*, September 18, 1870.

37. Ibid., May 26, 1866. The Fourteenth Amendment later put the extension of citizenship on a constitutional basis.

38. *14 Stat.* 27-30. See also Loren Miller, *The Petitioners* (New York: Random House, 1960), pp. 88-89, 98.

39. Assembly, *Journal,* 1867, pp. 11, 126, 133.

40. Senate, *Journal,* 1867, p. 143.

41. Ibid., p. 152.

42. *Statutes,* 1867, Assembly Resolution 2, pp. 180-181. The 1867 legislature ratified the Fourteenth Amendment on January 22, early in the session. *Statutes,* 1867, Assembly Resolution 4, pp. 136-137.

43. *Second Biennial Message of Gov. H. G. Blasdel,* p. 3.

44. *Territorial Enterprise,* May 23, 1866.

45. Ibid., February 20, 1867.

46. Quotations in this section are from the minute book of the United States District Court for Nevada, pp. 93-96, 123-124, in the District Court Clerk's Office, Reno, Nevada. The charge to the jury was noted by the *Carson Daily Appeal,* March 20, 1867.

47. See Robert K. Carr, *Federal Protection of Civil Rights* (Ithaca, New York: Cornell University Press, 1947).

48. *Statutes,* 1869, chap. 112, sec. 376, and *Statutes,* 1881, chap. 55.

49. *Territorial Enterprise,* August 7, 1866.

50. Caleb B. Burbank was one of the three district judges elected in Storey County in 1864, all of whom served until 1867; he was not re-elected in 1866. Angel, *History of Nevada,* pp. 98-99, 337.

51. *Territorial Enterprise,* June 8, 1866.

52. Walter Van Tilburg Clark, ed., *The Journals of Alfred Doten, 1849-1903* (Reno: University of Nevada Press, 1973), p. 889.

53. *Territorial Enterprise,* June 8, 1866.

54. Senate, *Journal,* 1866, pp. 109-114, 147, 217-218, 252-253.

55. *Statutes,* 1867, chap. 69.

56. *Territorial Enterprise,* March 3, 1867.

57. Ibid., March 5, 1867.

58. *Gold Hill Daily News,* June 10, 1867.

59. *Statutes,* 1869, chap. 59.

60. State ex. rel. Nevada Orphan Asylum v. J. F. Hallock, 16 Nev. 373 (1881-1882).

61. *Elevator,* December 13, 1873 (letter from Mrs. D. D. Carter).

62. Chinese and Indians were another story; the 1880 state constitutional amendment specifically asserted that the right to vote was not being extended to a "native of the Chinese Empire." Most Chinese were aliens ineligible to become citizens by naturalization at this time, and it is not clear whether the few who were United States citizens were allowed to vote. Indians were largely excluded from voting by the fact that they were not citizens and by the fact that "uncivilized American Indians" were exempted from payment of the poll tax, which was a condition for voting.

63. *Territorial Enterprise,* April 5, 1870.

64. *Elevator*, June 17, 1870.

65. Ibid., July 8, 1870.

66. *Territorial Enterprise*, August 30, 1871. Berry was identified by the 1870 census as a thirty-one-year old laborer born in North Carolina, with a personal estate of $1,000. He was then living in Hamilton in White Pine County with two white men, the owner and clerk of a hardware store. It is not clear what his occupation was at the time of his conviction, but the *Territorial Enterprise* remarked that, because of his forty-seven dollar fine, "he will have to sell a good deal of hot corn to get even—not less than 470 ears at the ruling rate." Ibid., p. 3.

67. *Elevator*, February 28, 1874; *Pacific Appeal*, April 6, 20, 1878.

68. The 1875 legislature had appointed Jacob Yates, "a colored man," as a legislative messenger. See *Pacific Appeal*, January 30, 1875.

69. See Ella Lonn, *Reconstruction in Louisiana after 1868* (New York: G. P. Putnam's Sons, 1918), pp. 269-275, 278-291, 295-298.

70. *Statutes*, 1875, Senate Resolution 11, pp. 177-178. A number of state legislatures, including some in the North, censured President Grant for his actions in the Louisiana legislative dispute. See Lonn, *Reconstruction in Louisiana*, p. 304.

71. *Virginia Evening Bulletin*, November 16-18, 1863.

72. Ibid., October 1, 1863 (my italics). The same newspaper was at this time telling dialect stories about "niggers" in the South, emphasizing what it was obviously assumed would be regarded as comical behavior by whites. Ibid., October 28, 1863, January 5, 1864.

73. *The Celebration of the Eighty-eighth Anniversary of the Declaration of Independence, July 4th, 1865, at Virginia and Gold Hill, Nevada* (San Francisco: Commercial Steam Presses, 1865), p. 31. Reprinted from *Virginia Daily Union*, n.d.

74. Clark, *Journals of Alfred Doten*, p. 842.

75. *Territorial Enterprise*, July 6, 1865.

76. *The Celebration of the Eighty-eighth Anniversary*, p. 28.

77. Paul Fatout, *Mark Twain in Virginia City* (Bloomington: Indiana University Press, 1964), p. 180, and Arthur G. Pettit, "Mark Twain's Attitude Toward the Negro in the West, 1861-1867," *Western Historical Quarterly* 1 (January 1970): 51-62.

78. Most of the surviving newspaper articles and letters bearing on this incident have been collected by Henry Nash Smith, ed., *Mark Twain of the Enterprise* (Berkeley: University of California Press, 1957), pp. 187-205.

79. Pettit, "Mark Twain's Attitude," p. 56. Effie Mona Mack virtually ignores the miscegenation part of the incident in her discussion of Twain's last days in Nevada, while Arthur G. Pettit omits mention of Twain's quarrel with the *Union*, which did not have a racial component. More balanced treatments are to be found in accounts by Paul Fatout and Henry Nash Smith. See Effie Mona Mack, *Mark Twain in Nevada* (New York: Charles

Scribner's Sons, 1947), pp. 307-326; Pettit, "Mark Twain's Attitude," pp. 51-62; Paul Fatout, *Mark Twain in Virginia City,* pp. 196-211; and Smith, *Mark Twain of the Enterprise,* pp. 187-205.

80. *Biennial Report* of the Warden of the Nevada State Prison, 1867-1868, pp. 6-7.

81. Senate, *Journal,* 1869, pp. 266, 278; Assembly, *Journal,* 1869, pp. 265, 267.

82. However, a Mason had to be "free-born, neither a slave nor the son of a bondwoman," a requirement which would have disqualified many nineteenth-century blacks. See John Stewart Ross, *Compilation of Approved Decisions and Regulations of Free and Accepted Masons of California* (San Francisco: Published by order of Grand Lodge, 1932), p. 75.

83. Ibid., pp. 74-78; William J. Whalen, *Handbook of Secret Organizations* (Milwaukee: Bruce Publishing Co., 1966), p. 115. Other reference works consulted are Albert C. Stevens, comp. and ed., *The Cyclopedia of Fraternities,* 2d ed. (New York: E. B. Treat and Co., 1907), pp. 72-78, and Arthur Preuss, comp., *A Dictionary of Secret and Other Societies* (St. Louis: B. Herder Book Co., 1924), pp. 324-328.

84. See Theron Fox, ed., *Mother Lode Race Incident* (San Jose, California: Harlan-Young Press, 1966).

85. The laws specifying that attorneys had to be white and restricting militia service to whites were not repealed until 1893. See *Statutes,* 1893, chap. 3, 40. The antimiscegenation law was not repealed until 1959 after it had been declared unconstitutional by a state court. See *Statutes,* 1959, chap. 193 and Case No. 177539, Department No. 3, 2d Judicial District Court of Nevada (Washoe County), December 9-10, 1958.

—4—

"We Demand Our God-Given Inalienable Right"

In the late 1850s and early 1860s black leaders in the West had almost given up in despair their attempts to secure "simple justice" by the repeal of racist laws. At the point of greatest disillusionment, however, the events set in motion by the Civil War started a process that led to the abolition of slavery and beyond it to an attempt to repeal most of the worst laws and to allow blacks more freedom. In this new environment, black leaders once more began to organize to assert their rights and to work actively for the repeal or modification of racist legislation. A growing militance and optimism in the black community seems evident in California and Nevada; this mood culminated in the great celebrations of the ratification of the Fifteenth Amendment in 1870 and, in Nevada, led to the greatest triumph of black activism in the state, the overturning of the racist school law. It is probably safe to say that most black leaders in Nevada thought by the early 1870s that they had attained equality before the law and effective equality in most other areas. The significant exception was "social equality"; the antimiscegenation law remained on the books without effective challenge, and many blacks did not advocate equality for their race when it came to marriage with whites.

Throughout the 1860s and 1870s Nevada's small black population remained linked to black communities in California in several ways. Again, as in earlier years, the first stop in the West for many of the most able and active blacks was California, and they then spread out to Nevada and other western states. Thomas Detter is an excellent example of this process but there are others. William H. Hall, who had been active in black conventions and similar activities in New York before coming West, was president of one of the California colored conventions of the 1850s and an active participant in the 1865 convention in that state. He was in Nevada for several years in the late 1860s and participated in the mining boom at Treasure Hill.

Charles Wilson, another California leader of the 1850s, also went to Nevada, and the poet James M. Whitfield spent at least a year in the state at the end of the 1860s. For several decades after the early 1860s there were black weekly newspapers in San Francisco that served to link the black leaders of the West; blacks in Nevada as well as other western states read these papers and contributed to them. The *Pacific Appeal* was founded in 1862 and continued into the 1880s. For its first three years, its publisher was Peter Anderson and its editor was Philip A. Bell, who had edited black newspapers in the East before coming to California. In 1865 Bell founded his own newspaper, the *Elevator*, and from this point on there were two principal weeklies in San Francisco, with Anderson editing the *Pacific Appeal*. Probably the California black community was looked to for leadership to some extent because leaders there had had longer experience with civil rights efforts, even though, in cases such as school discrimination in Nevada, California was behind other states.

"TO PETITION FOR EQUAL RIGHTS BEFORE THE LAW"

Even before Nevada became a state, blacks petitioned for an end to racist laws and sought through legal action to accomplish the same result. Although their efforts evidently had little effect, with the exception of their assault on the school law, until national laws and constitutional amendments overrode state action, their efforts, which began in 1863, were persistent and able for several years.

In July 1863 a letter from a correspondent in Virginia City to one of the black papers in San Francisco called for a convention of blacks in Nevada, chiefly to secure the right for blacks to testify from the territorial assembly, which was scheduled to meet in 1864.[1]

A meeting of black residents was held in Virginia City on December 1, 1863, to plan a celebration of the first anniversary of the Emancipation Proclamation for January 1, 1864. The meeting, chaired by R. H. Scott, adopted the following resolutions:

> That we heartily tender our thanks to Abraham Lincoln, . . . for the liberation of many of our enslaved brethren in the southern portion of the United States. . . .
>
> That the Emancipation Proclamation of Abraham Lincoln has created in us a strong desire to become men among men—to prove ourselves worthy of the gift of God to man, Liberty . . . by going forth to battle against the enemies of God, Liberty and Union.[2]

The planned meeting was held on January 1 in the First Baptist Church. In addition to a major address by Thomas R. Street, the celebration included the reading of the Emancipation Proclamation, music by a brass band, the reading of an original poem by S. Shifton, various other remarks, the singing of "John Brown," and supper and a dance in the evening.

Street's address partly gave thanks for the Emancipation Proclamation, which he saw as the beginning of the end of slavery everywhere. The nineteenth century had begun with slavery a widespread institution, he said, but it had since been abolished in the British and French West Indies and in several of the United States, "and it is not unlikely that the sun of 1870 may shine upon a mighty nation, whose soil no bondsman's foot shall ever again be pressed. Slavery . . . has met the all conquering hosts of freedom, and the end is before us." He was more realistic about the reasons why the Emancipation Proclamation had been issued than many subsequent orators have been: "The principle which it embodies and utilizes, is the outgrowth of the advancement of the age, but it is nonetheless welcome to its recipients . . . because of its being acquiesced in by a majority of the American people as a military necessity."

Street also strongly endorsed a goal of full liberty for "colored" Americans, citing the Declaration of Independence as an ideal, although disavowing any interest in "social equality."

> I speak of the rights of the colored race; it is a subject about which there has been much of misrepresentation and much of unseemly ridicule. We do not ask from the Anglo-Saxon what he calls social equality. We have as little desire for social equality with him, as he can have for social equality with us. . . . We prefer to mix with our

own people, to form our own society, to have our own customs, our own manners and our own destiny. . . . The rights we ask are those which properly belong to every member of the human family, of whatever country or race, the right to eat what we earn, to enjoy unmolested our lives, liberty, and property, and to be justly protected in the exercise of those rights by the Government which we aid in supporting and preserving. We demand for ourselves and for our posterity only that liberty which is our God-given inalienable right.

Specifically he noted that California had just repealed a restriction on the right of blacks to testify, and he expressed his "hope that the first Legislature of the dawning State of Nevada will adopt a similar measure for our civil and criminal Code."

Citing Hannibal, Ptolemy, and other historic figures, the orator asserted that "the pages of classic history blaze with the achievements of men upon whose brows the sun of Asia and Africa burned a dusky hue." Finally, he expressed succinctly a pride of race and of nation and a general expectation of progress. "I am proud of my race and my country, and I am led to believe that we shall not prove unworthy of our advancement and our destiny."[3]

Street participated in the celebration of ratification of the Fifteenth Amendment in Virginia City in 1870; he died in Reno in November 1873.[4] He does not appear to have been enumerated by census takers in 1870.

Whether any effort was made during the 1864 legislative session to petition that body for legislative changes is not clear, but a petition was introduced in the 1865 legislature, the first under statehood. On February 28, 1865, Senator Charles A. Sumner of Storey County presented to the senate a petition "praying for the passage of a law allowing blacks and mulattoes testify in the courts of justice of this State." Probably the petition was the work of black citizens.[5]

In mid-1865, a series of meetings in Virginia City led to the formation of the Nevada Executive Committee, designed to press for legal equality. The first meeting was held in the First Baptist Church on June 19, 1865, and included "Colored People" from Virginia City, Gold Hill, and Silver City. The purpose of this meeting was to organize a state executive committee, "whose object it shall be to take steps to petition the next Legislature for the Right of Suffrage and equal rights before the Law to all the Colored Citizens of the State of Nevada." The meeting was called to order by R. H. Scott, but Dr. W. H. C. Stephenson was appointed chairman. A nominating committee was appointed, and it proposed a seven-member executive committee; however, it was decided to wait for another public

meeting before electing this committee.[6] The next meeting was held on
June 29; at that time the slate presented earlier, with one substitution
caused by the fact that one of the nominees had left Virginia City, was
approved. The first meeting of the executive committee was on July 5. At
this meeting Dr. Stephenson was chosen permanent president, Reverend
John T. Jenifer was named secretary, and Samuel T. Wagner became
treasurer. Subcommittees on resolutions and petitions, finances, and
expenses and printing were appointed, and a public meeting was called
for July 12 to be held at the AME church. At this meeting, several resolutions were adopted. The first referred to the participation of blacks in
the Fourth of July parade:

> That the recent dissatisfaction manifested by some of the white citizens
> of California at the invitation extended to the colored citizens, to
> participate in the celebration of the Fourth of July, as well as the in-
> difference with which they were treated in this city, is but the exhibition
> of prejudice against the colored man, and the relic of the principles of
> slave power and Copperhead Democracy.

A second resolution pledged cooperation with the California executive
committee, and the final resolution expressed the aims of the Nevada
Executive Committee in broad terms:

> That the present and future prospects of the colored citizens of the
> United States demand renewed efforts on their part in the redress
> of their grievances and the maintenance of civil and political rights.
> Our watch-word should be; "Equality before the Law."

A subsequent meeting of the executive committee on July 19, 1865,
discussed the "past, present and future condition of the colored people
in the United States." A letter from Chief Justice Salmon O. Chase to a
committee of "colored" men in New Orleans was read "with pleasure."[7]
   Whether this committee met between July and December is not clear,
but on December 5, 1865, a convention was held at the First Baptist Church
in Virginia City. Dr. Stephenson presided, the minutes of some previous
meeting were read, and the delegates from Virginia City were confirmed
(there were no delegates from other cities). A committee was appointed
to "prepare business," and while it was deliberating Dr. Stephenson and
others addressed the convention. On the advice of the first committee,
standing committees on petitions and resolutions, finance, and publication

were appointed. The next evening another session of the convention heard Dr. Stephenson report on petitions and resolutions plus an "Address to the People of Nevada" from the committee; it adopted the address, with instructions to have it published in the press of the state. A petition, "Equality before the Law," was also read and adopted, and plans were made to circulate it for presentation to the 1866 legislature.[8]

On January 1, 1866, a celebration of the anniversary of issuance of the Emancipation Proclamation was held in the First Baptist Church in Virginia City. Reportedly the audience was "three-fourths white" but blacks provided the program. David W. Sands, president of the day, read a poem, "America" was sung by his wife Laura Sands, the Emancipation Proclamation was read, followed by "unbounded applause," and there was an oration by Dr. Stephenson.[9]

While he paid much attention to recounting the history of the Civil War and the abolition of slavery as a result of that war, Dr. Stephenson also asserted boldly that blacks wanted and expected to receive the full "God-given" rights of American citizens. He optimistically asserted that "the cause of humanity, the principles of liberty and justice, the question of every man's right to compensation for his labor, has been settled in this nation forever." The Emancipation Proclamation, he said, was

the entering wedge to the destruction of all those disabilities, the offspring of slavery, which a portion of the citizens of this Republic endure—the offspring of oppression, but not of complexion. . . . In the death of slavery will eventually follow the investing of all men with civil and political rights. The Declaration of Independence must and will be recognized as the law of the land.

The role of black citizens in achieving the implementation of these rights was not to be a passive one. Dr. Stephenson told his predominantly white audience:

The prospect of our oppressed race is a glorious future. It is for colored men to show themselves equal to the emergency—to fearlessly meet the opponents of justice, and contend for rights and privileges which might withholds from them. . . . Let colored men contend for "Equality before the Law." Nothing short of civil and political rights.[10]

The petition drawn up at the January meeting and an accompanying memorial were presented to the legislature in February 1866. On the

forty-fourth day of the session, February 13, 1866, Senator Charles
Sumner presented these documents to the senate. They were not printed
in the senate *Journal*, but the summary of them there indicates that the
"colored citizens" prayed for "an amendment to the Constitution allowing
colored people to vote; also, that the Civil Practice Act be so amended as
to allow colored people to testify in civil cases, in Courts of this State;
also, for their proportion of the school moneys." The *Journal* indicates
that the petition and memorial were "laid on the table."[11]

The memorial, which was described as "a model document" by a
Virginia City correspondent, was signed by Dr. Stephenson, D. W. Sands,
Moses Elliott, William T. Courts, John Waters, and Joseph Price. It asked
the legislature to allow persons of African descent to vote, to testify in
civil cases, and to be allowed to use the public schools. Specifically, the
legislature was addressed as follows:

> The Colored Citizens of the State of Nevada, in Convention assembled,
> respectfully pray your honorable body, that this Petition and the
> Address which accompanies the same, showing forth honorable notice
> that we are an industrious, moral and law-abiding people. We most
> respectfully pray your honorable body, in view of the above merits,
> and those set forth in the Address, to your honorable notice, an
> amendment to the Constitution of the State of Nevada, . . . to the
> end that American citizens of African descent, and such other persons
> of African descent as may . . . become citizens, may be admitted to the
> right of franchise and citizenship of the State of Nevada.
>
> We also pray your honorable body, an amendment to an Act to regulate
> civil cases in the Courts of Justice in Nevada, approved November 29th,
> 1861, Title 11th, Chapter 1st, part of Section 342, to the end that
> American citizens of African descent, in common with others, can avail
> themselves of the privileges of the Public School Fund. We in duty
> bound will ever pray.

The address to the citizens of Nevada was signed by Dr. Stephenson,
Courts, Sands, Waters, T. A. Lee, and Cicero Miner. Pointing out that the
"God of Battles" had decided the question of slavery, the address asserted
that "relics of its barbarism . . . are to be found . . . written on the statute
books of many States. They are imprinted in the statute books of the
State of Nevada." The address was specific about injustices to blacks:

Taxation without representation; with no voice in the selection of those who govern; denied admission to, and even the privilege of collecting our just dues through the Civil Courts; our children shut out by statute law from all avenues of obtaining instruction, are grievances of which the colored citizens in the State of Nevada have just reason to complain.

It pointed out that black citizens contributed through taxation to the support of the schools and the government, but "we do not share its benefits. Is it right that the colored citizen should be compelled to pay taxes for the education of a class, while their own are doomed, by your laws, to grow up in ignorance?" Asserting that the "colored citizens" were loyal to the state and nation and "industrious, moral and law-abiding," the address claimed that black property owners paid taxes in 1864 on "real and personal property in the state valued at over two hundred thousand dollars" and that the reduction in property values in 1865 among them was no greater than the reduction of such values among the white population. The address ended with an appeal for the end of "odious and oppressive laws . . . incompatible with free institutions, repugnant to the spirit of Christianity, in violation of the law of God, a foul blot upon the escutcheon of any people."[12]

It is not clear whether these group efforts continued in 1866 and 1867, but Dr. Stephenson made some efforts to secure repeal of the law on civil testimony during the 1867 session. The 1866 Civil Rights Act passed by Congress declared that blacks possessed the same rights as whites, but the exact meaning of this law, as well as its constitutionality, was in question. A bill was introduced in the 1867 session of the Legislature to apply the Civil Rights Act to Nevada. (The course of that bill through the legislature has been described in chapter 3.) Although it passed the assembly, it was eventually killed when Republican Senator Charles A. Sumner and Democratic Senator F. M. Proctor of Nye County raised objections to it. After the bill had been referred to the judiciary committee because of Sumner's and Proctor's objections, Dr. Stephenson published a letter in the *Territorial Enterprise* that vigorously attacked these two men. After pointing out that he was a physician who had been practicing medicine in Virginia City for five years, Dr. Stephenson went on to say:

I pay a United States Revenue tax, a city license tax, a city real estate and personal tax, a State and county real estate and personal property tax, a school tax and a hospital tax, and I desire to meet the two gentlemen at any place they may appoint, (I paying all expenses) to discuss upon what principles of right, justice, or equity, I shall be debarred by an enactment of the State from collecting my just dues, in order that I may meet my obligations, as a good citizen, willing to contribute my portion to carry on the machinery of the State and Federal governments.

Specifically he asserted:

> I have three thousand dollars due to me, in this State from Anglo-Saxons, for professional services, which I can only collect through sufferance; and this, in sums of ten to forty dollars, is a dead loss, from the fact that the parties have shielded themselves through an Act of the State which leaves me no redress.

He suggested that Sumner and Proctor "retire to private life. An enlightened public will soon demand it." The newspaper supported Dr. Stephenson's position, stating editorially that

> if these gentlemen can give a rational reason why he should be debarred the privilege of collecting his debts in a Court of Justice, let them come forward and publicly proclaim it. . . . The fact that he is a colored man cannot be received as an excuse on the part of the gentlemen named for failing to make the explanation demanded. He is a citizen of the State and of the United States, and pays more tax than either of them—than both of them, no doubt.[13]

Perhaps Dr. Stephenson's letter and the reactions it stirred up had some effect, although no bill in this area was ultimately passed. The senate judiciary committee later reported a bill to repeal the ban on both civil and criminal testimony by blacks as a substitute for Assembly Bill 71; however, this bill was indefinitely postponed by a vote of nine to eight.

No evidence of subsequent lobbying efforts by Nevada blacks in the nineteenth century has yet come to light, but it seems likely that there were such efforts. By the 1880s most discriminatory laws had been repealed and/or overruled by national action, and it is quite likely that Nevada blacks felt less need for legislative action than they had during the 1860s.

Two comments about an obscure legislative proposal in 1873 indicate some alertness about legislative happenings on the part of the black community although also some ignorance of existing law, the latter perhaps shared by legislators. On February 14, 1873, Assemblyman P. L. Shoaff of Lincoln County introduced a bill, "An Act to prevent miscegenation."[14] It is not clear what this bill referred to since there was still a general anti-miscegenation statute on the books, but a black correspondent in Carson City, signing himself "Wilse," noted that the bill (which was never passed) would have made the marriage of a black man to a white woman illegal. (The bill was never reported by the committee to which it was assigned.) "Wilse" sarcastically regretted that the bill did not pass, so

> that future generations of unborn maidens would have hailed the mention of his name with loud hosannas. Mr. Shoaf exhausted himself with that effort, and since then has only been equal the task of drawing his pay, which duty he performs weekly with an alacrity which is really surprising in one of his age.[15]

Later that year, Mrs. D. D. Carter of Placerville, a frequent contributor to the San Francisco black newspapers, made a visit to Carson City. As she reported it, she went to the Capitol, stood in the empty assembly chamber, and

> we brought our imagination into play, and had before us the very smart man who introduced the celebrated bill against miscegenation and we felt all the horror he did, only it was on the other side—we being filled with a great desire to present before the honorable body a bill compelling all white men to marry colored women, squaws and even Chinawomen who were mothers to their children, and so help to support and educate their own flesh and blood.[16]

There is an incomplete record of another attempt by blacks in 1868 to secure rights by litigation. George Cottle, owner of a hotel in Virginia City, got in a dispute over possession of some property claimed by a white man. At a proceeding in connection with this dispute, Patrick Lanman, a constable who was acting as a judge, ruled that a black witness for Mr. Cottle could not testify because of the state law forbidding testimony of blacks in civil cases. A meeting of black citizens was called and a committee to fight for the right to testify was formed, with Cottle as chairman and William A. Vincent as secretary. The committee raised fifty dollars on the spot to defray expenses and appointed a committee of three to correspond with blacks in other Nevada towns to raise more money. This meeting also authorized Dr. Stephenson to seek the arrest of Lanman, and this he did. Lanman "was arrested and held to appear under $2,000 bail to

appear before the Grand Jury on the first Monday in March." Presumably the
effort was made to show that Mr. Lanman had violated the Civil Rights Act.
    The outcome of this action is not known, but the efforts this committee
undertook may have had some effect on the 1869 legislature, which
repealed the testimony law in civil cases. In any case, it showed, as William
Vincent of the defense committee stated, that "being fully aware of our
rights, we are not willing that the decision of Mr. Patrick Lanman shall be
suffered to remain uncontested."[17]

"WE VALUE OUR BLACK BABIES AS
WELL AS OTHER FOLKS DO THEIRS"

    It has been noted that when Nevada became a state, by law "Negroes,
Mongolians, and Indians" were excluded from the public schools unless
separate schools for these nonwhite children were established. For various
reasons, it appears that only one school for black children actually operated
for any length of time. Most of the time, therefore, black children simply
did not attend school at all. Evidently an occasional child was permitted
to attend, either because a local school board was ignorant of the law or
thought the law had been invalidated by national civil rights action, but
the number must have been small. The 1870 census of population reported that three black children of school age had been in school during
the preceding year; since these three children lived in three different
counties, it was clear that there were no schools for black children during
1870. From Eureka, Thomas Detter reported bitterly that "no children
are admitted except those who wear white skins. We have several colored
children here who are growing up in ignorance, all on account of the white
man's prejudices. I ask, when will 'man's inhumanity to man' cease?"[18]
    One of the black children permitted to attend school in 1870 lived
in Elko County; evidently this was because blacks there had been able to
persuade the school board that the Fourteenth Amendment had annulled
the discriminatory state law. In June 1870 F. G. Grice, a barber originally
from Haiti, wrote from Elko to report that "a colored boy made his appearance in the public school in this town, as one of the pupils, who was
accepted by the gentlemanly teacher, Mr. Stone." Grice indicated that
the editors of the *Elko Independent*, a Democratic paper, had "tried with
all their little might to raise the prejudiced passions of the people against
Mr. Stone, and the Board of Commissioners" but without success; "the
boy is still a regular attendant of that school."[19] In 1874 another Elko
correspondent, signing himself "Whiskiyou" (who probably was Charles
Wilson), reported:

Early in 1870, shortly after the establishment of the common schools, your humble servant went before the School Board and took the position, that under the provisions of the 14th Amendment, colored children were entitled to admission to the common schools. After weighing the matter carefully, they coincided with me, and immediately gave orders for the admission of colored children into the schools.

Whiskiyou also reported that there was general support in Elko for this position of the school board with no "protest" by either Republicans or Democrats.[20]

There is evidence that many Nevada blacks highly valued education and wanted their children to attend school. In addition to their numerous efforts to secure education for their children and the statements of various speakers at public meetings, there were other comments by various persons writing in the San Francisco newspapers. For example, a letter from Cosmorama in Silver City in 1865 asserted that those without formal education should teach themselves and others: "Again I say to you, try and elevate your race, and *all* who are ignorant."[21] Reverend John T. Jenifer wrote from Virginia City in August 1865 that "if our people ever are to be raised from the dust into which they have been crushed and ground for two hundred and forty-five years, it is to be done by that potent lever, education, and especially among our youth."[22]

Black citizens and groups were vocal in their protest against the exclusion of their children from the public schools, and they attempted, in at least one instance, to provide their own school. Eventually, their efforts resulted in the overturning of the racist school law.

Apparently only in Storey County did whites try to provide separate schools for nonwhites , and then only sporadically. What can be learned of their efforts sheds some light on the reasons why a separate school system for nonwhites was not established permanently.

John A. Collins was superintendent of schools in Storey County from 1862 until 1867 and probably was responsible for the only efforts made before the repeal of the racist law to educate nonwhites. Although he was not one of those who made antiracist motions and statements in the 1863 and 1864 constitutional conventions, to both of which he was a delegate, Collins had been active in the Massachusetts Anti-Slavery Society before going West and while in California "his anti-slavery sentiments militated against his election to the . . . legislature."[23] Evidently after the passage of the discriminatory school law of 1865, Collins labored to find a means to provide education for nonwhites, especially blacks.

In his school report for 1864-1865, Collins spoke of the problem and specifically attacked the unfairness of the law as it applied to blacks:

> Some law more efficient than now exists, should be framed, to secure educational facilities to the children of negroes, Indians and Mongolians. A severe penalty is attached to any district that will admit children of any of the proscribed races into the Public Schools of this State—denying any School District even by a unanimous vote of its citizens, the right to admit one of these unfortunates.

Collins then went on to assert:

> From the organization of the Territory to the present time the property of the negro has been taxed for the support of Public Schools. The Assessor's books for 1863, show that the taxable property of the colored people of Virginia City, for that year, amounted to the sum of $82,000. Upon this amount a school tax of two-fifths of one per cent was paid into the County School Fund. This is gross outrage upon a helpless class—our self-respect, if not our sense of justice, should counsel us to terminate or modify this system of wrong.[24]

If his figures are correct, the blacks of Virginia City must have paid a school tax of $328 in 1863 for which they received no educational benefits for their children.

Several factors militated against establishing separate schools for nonwhites. One was the small number of such children, combined with the fact that, from 1865 to 1867, the school law provided that a school for nonwhites could be operated only if there were at least ten students. Collins' school report indicated that the census marshal had counted either seven or nine black children between six and eighteen (two different figures are given in his report at different places), plus thirteen Indian and fifteen "Mongolian" students. The Virginia City School Board evidently wanted to set up a school for Chinese and black children, probably to meet the requirements of ten children as well as to provide a stronger justification for spending the necessary money to operate the school. In September 1865 the school board ran advertisements in Virginia City newspapers seeking to find Chinese children whose parents might want them to attend a nonwhite school. The advertisements asked that "all parents of such Mongolian Children, desirous of having their children attend such school, are requested to notify the Board at once."[25]

Probably some parents of black children objected to having their children attend school with Chinese children; in the school report that has been quoted above, John A. Collins said that "the Board of Education have expended much, both of time and earnest labor, to organize a Public School for . . . [the] benefit" of children of all three races; "but there are mutual prejudices existing of one race against another, almost, if not quite, as strong as that of the superior race, which bolts the doors of educational halls against them all." He then went on to say that the board had not found a way to educate these groups "without incurring a much greater outlay of money, than the occasion, in their judgment, seemed to justify."

At the end of his report, Collins appended a note to the effect that, since the writing of the report, W. W. Waterman, the former teacher of the third ward school, "has charge of the school for colored children" and that another teacher had been assigned to the third ward school. It is not clear whether an attempt was made in the fall of 1865 to operate a school for blacks and/or blacks and Chinese, but this may have been the case. The only school known to have been conducted for nonwhites was run for several months beginning in February 1866 and taught by Waterman, but two sources state that other schools were attempted. At any rate, the school Waterman conducted evidently was for black students only. A black correspondent in Virginia City wrote the *San Francisco Elevator* in March 1866 with the information that "the school for the education of colored youth opened three weeks ago with sixteen pupils, and is at present in successful operation." He also reported that "a school for adults has been opened in the evening, for all who desire to avail themselves of its privileges," but that "so far as regards our adult population, very little interest has been manifested. The culture of the mind, with them, is of a secondary consideration."[26] After the school had been in operation for several months, an account in the *Territorial Enterprise* reported that the school was located on E Street in the Oriental Hotel and that Mr. Waterman instructed approximately fifteen children during the day and fifteen adults at night. At a party given in the schoolhouse,

a little boy, five years old, who, only five weeks ago, did not know one letter of the alphabet from another recited a poem of several verses with only one prompting, and reads in the First Reader. Others of a larger growth gave creditable recitations, and all the scholars present were exercised in music, in which they justly elicited applause.[27]

Evidently the Storey County School Board made another attempt to set up a school for nonwhite children during the following year but without success. A news item in the *Gold Hill Daily News* in June 1867 reported the opposition of "colored" parents in Portland, Oregon, to plans for a school for their children plus Chinese and Indian children. The *News* commented, "We were told last year, by some of our own county school authorities, that the reason why there was complaint about the Board's not making colored school arrangements was because the negroes objected to co-educate with the Chinese, and it was impossible to get the Indians to associate with either!"[28] This statement brought an immediate reply from Dr. Stephenson who said that blacks in Virginia City had objected to plans for a school to include Chinese and Indian children because there was no effort to restrict the attendance of children who were not "civilized." He said:

> In conversation with the County Superintendent, and in presence of a friend now in the East, I favored a mixed school, with no objections to Chinese or Indian children, provided they lived in good, honest, respectable white families. As the race with which I am identified is civilized, I informed him that color of the skin was not the barrier; and neither should it be a reason to compel my race to associate and mingle with idolatrous heathens, or the scum of the community, let them be white, black, yellow or red. Among all races there are some who are dissolute, vile and immoral, as well as the upright, virtuous and just. Society is so constituted that men and women, like water, seek a level.[29]

In 1870 Dr. Stephenson once more protested the "monstrous injustice" of taxing black parents while denying their children the benefits of public education. Asserting that segregated schools were acceptable to the black community, he stated strongly that providing no public education at all for their children was wrong. He wrote:

> It is not a question of admission to the white public schools which the people of color have contributed to erect and support, but whether, as at the present time, are they, as human beings, entitled to any school privileges whatever. . . .
>
> To colored or separate schools, the people have raised no objection; but school privileges they claim as a matter of right and justice.

Dr. Stephenson hoped that adoption of the Fifteenth Amendment would give blacks the leverage to change the situation. He also asserted that it was "just" to exclude Indians from the schools because they did not pay taxes; further, he asked whether it was proper to tax blacks for the education of Indians as well as whites. Blacks, he said, should not be criticized for objecting to having Indians and Chinese in their schools when whites would not accept the same races in their schools. He ended by returning to his original theme: "I do not consider every white man a proper associate for me, neither every colored man. Socially, the colored race demands respectability. Mr. Lynch [editor of the *Gold Hill News*] and his race will not claim less."[30]

There may have been another attempt to set up a school for nonwhites during the 1867-1868 school year in Virginia City. State Superintendent of Public Instruction A. N. Fisher wrote in his report for that year that "but one colored school has been attempted in the State during this year, and it was soon discontinued on account of extraordinary expense."[31]

The black population of Carson City, which was the other center of black population in Nevada, went to great lengths to secure an education for their children in spite of white refusal to admit them to the public schools; they finally secured the annulling of the state law. In September 1867 the *Carson Daily Appeal* reported that the "colored men of Carson" were trying to "build a suitable school house for the use of that class of persons. The proposed building could also be used by them as a place of worship." Reportedly two hundred dollars had been raised "by some of the principal business men of this place. A lot has already been donated whereon to erect such a structure. The location of this ground is at the head of Second street, to the west of the city." Noting that "inasmuch as the colored children of Carson, we believe, are not permitted to attend the public school, our citizens should contribute liberally" to the school house fund. The newspaper reported that a lecture was to be given as a benefit for the school, but details of the event were not yet available.[32]

In November 1867 the trustees of the "colored school house property, now known as the 'Literary and Religious Association of Colored Citizens,'" announced that the building was "finished and paid for, with the exception of a few dollars." After thanking the "numerous friends and citizens of Carson" who helped them with the building and suggesting that "we value our black babies as well as other folks do theirs," the trustees expressed a "hope" that the school commissioners would "help us to pay a teacher for the colored school."[33] It is possible that funds for a teacher were provided by the public school system (evidence of this has not yet come to light), but it is extremely unlikely. In 1871 the black population of Carson City launched a legal attack on the school law in the courts. In the ensuing action, there is no mention of any previous public support of any kind for the education of black children in Carson City. Another reason for supposing that a teacher for a separate school was not funded is the small number of black children involved. In 1868-1869, the school census marshal reported only four black children in Carson City.

In 1867 State Superintendent of Schools A. N. Fisher, who was also a Methodist minister, began to criticize the school law on the ground that it in effect denied public education to black children. In 1869 he repeated his objections to the law, asserting that, because separate schools were not required, "colored children are without educational privileges."[34] The legislature did not respond to these requests, however, and the school law was not changed until the state supreme court invalidated it as unconstitutional in 1872.

Evidently the legal challenge to the school law was a group effort, although details are lacking. A Carson City newspaper not sympathetic to their cause reported in April 1871 that "the Negroes, we understand, will appeal to the Courts, and have already employed counsel for that purpose." It also suggested that the issue was considered of some importance by white leaders of Carson City. Reporting that the county superintendent of public instruction had appointed two new members to the board of school trustees to replace two men who had resigned, the newspaper went on to say: "It is understood that the appointees, together with Mr. James Duffy of the original Board, are opposed to the admission of negro children to the public schools, the Board now being unanimous on the subject."[35]

The case arose on the application of a seven-year-old black child, David Stoutmeyer, to attend a public school in Carson City. His father, Nelson Stoutmeyer, a laborer who owned real property but could not himself read or write, had filed suit against James Duffy, S. H. Wright, and N. C. Gardner, trustees of school district no. 1 of Ormsby County, after they had turned down a written request that his son be admitted. On April 21, 1871, the state supreme court ordered the trustees either to admit David Stoutmeyer or to appear before the court on April 29 to show cause for not admitting him.[36]

A brief was filed for David Stoutmeyer on August 8, 1871, by attorney T. W. W. Davies. It argued that the school law was unconstitutional on several grounds.

The first argument, which was essentially accepted by two of the three justices of the state supreme court, was that the state laws apportioning state aid to schools did so on the basis of the number of children, regardless of the race of the children. This being so, the school apportionment laws "would be unequal, unfair and unjust unless *all* the children, for whom money is received, are allowed the benefits of instruction in the public schools, supported and maintained by such moneys."

The second argument was that the state school law excluding blacks from the public schools was "unconstitutional and void" because it was in conflict with the Fourteenth Amendment to the United States Constitution. It was specifically asserted that Nevada's school law was in conflict with all three of the major clauses of this amendment—the privileges and immunities clause, the equal protection clause, and the due process clause— and also with the civil rights acts passed in 1866 and 1870.

The constitution of Nevada was allegedly violated by the law because the constitution provided for a uniform system of public schools. Citing the debates in the constitutional convention of 1864 over racial criteria for admission to the state university, the Davies brief maintained that "it was the design of the Convention to establish educational institutions on liberal principles, for the benefit of *all the children* of the State."

A third ground of attack on the law was that "it legislates against a race or class of citizens on account of their color." Admitting that the school board could exclude "obnoxious persons" from the public schools, it was argued that the school children involved were excluded solely for another reason, their race. Upholding this statute, Davies went on to argue, would mean that the legislature would have unlimited power in this field so that "the colored citizens may be excluded from holding offices, sitting on juries, visiting places of public accommodation, entertainment, and the like."

To the possibility that the law merely provided for segregated public schools, the Davies brief replied that the legislature had no authority to establish public schools on a racial basis and that therefore such schools were illegal. Further, "although the instruction in the public schools and these separate schools may be precisely the same, a school exclusively devoted to one class must differ essentially, in its spirit and character, from that public school known to the law, where all classes meet together in equality." The brief went on to assert that separating school children by race is detrimental to children of both races because "it tends to create a feeling of degradation in the blacks, and of prejudice and uncharitableness in the whites."

Still another claim was that black parents of school children were taxed "the same" as parents of white children, while aliens who paid no taxes could still send children to the public school. "This," charged Davies, "is virtually endorsing the obnoxious doctrines of 'taxation without representation.'" A similar claim arose from the fact that much state support for the public schools came from the sale of public lands; thus, the state was not entitled to discriminate against any citizen of the United States.

It was also argued that excluding blacks from the public schools deprived them of beneficial contacts with the "superior" race.

Men derive their characteristic features from the books they read and the people with whom they associate, and if the white race is the superior race as claimed and admitted, the denial of admission of the colored citizens to the public schools, is a denial of the benefits which would necessarily result to them from contact and association with the whites on terms of equality.

The brief closed with a number of arguments designed to show that Nevada's school law was "not only illegal, but unwise, unjust and unnecessary." Pointing out that there were black members of the federal Senate and House of Representatives and blacks in many other local, state, and national governmental offices, the brief implied that excluding them from public schools was absurd.

Since "republican" government assumed an educated citizenry, Davies asserted, the states had an obligation to educate all their citizens. He also asserted that the national government had a policy of encouraging education and that states were without power to thwart this policy. Another argument for making education available to black children was that they "had recently been vested with the great rights of citizenship," such as the right to vote, to hold office, to testify in court, and to sit on juries, and "they should be afforded every possible facility for moral and intellectual improvement, to enable them to qualify themselves for the intelligent and efficient discharge of the various important duties lately devolved upon them."

Davies' final argument was that Nevada's racial discrimination "comes with especial bad taste." He pointed out that the state had supported the abolition of slavery during the Civil War, ratified "with the utmost alacrity" the Thirteenth, Fourteenth, and Fifteenth amendments, and supported by resolution the Reconstruction policy of the Congress.

In March of the year following the beginning of the suit, the state
supreme court issued a writ of mandamus ordering that David Stoutmeyer
be admitted to the school and an opinion holding that the provision of
the state school law that had been cited to justify his exclusion was unconstitutional.[37] However, the court was divided along partisan lines. The
two of the three justices who were Republicans held that the exclusion
of black children was unconstitutional, although their reasons for so
holding were somewhat different, and neither followed Davies' brief very
closely. The third justice, a Democrat, wrote an opinion arguing that the
school law was constitutional.

Justice B. C. Whitman concluded without giving reasons that the·
statute was not in conflict with the federal Constitution and laws, stating,
"While it may be, and probably is, opposed to the spirit of the [United
States Constitution and laws] still it is not obnoxious to their letter."
He then went on to argue that the exclusion of blacks from public schools
violated the state constitution. His reasoning was that the constitution,
in two provisions authorizing the legislature to establish a "uniform system
of common schools" and providing for state support for these schools,
had intended to provide for the education of all children. "If the constitution provides anything in the language quoted," he said, "it provides
for the education of all children of the state." Justice Whitman did say
that the school board could operate segregated schools if it chose to do so:

> This general position, is, however, to be taken subject to the very
> great powers of the trustees to arrange and classify the schools as
> they deem for the best interest of the scholars. While on the one hand
> they may not deny to any resident person of proper age an equal
> participation in the benefits of the common schools, and while in the
> present case upon the facts presented, the defendants should have
> admitted the relator into the public school in question; yet, on the
> other hand, it is perfectly within their power to send all blacks to one
> school, and all whites to another. . . .

Chief Justice J. F. Lewis, while concurring with Justice Whitman in
the issuance of the writ of mandamus, did so for different reasons. Without discussing the relation of the Constitution to the issue, he found the
state law in question in violation of section XXI of the state constitution,
which required the legislature to enact only "general" laws. The purpose
of this requirement, he held, was

> to give to all citizens the equal advantage of the laws, to deprive the
> legislature, as far as possible, of the power of creating distinctions,
> and granting immunities and exemptions to one class of citizens over
> another. Nothing can be conceived more obnoxious or antagonistic
> to this principle than the law in question. It deprives an entire class of
> citizens of one of the most inestimable privileges of political organiza-
> tion; makes the most invidious discrimination against them, exacting
> a revenue from their property for the organization and support of
> public schools, and denying them their advantages, holding them
> amenable to the law, but withholding from them its highest privileges.

He argued that a legislative classification by race was unconstitutional;
"the legislature has no more right to designate a class by the color of
the skin, than by the color of the hair." He pointed out that blacks were
citizens and asserted that "no law now in force, or which we are bound
to recognize, places them in any different position, so far as citizenship
is concerned, to any other class of citizens." He held that the state constitutional amendment denying them the vote was unconstitutional because
of the Fifteenth Amendment and that

> they follow the same pursuits, are engaged in the same employments,
> may be members of the same professions, are in fact in no way marked
> or distinguished as a class, except by the one physical characteristic
> mentioned . . . the mere matter of color does not place a Negro in a
> condition or situation which, in legal contemplation, is different from
> other citizens.

Chief Justice Lewis concluded by agreeing with Justice Whitman that
segregation of blacks by the school board would be constitutional, however: "So long as the same advantages of education are given to all, such
classification could not interfere with the constitutional principle upon
which I place my conclusion."

Justice John Garber dissented from the order granting a writ of mandamus
and also disagreed vigorously with both lines of reasoning his colleagues presented. He agreed with Justice Whitman that the United States Constitution was not in conflict with the law, specifically citing the three main
clauses of the Fourteenth Amendment. He disagreed with Whitman, however, on the meaning of the state constitutional provisions regarding
education, holding that they could not be read to require the admission of
all children, for if this were the case, "the blind, the idiotic, the insane,

the vicious and the diseased must all be admitted." Further, he ridiculed
Justice Whitman's contention by arguing that his interpretation would
void the entire school law "because it fails to accord to the Shoshone
infants their constitutional privilege of compulsory education."

The main thrust of Justice Garber's dissent was that legislative classification by race was indeed reasonable and constitutional because it accorded with basic realities of racial differences. To sustain this point he
quoted at length from a Pennsylvania opinion which asserted that "the
natural law which forbids [the] intermarriage [of blacks and whites] and
that social amalgamation which leads to a corruption of races, is as clearly
divine as that which imparted to them different natures." Justice Garber
pointed out that "at the time this statute was enacted, the Negro was not
a voter; he could not hold office; he could not testify in a civil case where
a white was a party; and the intermarriage of the two races was unlawful,
and the solemnization of such a marriage a misdemeanor." He concluded
that the statute should be read as requiring the establishment of separate
schools for blacks and that their exclusion from the public schools should
be held to be constitutional.

The *Territorial Enterprise* and the *Carson Daily Appeal*, both Republican papers, believed that partisanship had a great deal of bearing on the
case. In an editorial the *Enterprise* said:

> There are men—we do not say that Judge Garber is one of them—who
> have been reared and suckled by black nurses, whose companions have
> been black children, whose mistresses have been black women, and yet
> who protest with horror against white and black children reciting their
> lessons under the same roof. They will eat with the negro, talk with
> the negro, and sleep with the negro, yet they will not read with the
> negro. There may be Democracy in this, but there is very little reason.[38]

An editorial in the *Appeal* opposing a Democratic nominee for the supreme
court in 1876 stated, "We believe that if he had been on the bench with
Garber, he and Garber constituting a majority of the Supreme Court, the
colored children would never have been admitted to the schools."[39]

Apparently the decision was promptly obeyed. A contemporary newspaper reported soon after the decision that "the colored children were
yesterday admitted to seats in the public schools. They appear intelligent
little fellows and were tidily dressed."[40]

Superintendent Fisher stopped giving statistics for black children in
his next report because, he said, "practically, the children of all citizens

are now free to attend our public schools. . . . I believe that this ruling
has been cheerfully complied with throughout the State, and that the
privilege it secures is eagerly enjoyed by the hitherto proscribed race."[41]
In 1873 the legislature repealed the entire statute, making no attempt to
preserve segregation; the small number of black children made separate
schools impractical.[42] In March 1873 a letter from Carson City to a San
Francisco black newspaper reported that black students "are doing so
well in learning and deportment that they receive the highest encomiums
from their teachers and compel respect from the other scholars." This
correspondent reported that there were ten black children "in all the
departments from the primary to the high school" and that in the high
school "the names of Freddie Bullock and Charlie Edwards have been
mentioned in the roll of honor" published monthly in local newspapers,
and "each time they have been classed as No. 1."[43] In the fall of 1873
Mrs. D. D. Carter, a black visitor to Carson City, wrote: "It did my soul
good to see our children going with the white children to the same
schools, and to see their names on their roll of honor. Every department
of the public schools has colored children in it, and the war of races,
which so many prophesied and desired to see has not been seen, but
contrawise [sic] all is harmony."[44]

Nevada was ahead of California in opening public schools to blacks
on a nondiscriminatory basis. In 1874 the California Supreme Court
upheld a law similar to the Nevada law invalidated in 1872 although
it ruled that it could not be applied to exclude black children altogether;
however, it was constitutional in that state after this decision to operate
racially segregated schools.[45] The San Francisco school board voluntarily
integrated its schools in 1875, but by 1877 there were still separate
schools for black children in Stockton, Sacramento, and San Jose.[46]
Black citizens of Nevada and visitors from California frequently commented on the difference between the two states. The Carson City correspondent quoted above also wrote, "I must say we are a little ahead
of you in . . . that respect, as our children are attending the school."[47]
On a visit to Carson City and Virginia City, editor Philip Bell of the
San Francisco Elevator noted, "There are no proscriptive schools in
Nevada, and as I learn, the colored pupils have equal advantages with
others." He asked: "When will California be as liberal and as just?"[48]

"THE OBJECT IS UNITED POLITICAL ACTION"

Blacks could vote in Nevada in 1870 and subsequently, and it is quite
clear that they voted overwhelmingly Republican because they saw this

party as responsible for the end of slavery and for the national effort to
extend other rights to them. Nevada was typical of other northern states
in this respect.

The fact that almost all Nevada blacks took for granted their Republicanism is well illustrated. W. H. Hall, the orator at the celebration of the
ratification of the Fifteenth Amendment in Virginia City in 1870, stated:

> We feel justified in asserting that every colored man, from the frozen-
> bound confines of Maine to the genial borders of redeemed Florida,
> is under a never-to-be-forgotten debt of respect and gratitude to the
> great Republican Party from the auspicious time they enunciated·
> the dogma of no more extension of slave territory to the completion of
> the grand event we are commemorating here today.[49]

An unknown correspondent from Unionville, Nevada, who signed himself
"Sage Brush" put it more succinctly in urging the reelection of President
Grant in 1872: "I hope our people will not forsake the party which made
them men."[50]

In 1868 Orion, in a letter from Virginia City, described a large Union
party election rally, commenting, "It was the emphatic decision of the
meeting that the civil and political rights of the freedmen must be maintained" by electing U. S. Grant president. The letter went on to speak of
other meetings in Gold Hill, to assert that the Union party was united in
Nevada, and to predict victory in November.[51] No details were given about
black participation in these party activities, but Orion must have been
present as a spectator at least.

A Hamilton newspaper reported that, at the municipal election held
in that city on June 6, 1870, "for the first time the colored citizens of
this city exercised the right of voting. . . . There were 53 registered, and
all, without a single exception, voted the straight Republican ticket." It
was reported that their voting produced no excitement or opposition.
"Neither violence or jeering was interposed against the newly enfranchised
citizens from any quarter, and as a rule they came up in twos and threes,
deposited their ballots unostentatiously, and departed in peace."[52]

During the 1870 general election campaign, it was reported that half
a dozen "colored citizens" attended a Republican rally at the Stone
Saloon in Hamilton.[53]

A small notebook now at the University of Nevada in Reno, which
evidently is a record book of a Republican worker in Ormsby County
in 1880, contains the printed precinct lists for that county for that

year with some added notations, identifying the party and ethnic group
of many voters. Twenty-two names were identified as "Colored"; all
but two of these were listed as Republican. One has the handwritten
notation, "Votes at Republican primaries," and one is not identified
by party.

Blacks could vote in Nevada for the first time in 1870, and evidently
they were quick to organize Republican groups for the purpose of maxi-
mizing their voting power. Dr. Stephenson seemed confident that the
right to vote was the key to gaining other rights. In February 1870 he
wrote the *Territorial Enterprise* that ratification of the Fifteenth Amendment was no longer in doubt and would occur in five or six weeks; consequently black citizens would vote for the first time at the next city
election in Virginia City and the next state election. He predicted that
if the Virginia City elections were competitive as they had been in the
past, "the colored voters in this city and county hold the balance of
power." He urged black voters to "exercise the right of a free man as
becomes one" and "no longer submit to the payment of a regular and
special school tax, wherein we are deprived of all benefits." He ended
by asserting, "We shall have something to say to the political office-
seekers, and to the political parties, in this matter."[54]

"R. H. S." (probably Robert H. Small, a barber from Maryland) from
Wadsworth wrote a strongly Republican letter, which was printed in the
Territorial Enterprise during the 1870 campaign. "It is true," he wrote,
that "we constitute but an inconsiderable minority; still, by a determined
and united effort, we will not only make our 'three hundred' votes felt,
but will prove our gratitude to the party that redeemed us from a servitude,
the horrors of which we cannot, we must not, and dare not forget." Citing
the battles black soldiers participated in during the Civil War, the New
York riots of 1863, and recent actions of the California legislature,
R. H. S. said: "We are not yet secure in our God-given rights, and by no
dereliction on our part must we allow our ancient enemies to ride into
power." He particularly urged a vote for Congressman Thomas Fitch on
the ground that a Democratic capture of the House of Representatives
was possible.[55]

In Virginia City, the Lincoln Union Club was organized at a "mass
meeting of the colored citizens of Virginia City" on February 16.
Dr. Stephenson was elected president for the first six months, George
Cottle vice-president, and Samuel Wagner treasurer; three other officers
were also elected. A member of the club wrote, "The object of our club
is for united political action throughout the State, in view of the good

time coming." The club initially had fifty-two members,[56] and it participated in the Emancipation Proclamation celebration in Virginia City in
that year.

In Elko, early 1870 brought the establishment of a "literary and
political club, under the title of 'Elko Republican Club.'" Regular weekly
meetings were held. At the meeting of June 21, there was a two-hour
debate on "Women's Enfranchisement," with the successful affirmative
position argued by Charles M. Wilson and F. G. Grice and the negative
position argued by George W. Jackson and W. A. Scott. A subsequent
meeting was to discuss "San Domingo Annexation to the United States."[57]

Also in 1870, William M. Bird, one of the earliest black residents of
Virginia City, ran for mayor. Bird was well known in Virginia City, and
this bit of doggerel gives two of the reasons:

Billy Bird, the coon barber, who once ran for Mayor,
Who sold a hair tonic that would not grow a hair,
On his own bald pate his locks he would pull,
Saying: "Dis is for hair, sah; it does not grow wool."[58]

In advertisements in the *Territorial Enterprise*, which began in 1866 and
continued into the 1870s, at least, Bird advertised his Imperial Hair Restorative or Capillary Fertilizer, available at his shop or by mail. He claimed that
his hair restorative was "without a rival" for "speedily restoring new hair on
Bald Heads and imparting new life and vigor to the old hair."[59]

In April 1870 in an advertisement headed "Does the World Move!"
Bird announced his candidacy for may or of Virginia City as an independent. He pledged himself, if elected to the office, "to perform its
important functions with integrity and ability."[60] There were charges
that Bird ran in an attempt to reduce the winning margin of the Republican candidate for mayor, although he cannot have been intending
to elect the Democratic candidate, since there was none at this election.
The *Elko Independent*, in reporting that the plurality of Republican
W. T. Eaves for mayor was 283 votes while other Republican candidates
running city-wide had pluralities of 763, 788, and 794, stated, "What
cut down Eaves' majority was W. M. Bird, Independent colored candidate,
getting 320 votes."[61]

The *Carson Appeal*, a Republican paper, stated when Bird announced
his candidacy: "'It is a dirty bird that befouls its own nest'—and of this
man we have but to say that the colored men in the State repudiate him
utterly."[62] Probably most black men were shocked that he would run

against a Republican. The *Elevator* commented that it hoped blacks would not vote for him, suggesting: "He is evidently put forward by Democrats in hopes of securing the colored vote, and thereby defeating the Republican nominee. Mr. Bird is probably as well qualified for the position as any other man, but we believe his political antecedents are unsound."[63] A correspondent from Hamilton, signing himself "Undertaker & Co.," commented satirically on Bird's candidacy. The correspondent stated that "the lamentable political suicide of our fellow citizen, Hon. Bill Bird, would-be Mayor of Virginia City, was the cause of great regret to the colored citizens of Hamilton, and we were determined to give his remains a fitting funeral demonstration." The details of the "funeral procession" and graveside ceremony were given, and the letter ended: "After the impressive oration, the Professor was buried with all dishonor, and the procession returned to the City."[64] In 1873 Philip A. Bell referred to this election in recounting his meeting with Bird on a visit to Virginia City but said that he had forgiven him, because "all is fair in love, war and politics."[65]

Nevada blacks were active politically during the presidential year of 1876. In Carson City there were separate white and black Hayes and Wheeler clubs but also some joint activities. The *Carson Daily Appeal* asserted, "There are 47 colored men registered in this county and we believe they are all members of this club."[66] The Colored Hayes and Wheeler Club held at least five public meetings in October and November 1876. These meetings were addressed by various white Republicans, including former state Senator Charles L. Varian of Humboldt County, attorney George R. Ammond, Dr. Munckton, a druggist, and C. S. Mott, as well as speakers from their own membership.[67]

A large rally was held at Empire, near Carson City, a few nights before the election, with significant participation by both Hayes and Wheeler clubs. Several railroad cars brought people to swell the "great crowd," which was "accompanied by the Carson Brass Band, the white glee club . . . and the colored glee club." Amid blazing bonfires, seven addresses were given, one by George H. Rogers, "the well known colored orator." About 10 P.M., the crowd came back to Carson City "and marched down Carson street to the County Committee's headquarters, the band playing at the head of the column."[68]

The evening before the election, the White Hayes and Wheeler Club held a rally at the theater. The colored club had planned a rally following this at the Turn Verein Hall, and the two groups evidently merged after the white meeting. "At the conclusion of the exercises at the theater, the crowd, responsive to the invitation extended by President Grinage of the Colored Club, repaired in great numbers to the Turn Verein Hall."

Speeches, songs, and musical selections alternated for much of the night. Commented the *Appeal:* "We have never seen a more ardor-inspired election eve than this."[69] Evidently the election helped break down some of the barriers between blacks and whites.[70]

In 1878 the black citizens of Carson City, apparently without consultation with black voters in Virginia City, formed a "Nevada Union Colored League." A meeting of "colored citizens" of Virginia City and Storey County discussed this action and passed a resolution stating that, because the Carson City group had not consulted with them, "we do ignore and repudiate the said Nevada Union Colored League, and denounce the action of the colored citizens of Ormsby County, as an usurpation upon the rights of the colored voters of Nevada at large."[71]

An article referring to an edition of the *Virginia City Chronicle* that no longer seems to exist refers to a partisan meeting of blacks in 1879. "Indignation meeting of colored republican voters, to secure justice at the state capital, nearly broke up in a fight." The reporter went on to say that "there was much hard feeling, and many black looks."[72]

Black residents of Eureka held some kind of a political meeting in 1880 and probably had a partisan organization in that year. A newspaper in that city reported that "pursuant to an adjourned meeting, the colored citizens met last night at the residence of Mr. Chas. Williams. They had a very spirited meeting, and the political issues of the day were very ably discussed by Messrs. J. B. Parker and the veteran Thomas Detter. They meet again on Tuesday evening at the same place."[73]

In August 1880 a meeting of black voters in Virginia City, chaired by R. A. Brown, voted not to establish a separate Garfield and Arthur club for that election; instead, blacks were encouraged to affiliate with the existing white clubs organized in each ward. Brown reportedly made remarks to the effect that "it would look more square and manly for the colored Republicans to join the clubs already formed. . . . He was satisfied they would be accorded the same rights and privileges as white members. Should they form a separate club there would be sure to be persons who would say it was a 'sell-out' club."[74]

The next night another meeting of black voters organized a separate Garfield and Arthur Club, with J. H. Price as president and T. A. Lee as secretary. The club members signed a pledge to do everything within their power by "honorable means" to elect Garfield and Arthur and the entire Republican ticket.[75] This group had a "clubroom" and met there several times before the election. Speakers before the club included Judge J. K. Brown, Colonel R. H. Taylor, D. O. Adkison, and other white politicians.[76] M. Howard's saloon may have been their meeting place.

"I CLAIM THAT THE BLACK MAN
HAS ALWAYS BEEN AMERICAN"

In 1870 there were elaborate celebrations of the ratification of the Fifteenth Amendment in several Nevada cities, as well as in neighboring California. Whites as well as blacks participated in them in Virginia City, Elko, and Treasure City.

In Virginia City, a meeting of "colored citizens" held on February 3, 1870, resolved to celebrate the ratification of the Fifteenth Amendment, whenever it should occur. A committee headed by Dr. Stephenson tendered an invitation to speak at the celebration to William H. Hall, then in Hamilton, who was promised expenses and "remuneration" if he would accept. A one-hundred-gun salute was planned for the morning of the day of ratification, and a total of $227 was collected at the meeting to defray expenses, with $175 more subscribed. A general committee made plans for the celebration while a finance committee raised more money. Advertisements of the coming event were placed in local papers.[77]

The first event was a parade through Virginia City to Gold Hill. The parade formed at the "Hall of the Lincoln Union Club" on April 7, 1870, actually a few days after the amendment had been declared ratified. The celebration was so close to the ratification that the secretary of state's document of ratification and an accompanying statement by President Grant did not arrive in Virginia City in time to be read at the celebration.[78] The parade, preceded by an American flag and the Virginia Brass Band "playing popular patriotic airs," contained a "fine silk flag" made by the black women of Virginia City and later presented to the Lincoln Union Club. On one side of this flag were the words "Justice is slow, but sure" arranged elliptically around a figure of Justice. On the back were the words: "Lincoln Union Club. Organized March 1st, 1870."[79]

The parade consisted of about fifty men walking, followed by twelve carriages containing men, women, and children. "All were well dressed, and the Marshals rode on horseback. In all, the procession numbered nearly or quite 150 persons." As it marched by Fort Homestead into Gold Hill, the flag was raised on the fort and a thirty-nine-gun salute was fired. In front of the offices of the *Gold Hill News*, the parade stopped and "gave three hearty cheers for the GOLD HILL NEWS, three more for the Republican party, and three for the Fifteenth Amendment."[80] In Virginia City, the parade also stopped and cheered the *Territorial Enterprise*, which commented that no praise was ever received "with greater pride and pleasure. Colored citizens, we thank you."[81]

Exercises at the Athletic Hall were extensive. The banner carried in the parade was given to the Lincoln Union Club by Miss A. E. Vincent, "in behalf of the ladies of Virginia," and there was a response by Thomas R. Street. Joseph Price read a prayer expressing gratitude to God and the Republican party for enabling blacks to be "citizens of this our native country." He asked for God's help "so that we may prove to and assure the world of our realization and appreciation of the just and righteous acts of our fellow countrymen in constitutionally securing to us that which has always been our just rights."[82] Theodore A. Lee read the Civil Rights Act, since the proclamation of ratification of the amendment had not yet arrived. David W. Sands and J. M. Whitfield then read poems they had written. J. M. Whitfield's poem was a comment on slavery and a plea for freedom. There were musical selections by the Virginia Brass Band and two addresses. Dr. Stephenson made a brief speech in which he discussed the Civil War, declared that the Fifteenth Amendment was an "act of justice . . . cemented by the blood of the martyred friend of the oppressed, Abraham Lincoln," and ended by thanking God "for this triumphant victory of right over might—of liberty over oppression—of christianity over barbarism."[83] The principal address, however, was by William H. Hall, who had been persuaded to come all the way from Hamilton in eastern Nevada for the occasion. Hall's address was evidently well regarded by a number of local white businessmen who asked him to give another public address a few days later.[84] On April 10, 1870, Hall delivered this second address, "The future of the African Race, under a Republican form of Government."[85] (The 1870 celebration in Virginia City is the only incident involving blacks in nineteenth-century Nevada that is mentioned in the Harold's Club popular history *Pioneer Nevada*.)[86]

A similar celebration was held in Elko. F. G. Grice, writing from Elko, stated before the event, "We intend to shake Elko with the firing of thirty-seven guns."[87] However, he reported later that, since there were no cannon in Elko, "we used two large anvils for that purpose." The salute was at noon and "literary exercises" began at 1 P.M. in the courthouse, with more people in attendance than the building could accommodate. While there was no precise observation on this point, obviously many white people were among the audience.

One of two major addresses of the day, by Charles M. Wilson, indicates quite fully the needs and desires of many black leaders of Nevada at that time. While praising the Republican party for its role in emancipating

the slaves and adopting the three Civil War amendments to the Constitution, Wilson displayed a realistic attitude about the reasons for these
actions. He argued that "the first great act of Freedom's drama as performed by President Lincoln, in giving freedom to the slaves was, to a
great extent, a war measure based on military necessity, of which the
Civil Rights Bill, the Thirteenth, Fourteenth, and Fifteenth Amendments
were the logical consequences based on political necessity." He believed
that slavery would still exist if the war had ended before 1863 but that,
once the slaves were free, it was necessary to ratify that freedom by passage of the Thirteenth Amendment, to extend other rights to them through
passage of the civil rights bill and the Fourteenth Amendment, and
finally to ratify the Fifteenth Amendment "in order to secure to them
their self-protection." He noted that even the South had ratified the last
amendment "as an act of justice to the black man, . . . and as a token of
a nation's gratitude" and also "for the purpose of preserving a political
equilibrium."

Wilson's main point focused on the present goals of blacks. He asserted
strongly that blacks were simply Americans who had been discriminated
against. "I claim, fellow citizens that the black man has always been
American in his ideas, his sentiments, and his affections . . . speaking the
same language, imbibing the same inspirations, revering the same customs
and worshipping the same God." This being so, the black man had always
wanted legal equality. "I have ever claimed for him EQUALITY BEFORE
THE LAW. This is the end and aim of our aspirations and our ambition
soars no higher." Wilson denied that "social equality" was desired or
could be legislated. Pointing out that "everything is attracted to its
kind" in all human societies, he asserted that "the laws which govern
human society are based on certain attributes and qualities of the mind,
on moral and intellectual worth, on pride of birth, and to a great extent,
on the material conditions of life." This being so, social equality is
"beyond the control of human legislation. . . . The black man being well
aware of the laws which govern human society, seeks to alter no social
law, but is content and satisfied with his own social condition."[88]

Thomas Detter delivered the second major address at the Elko celebration. He too praised the Republican party but also attacked the Democrats, urging them to "adopt new and liberal platforms, and prepare
[themselves] for the new order of things." He too pointed out that the
Civil War was the cause of the abolition of slavery and the indirect cause
of the passage of the Thirteenth, Fourteenth, and Fifteenth amendments.

Quoting Lincoln, Alexander Stephens, Stephen A. Douglas, and Andrew Johnson, he asserted that the South had made the decision to abolish slavery by going to war against the Union. Emphasizing that the nation was founded on the principles of the Declaration of Independence, Detter said: "We rejoice that slavery is dead and that Constitutional Liberty is the leading issue of the day." He gave advice to "Colored citizens of African descent" to "go forth in the great battle field of life, and with your ballot, guard well your liberties. . . . Seek often those acquirements that make nations great—get knowledge and money."

Detter's talk made it clear that he did not feel that blacks had gained all their rights. "My white fellow citizens, we want you to conquer your prejudices. Give us even justice—open wide the doors of your common schools to our children; give us our chance . . . in the great race of life." After quoting Washington and Patrick Henry, Detter ended his speech by quoting the reply of Toussaint L'Ouverture when threatened with the beheading of his sons if he did not cease his rebellion: "It is better for two to die than a nation to be enslaved." Detter closed with these words: "Personal and constitutional freedom is what he died to secure. These are my sentiments, I am responsible for the same."

W. A. Scott, president of the day, made some brief introductory remarks. He was pointedly partisan: he thanked "God and the Republican party" for the Emancipation Proclamation and the Fifteenth Amendment and indicated that blacks would prove they could "exercise the elective franchise intelligently, which will never! never! and never be for that party which haughtily rejected to sanction our manhood and the dignity of our God."[89]

A band played "America," "Yankee Doodle," and the "Star Spangled Banner," a Miss Honeywell sang "Marching Through Georgia," and A. C. Dallas read a poem by J. M. Whitfield. In the evening there was a "social ball" at the home of Thomas Detter, which included some black residents of Carlin.

A Fifteenth Amendment celebration was also held at Treasure City in the remote and recently developed White Pine mining area of eastern Nevada. "The day was ushered in by the firing of one hundred guns, and another salute was fired at sundown. About 7 o'clock in the evening the torchlight procession numbering about sixty, headed by a brass band of music, formed on Dunn street, and proceeded to march through the principal streets of the city." There were flags displayed along the route,

Marshal O'Keefe kept order, and spectators cheered the parade. Among the transparencies carried in the parade were ones with these slogans: "We tender our thanks to our political friends," "Boys in 1869, men in 1870," "Political equality—social equality regulates itself," "We have fought with you—we will vote for you," a quotation from a Governor Andrews, and one from President Grant: "No consummation since the war has given me so much pleasure as the ratification of the Fifteenth Amendment."[90]

After the parade a number of speeches were delivered "in the hall of the colored folks on Treasure street." "A large number of white spectators witnessed the proceedings at the Hall with respectful attention." Most of the speakers were black; they included H. Hudson, Isaac Starkey, William Nibblet, and S. T. Wilcox, but ex-Governor Miller of Minnesota also spoke. A white paper commented, "Some of the speeches of the colored orators were not surpassed by Governor Miller, who ranks as one of the 'Grey Eagles' of western oratory."

The speech Hudson gave repeated a number of themes found in speeches by other black speakers in other parts of Nevada. He dwelt on the "record you [blacks] have made on the battle-field," referring to Civil War battles at Port Hudson, Wagner, and Antietam, praised Lincoln, the "illustrious martyr," and hailed the Republican party as the party of "equal rights . . . regardless of color." He expressed gratitude for the ratification of the Fifteenth Amendment but also noted that it was "an act of retributive justice."

Hudson specifically lauded education and connected education with material advancement. Speaking to blacks he said: "Let me urge upon you the importance of acquiring education." He urged blacks to educate their children and themselves in order to "move from menial employments to avocations of a higher order. . . . It is the worldly standard by which we are all judged. The possession of wealth is regarded by the majority, as an evidence of superiority."

Finally, Hudson expressed a basically optimistic view of the future:

> In looking into the far distant I see peace and plenty in abundance;
> I see the colored citizens of the Republic in common with others
> filling high positions of Church and State. I see Cuba and others of
> the West India Islands annexed to the United States. In short I see
> the best and finest government the world has ever produced, and
> asylum for the oppressed of all nations of every clime.[91]

These celebrations have been described at some length and speakers have been copiously quoted for several reasons. There seem to be significant parallels in the events in these three widely separated parts of Nevada. First, the initiative for the celebrations clearly came from the black community, small as it was, and most of the parading, speech making, and musical and poetic exercises were planned and carried out by blacks. Second, the celebrations demonstrated a considerable degree of ability present in this small population. The quotations from speeches indicate that the addresses were intelligent and articulate, and it is clear that many whites in these three cities acknowledged this achievement. Third, all three celebrations involved white participation—to a minor extent in planning and carrying out programs and to an undetermined but substantial extent as spectators. Further, there is little evidence of white hostility to the celebrations or the blacks. Fourth, the black speakers seemed to agree on several themes. While expressing gratitude for the extension of the right to vote and the earlier abolition of slavery, a number of speakers made a point of noting that these acts had merely recognized blacks' preexisting rights, and other speakers emphasized the necessities, military and political, that had led to these actions. In other words, while the speakers clearly expressed gratitude, they were not obsequious or fulsome in their expression of this gratitude. All the speakers assumed that the Republican party had been their ally and would continue to be and that the Democratic party was their enemy. All were optimistic about the future, and most of them indicated that blacks had obligations to take advantage of the opportunities now extended to them—for example, by voting intelligently and/or diligently seeking an education. There was some difference among the speakers as to the degree of satisfaction with existing conditions, however. Some implied that their race had achieved all it wanted or could legitimately expect, while others pointed specifically or generally to disabilities that whites were called upon to remove. In no case, however, did the speeches have a tone of "Uncle Tomism"; in no case did the speakers seem to be saying what they thought white men wanted to hear. In some cases, such as Thomas Detter's speech at Elko, the speakers said things that they must have assumed whites would not applaud. In short, these celebrations in 1870 indicate an intelligent, articulate, vigorous black leadership group heartened by an extension of freedom, realistically grateful to the elements in white society that had produced these new freedoms, aware that more progress was needed, but basically optimistic about what the future would bring.

"OUR FREEDOM IS NOT COMPLETE
UNTIL WE HAVE EQUAL JUSTICE"

Thomas Detter was the most articulate of the remarkable blacks who lived in nineteenth-century Nevada and one of the most articulate in the West. Probably only editors Philip Bell and Peter Anderson left a more complete record of their ideas. Detter's ideas, expressed in letters to the black press, speeches, and his book, are useful as another indication of the thinking of important western black leaders of the last century.

In April 1863 Detter wrote that Jefferson Davis was a traitor who should be hung and closed with this bit of doggerel: "Jeff Davis used to think he would have some fun, but if he don't look out he will be hung. Jeff Davis' niggers have gone home, and left poor Jeff to kingdom to come."[92] He advised other blacks to persevere in their efforts to secure justice, noting that it took many years of work before the California legislature repealed the laws denying blacks the right to testify. Later that year, in suggesting that slavery had received its "death-blow" from the Emancipation Proclamation, Detter stated that black men had fought in every war for the United States and that it was time to do so again:

Liberty and natural justice are the great national principles that stimulate the colored man to battle. If they are to be obtained at any sacrifice, we should be willing to make that sacrifice. . . . Our enslaved brethren are calling to us to help them to throw off the fetters that bind them down. May we indeed do all in our power to crush the tyrant and liberate the captive.[93]

In October 1866 Detter argued that American citizenship should carry with it the right to vote: "No man is a citizen in its true meaning who is deprived of the ballot." Pointing out that the 1866 Civil Rights Act did not extend the suffrage to blacks, he noted that blacks were "exceptions to the favored classes."

If Congress has the power to declare us citizens, it should have secured to us the same rights and immunities that others enjoy. . . . I say we are American citizens with no political rights—natives, and are treated worse than alien soldiers, and we receive not the honor of soldiers.

Noting that the efforts of blacks in fighting to save the Union had not brought about the abolition of all discrimination, he stated a basic complaint: "We are Freemen and still oppressed in our native land. Slavery is fallen, but it is not dead. . . . Our freedom is not complete until we have equal justice with our white fellow citizens."[94]

In 1867 he returned to the theme of suffrage. Blacks, he said, were voting in some southern states but many northern states still did not allow them to vote; he asked: "Are not the blacks of the North as justly entitled to the ballot as those of the South, and as well qualified to exercise it? The time has come; the logic and reason of the age demand justice for all men, regardless of nationality, creed or color." In brief, he said, "I am satisfied that to secure justice fully for the negro, the North needs reconstruction upon a just and equal basis." He argued that Jefferson and Madison had agreed with blacks' claim to be citizens and that blacks had voted in the early years of the Republic. Detter closed with a plea for action by northern states: "We are often told to wait. Wait, when we ask for justice? We have waited until many of us have gone where justice is given to all, and yet here it has not come to us."[95]

A few months later, he returned to his plea for freedom and justice: "Color must cease to be a barrier and a badge of dishonor. Injustice, tyranny and oppression must be driven from this fair land, and the rights of all sheltered and protected. Hope on, Hope ever!"[96]

The suffrage theme was dominant again in a letter he wrote from Idaho City in June 1868. Noting that the northern Republican party was split over the question of black suffrage, he argued, "No man is indeed a Republican who is opposed to EQUALITY BEFORE THE LAW." He predicted victory for the party "that has the moral courage to rise above sectionality and prejudice of caste" and asserted that "there can be no lasting peace until justice shall become the rule of the nation." Another remark in this letter must have had a particular meaning for him. "Men must be measured according to their intellect, not their color."[97]

As the 1868 general election drew near, Detter commented, "Our hopes for the ultimate triumph of free principles are hinged upon the coming Presidential election." Asserting, "We claim this to be our country and our home, and nothing less than the rights of freemen will satisfy us," he complained, "We are still the subjects of a bitter prejudice; we are yet a bone of contention, and it seems hard for the white man to yield up his prejudices against us."[98]

After the 1868 election, he wrote a satirical letter posing as a Democrat and complaining that the Democrats had been "whipped" in California and the nation because of failure to endorse Reconstruction and black voting.[99] A similar satirical letter a few months later recorded a

conversation with Pat, a lifelong Democrat who complained that he had
been paid only two hundred dollars to vote in the last election although
he had voted six times for governor, three times for congressmen, and
ten times for sheriff. When informed that the Democratic party intended
to admit blacks, Pat said he did not "care a copper-half-penny for all
the niggers in the world," and if they accepted the Democratic party,
"they are bigger fools than he gave them credit for." Pat ended by saying,
"We are throwing white men overboard to make room for niggers."[100]

Commenting again on the 1868 election, Detter noted that even some
Republicans were alarmed at the idea of "negro equality" and frightened
by the "fearful ghost of Chinese suffrage, called up from the tomb by
Democratic Spiritualists to delude fainthearted Republicans." He predicted that black suffrage was coming and, after quoting James Madison
to the effect that emancipation must be followed by citizenship, he asked
whether the black man could justly be denied the privileges of citizenship.
He also argued that it was foolish to "deny the common brotherhood of
mankind." Noting that the creator had made some men darker than others,
he asked whether this was a legitimate basis for hate. "I ask the question,
if it is a crime to be black, who is amenable for said crime, the Creator or
his creatures?"[101]

As the general election of 1870 approached, Detter wrote a letter from
Elko, strongly urging that blacks continue to support the Republican party
and oppose the Democratic party. Pointing out that although some Republicans were "traitors" who "are opposed to every measure that tends
to elevate the colored man" and to associating with blacks "outside of the
polls," he nevertheless believed that these persons were not typical of
the party's true principles. "Let us adhere strictly to the genuine principles
of the party, and honor those who have been untiring in their efforts to
complete freedom's noble work," he urged. Detter showed that he was
well aware that the Democrats were using opposition to the Chinese as a
partisan weapon. The Democrats, he said, "use the *Chinese* improved
musket, intended to kill at long range."[102]

In November 1870 Detter wrote that the Republican "mission" was
incomplete and would not be completed until all the laws "for the
protection of human rights are as immovable as the Rocks of Gibraltar."

Detter gave a good analysis of the position of the black community
and of white prejudices in 1870. Acknowledging that slavery was dead, he
asked: "Who can deny that its wicked spirit still haunts us by day and by
night? Everywhere we see the hideous form of American prejudice—the
offspring of slavery, the twin of tyranny." Complaining that white prejudice

still survived, he said: "He [the white man] has nothing to support his
prejudice but the evils which slavery entailed upon us, or to establish his
theory of the colored man's natural inferiority to the white. . . . They
[the slaveholders] made us beasts of burden, and to keep us servile,
ignorant and secluded." He asked blacks not to forget the past because
of the need to "teach our children to hate tyranny and oppression, and
to love liberty" and urged them to use education, the ballot, and the
press as ways of securing freedom.[103]

A few weeks later, he denounced the Democratic party as the party
that "ever crushed us under the iron heel of despotism" and asserted
that "their policy is still the Negro should have no rights that a white man
should respect."[104]

From Eureka in 1872 Detter praised citizenship and the advances it
had brought but complained that true justice had not yet been achieved.

> The intent of the last Constitutional Amendment was to place the
> Negro in possession of every political privilege, and to abolish all laws
> founded upon caste; abridging the rights of States to legislate against
> our class because of color. But . . . men evade it and disregard the
> rights of colored citizens. We are still denied privileges which others
> can purchase.

He mentioned discrimination in hotels, restaurants, common carriers,
and the courts (except for the federal courts). The black man in the
South, he said, "is arraigned before a mob Court to hear his death warrant
read." Detter believed there were two reasons for this state of affairs:
whites were not yet sufficiently educated to respect black rights, and
there were still insufficient legal remedies. The Constitution, he said,
does not do enough; "it does not secure us legal redress for all grievances
inflicted upon us by persons who still believe in Negro inferiority and
white supremacy over the colored citizen."[105]

During the 1872 presidential election, Detter strongly urged black
voters to vote for Grant and other Republicans and not be deceived into
voting for Horace Greeley for president. Calling Greeley a "traitor," he
predicted that his election would merely return the Democrats to power,
and "their first aim would be to paralyze the strong arm of the Federal
Government upon which we relie [sic] for the protection of our rights
in States where they are fettered by local legislation. . . . The time is not
yet for us to experiment with our liberty and rights. They are none too
secure."[106]

Detter was not infrequently called upon to comment on the death of friends. In 1872 he eulogized Peter Keelingsworth, saying of him: "Though educated in the school of slavery, he was a man possessing much native talent, and labored as seriously to build up Zion, and to win souls for Christ; beloved and respected by all." At the same time he said of another friend he had known for nineteen years that he would not praise him because he had faults he would not name but that he was a "constant" friend and always cheerful.[107]

The death of Jeremiah B. Sanderson, a pioneer black educator in California, produced a funeral eulogy by Detter. He praised the deceased, whom he had known for twenty years, as a devoted friend and a devout Christian. Above all, he said, "society has lost a man who loved to worship at the shrine of the pure and just." Saying that Sanderson was well educated, "a profound thinker and a close observer," Detter praised most his passion for justice: "I have stood side by side with him upon the rostrum; he there pleaded nobly for the rights of his down-trodden race, until his face glowed like a furnace, and the fires of liberty burned upon the altar of his soul."[108]

The next year, while expressing pride that blacks had not deserted the Republican party to vote for Greeley and had consistently "fought for the same cherished principles as those of 1776 and 1812," Detter indicated disillusionment: "We are citizens, yet denied the privileges of citizens. Our civil rights are not respected; our children are forbidden to enter public institutions of learning; public patronage is withheld from us, especially on the Pacific. . . . Withal, [the black] is a victim of American prejudice. It is yet a crime not to be white." In this situation he even hinted that it might be wise not to vote for some Republicans: "Vote for no man who is doubtful; bring them square up to the point of justice."[109]

On the death of Senator Charles Sumner of Massachusetts, Detter wrote: "A nation bows its head in submission to heaven's stern decree. Charles Sumner convinced the civilized world of his devotion to human rights, freedom and free institutions. He boldly defended them." He suggested that all blacks should be proud to contribute to a monument to his memory and closed with a poem.[110]

In 1874, while discussing the prospects of passing a new civil rights bill and suggesting that it might prove impossible to do so, he said: "I regard the title of citizenship of little value in a Republican Government when it does not make all equal, and remove every political and civil disability. The great work of freedom is not completed. Nor is the mission of the Republican national party ended."[111]

With the defeat of the civil rights bill in 1874, he became discouraged and even suggested that it might be time for blacks to leave the Republican party. "Just think of it! An American citizen denied accommodations at a public inn—shelter, food and a bed; and proscribed on almost every highway. And still our political friends, who have the power to remedy the evil, wink at it. They lack moral courage." Suggesting that blacks should vote in future only for candidates clearly pledged to justice, he said: "I care not if the coming political contest is made outside of the Republican ranks, if by so doing we are to receive the rights of freemen."[112]

In 1875 Detter gave an address in San Francisco at a celebration commemorating the Emancipation Proclamation. By this time Detter was optimistic; Congress had passed the civil rights bill whose prospects had seemed dim the year before. He said: "I regard the passage of the Civil Rights Bill as the last act in the drama of human rights, fixing ever, I trust our political and social status in these United States. The negro is no longer a slave—he is a freeman. Now and forever in his native land he is an American citizen." Proudly he recounted the strides blacks had made since the end of the Civil War, to the point where "beneath the dome of the nation's capitol he stands contending with the ablest adversaries of his race." Recounting great struggles for freedom, he argued that blacks had fought in every war for freedom and had struggled with their ally, the Republican party, to expand freedom. He predicted that "no government founded upon oppression and caste can live."[113]

Overall Detter apparently did not develop his ideas beyond the area of race relations. There, although he was not a systematic thinker, he was a perceptive and thoughtful writer who could present his arguments well. Many of his comments on race relations are more accurate and perceptive than similar comments published in white newspapers of his day. Probably he had some effect in shaping the political responses of many western blacks through his contributions to the black press, his public addresses, and various unrecorded personal contacts. Detter seems to have had a consistent attitude toward race relations from an early age. He simply wanted to be treated by whites without reference to his race; while he was aware of black heroes, such as Toussaint L'Ouverture and Crispus Attucks, his major theme was the injustice of being treated as an inferior because of his race; the implication is that he would like to be treated exactly like white people. There is no indication that he thought his values and outlook were different because he was black. At the same time he clearly identified with other blacks of the West and the nation, and he saw his life as necessarily intertwined with theirs— but apparently only because of white prejudice, which denied all blacks basic rights.

REGIONAL AND NATIONAL
ACTIVITIES

Nevada blacks were largely cut off by distance and the cost and short-
comings of the various forms of transportation linking East and West
from substantial involvement with activities of the black communities
of the East and South; however, there is little question that many of these
leaders kept up with events affecting blacks in other parts of the country,
and a few of them were recognized by black leaders of the East and
South. Some of them may have attended national meetings held in the
East. (Philip Bell, who had been an editor of one of the earliest black
newspapers before going West, was known through his newspaper outside
the West. In June 1868 he printed a letter commending his work from
Frederick Douglass, perhaps the most distinguished national black leader
of the nineteenth century.)[114]

Charles H. Wesley, a historian of black labor, wrote about a Nevada
delegate to the National Labor Convention of Colored Men held in
Washington, D.C., in December 1869. Near the beginning of the convention,
he wrote, "Mr. William U. Sanders of Nevada made the motion for the
appointment of a committee on credentials." Later he reported that
Sanders was chosen vice-president of a National Bureau of Labor set up
by the convention.[115] There is no evidence of a Nevada black with this
name in 1870, and it is probable either that this was an error or that
Sanders held a proxy for a Nevada delegate. The call issued by an executive committee headed by Isaac Myers had listed William H. Hall and
Dr. Stephenson as possible delegates to the convention, although Hall
was identified as being from California.[116]

Although he could not attend the 1869 labor convention, Hall, who
was then in the Treasure Hill area, wrote a long letter "to the President
and Members of the National Labor Convention of Colored Men of the
United States." Among other things, he discussed his views on the
"Chinese question," specifically a proposal to import Chinese labor into
the South. He opposed it, on two grounds. One was that the Chinese were
not Americans and did not wish to be, while blacks were trying "to be an
integral part of the nation." His second reason was that the Chinese,
being able to live on much less than blacks, would force southern blacks
into "starvation" if they were introduced; consequently, a "war of races"
might ensue. He hoped the national convention would oppose the plan.[117]

Hall also proposed in this letter that a national executive committee
at Washington be selected to follow the progress of the race in the South

and made the interesting suggestion that a "general fund" to be built up from contributions by both whites and blacks be set up to buy land for the "laboring black men" of the South. The land purchased by this fund, he thought, could be resold to the freedmen.

In early 1870, a meeting of black citizens of Virginia City "nominated" Dr. Stephenson to represent Nevada "in the National Executive Committee at Washington." However, there is yet no information to indicate whether he could afford to attend a national meeting in the East.[118]

A national convention of blacks in 1873 apparently had no delegates from Nevada, although there were delegates from California, Oregon, and Utah.[119] Charles Wilson may have attended the National Convention of Colored Men called by the Colored Newspaper Men of the United States in August 1876; he was suggested as a delegate for Nevada. The executive committee appointed by the convention included Wilson, and this may mean that he attended it.[120]

Apparently only one black convention in western states was called in the nineteenth century, and it may not have been held. An 1870 convention of "Colored Citizens of the States and Territories of the Pacific Coast" was called by an executive committee in San Francisco, which listed possible delegates from various areas, including R. H. Small of Wadsworth, Nevada.[121]

From the early 1860s into the 1870s, a number of black Nevadans made vigorous and able efforts to change constitutional provisions or laws that denied them the right to vote, hold office and serve on juries, testify in either civil or criminal cases, and (in practice) attend public schools. Their activity was typical of and interrelated with similar efforts by blacks in other western states. By the middle of the 1870s, most of the Nevada racist laws had been repealed or annulled, although more often by national than by state action.

The continuing success in changing these laws, accompanied by an apparent improvement in their actual treatment, led to a change of emphasis for these leaders. In the 1870s there were celebrations of their victories; observances of the anniversary of the Emancipation Proclamation and the ratification of the Fifteenth Amendment were important events in the Nevada black community, and they received attention from white Nevadans. Some participants in these events even believed that racism had been defeated and that American blacks had gained the same rights as white people, with the important exception of "social equality." That this conclusion was unduly optimistic is obvious; in the 1960s blacks, in Nevada as elsewhere, once more had to demand that government protect their rights. Although a fully adequate account of the actual status of black Nevadans cannot yet be given, it appears that the general pattern was one of improvement in the 1860s and 1870s followed by a reversal of this trend and a decline in status in the latter part of the nineteenth century and the first part of the twentieth century.

NOTES

1. *Pacific Appeal*, July 11, 1863. As noted in chapter 6, much later M. Howard and Oscar Taylor were identified as leaders in the 1863 efforts. The writer of the letter calling for the first meeting, however, signed himself "J" and his identity is not known.

2. Ibid., December 12, 1863.

3. Ibid., January 23, 1864.

4. Ibid., November 29, 1873.

5. Nevada Senate, *Journal*, 1864-1865, p. 298.

6. *Elevator*, August 4, 1865.

7. Ibid.

8. Ibid., January 5, 1866.

9. Ibid., March 9, 1866.

10. Ibid., January 19, 1866.

11. Senate, *Journal*, 1866, p. 146.

12. *Elevator*, February 16, 1866.

13. *Territorial Enterprise*, February 24, 1867. The *Enterprise* had supported the bill before Dr. Stephenson's letter. Ibid., February 20, 1867.

14. Nevada, Assembly, *Journal*, 1873, p. 154.

15. *Elevator*, March 15, 1873.

16. Ibid., December 6, 1873.

17. Ibid., February 28, 1868.

18. *Pacific Appeal*, December 16, 1871.

19. *Elevator*, June 17, 1870.

20. Ibid., February 28, 1874.

21. Ibid., May 26, 1865.

22. Ibid., August 11, 1865.

23. Andrew Marsh, *Reports of the 1863 Constitutional Convention* (Carson City, Nevada: Legislative Counsel Bureau, 1972), p. 464.

24. *Gold Hill Daily News*, October 23, 1865, in Bancroft Scraps, vol. 95:2. Bancroft Library, University of California, Berkeley.

25. *Carson Daily Appeal*, September 9, 1865, reprinting an item from an unnamed Virginia City newspaper.

26. *Elevator*, March 9, 1866 (letter from Orion).

27. *Territorial Enterprise*, May 2, 1866.

28. *Gold Hill Daily News,* June 5, 1867.
29. *Territorial Enterprise,* June 8, 1867.
30. Ibid., February 2, 1870.
31. *Fourth Annual Report* of Superintendent of Public Instruction, p. 16.
32. *Carson Daily Appeal,* September 6, 1867.
33. Ibid., November 27, 1867. The trustees were J. W. Jackson, Washington, J. R. Brown, John Anderson, and Jacob Johnson.
34. *First Biennial Report* of the Superintendent of Public Instruction (1868-1870), p. 14. For his earlier comments, see *Fourth Annual Report* of the Superintendent of Public Instruction, 1867-1868, p. 16.
35. *Daily State Register,* April 9, 1871.
36. Records of Case No. 508, Nevada State Archives, Carson City. Subsequent material on this case, whose source is not identified, is from these records.
37. State of Nevada ex. rel. Stoutmeyer v. Duffy, 7 Nevada 342, 346 (1872).
38. Reprinted in *Pacific Appeal,* March 9, 1872.
39. *Carson Daily Appeal,* November 7, 1876.
40. *Gold Hill Evening News,* March 6, 1872, quoting *Carson City Register.*
41. *Second Biennial Report* of the Superintendent of Public Instruction, pp. 15, 16.
42. Nevada, *Statutes,* 1873, chap. 81, sec. 14.
43. *Elevator,* March 15, 1873 (letter from "Wilse").
44. Ibid., November 29, 1873.
45. See Ward v. Flood, 48 Cal. 36 (1874).
46. California school law provided for segregated schools until 1880. (Later, in the twentieth century, California law provided for segregated education for children of Indian or Oriental parents.) See Robert F. Heizer and Alan F. Almquist, *The Other Californians* (Berkeley: University of California Press, 1971), pp. 61-64.
47. *Elevator,* March 15, 1873.
48. Ibid., May 17, 1873.
49. Ibid., May 6, 1870.
50. Ibid., October 26, 1872.
51. Ibid., September 11, 1868.
52. *White Pine News,* June 7, 1870, reprinted in *Elevator,* June 17, 1870.
53. W. Turrentine Jackson, *Treasure Hill* (Tucson: University of Arizona Press, 1963), p. 107.
54. *Territorial Enterprise,* February 2, 1870.
55. Ibid., August 30, 1870. The *Enterprise* also drew the attention of "our colored electors" to the letter.
56. *Elevator,* March 25, 1870 (letter from Theodore A. Lee).
57. Ibid., July 8, 1870 (letter from Grice).
58. Jerome J. Quinlan, "As I Remember Them," photograph collection, California Historical Society, San Francisco.

59. For a sample, see *Territorial Enterprise*, February 17, 1869.
60. Ibid., April 23, 1870.
61. *Elko Independent*, May 4, 1870.
62. *Carson Appeal*, April 15, 1870.
63. *Elevator*, April 22, 1870.
64. Ibid., June 3, 1870.
65. Ibid., May 16, 1873.
66. *Carson Daily Appeal*, October 26, 1867.
67. One newspaper account of a meeting, after reporting the names of white speakers, mentioned "some colored gentlemen whose names we failed to learn." Ibid., October 12, 1876. At a postelection meeting speakers were the president, F.W.B. Grinage, B. Johnson, Theodore A. Lee, R. Sharehorn, William R. Brown, C. B. Cooper, George H. Rogers, B. Dodge, G. W. Dale, R. Elliott, and D. W. Sands, a visitor from the Virginia City Lincoln Union Club. Ibid., November 10, 1876.
68. Ibid., November 4, 1876.
69. Ibid., November 7, 1876.
70. In San Jose, California, the Colored Hayes and Wheeler Club was abandoned in March 1876; members joined the white club because they felt that segregation was undesirable. *Pacific Appeal*, August 26, 1876 (letter from J. Overto).
71. *Territorial Enterprise*, August 27, 1878.
72. *Nevada State Journal*, January 12, 1937, quoting an article in the *Virginia City Chronicle*, "58 Years Ago." There is no such article in the *Chronicle* for January 11 or 13, 1879, and the edition for January 12 is missing from the newspaper collection at the University of Nevada, Reno.
73. *Eureka Daily Sentinel*, October 15, 1880.
74. *Territorial Enterprise*, August 17, 1880.
75. Ibid., August 18, 1880.
76. Ibid., August 27, September 2, 16, 1880.
77. *Elevator*, March 25, 1870. See *Territorial Enterprise*, April 7, 1870, and *Gold Hill Daily News*, April 8, 1870.
78. *Territorial Enterprise*, April 8, 1870.
79. Ibid.
80. *Gold Hill Daily News*, April 7, 1870.
81. *Territorial Enterprise*, April 8, 1870.
82. Ibid., April 10, 1870.
83. Ibid., April 9, 1870.
84. Ibid.
85. *Elevator*, April 22, 1870.
86. Harold's Club, *Pioneer Nevada* (Reno: Harolds Club, 1956), II: 106.
87. *Elevator*, April 15, 1870.
88. Ibid., May 6, 1870.
89. Ibid.

90. *Daily Inland Empire*, April 8, 1870, reprinted in *Elevator*, April 15, 1870.
91. Ibid.
92. *Pacific Appeal*, April 25, 1863.
93. Ibid., June 13, 1863.
94. *Elevator*, October 26, 1866.
95. Ibid., December 27, 1867.
96. Ibid., May 22, 1868.
97. Ibid., July 3, 1868.
98. Ibid., October 2, 1868.
99. Ibid., December 4, 1868.
100. Ibid., May 7, 1869.
101. Ibid., October 29, 1869.
102. *Pacific Appeal*, September 17, 1870.
103. Ibid., October 8, 1870.
104. Ibid., November 5, 1870.
105. Ibid., March 30, 1872.
106. Ibid., September 7, 1872.
107. Ibid., October 12, 1872.
108. See Rudolph M. Lapp, "Jeremiah Sanderson: Early California Negro," *Journal of Negro History* 53 (October 1968): 321-333, and *Pacific Appeal*, October 9, 1875.
109. *Pacific Appeal*, November 8, 1873.
110. Ibid., March 28, 1874.
111. Ibid., May 16, 1874.
112. Ibid., October 24, 1874.
113. Ibid., April 24, 1875.
114. *Elevator*, June 5, 1868.
115. Charles H. Wesley, *Negro Labor in the United States, 1850-1925* (New York: Russell and Russell, 1927), pp. 177-178, 180.
116. *Elevator*, October 15, 1869.
117. Ibid., November 19, 1869. The proposal to import Chinese laborers into the South (a few were actually introduced) is discussed briefly by Wesley, *Negro Labor*, pp. 196-197.
118. *Elevator*, March 25, 1870.
119. Ibid., December 13, 1873.
120. *Pacific Appeal*, March 11, June 24, 1876.
121. *Elevator*, June 3, 1870.

James P. Beckwourth, mountain man. *Courtesy of Nevada State Historical Society.*

The writing on this photograph identifies it as a portrait of the first black child born in Virginia City. *Courtesy of Nevada State Historical Society.* According to the Census of Population of 1880, Joseph W. Tait was born in Nevada in 1861. In 1880 his parents, Benjamin and Julia Tait, were living in Virginia City, so this may be his photograph. The 1870 and 1880 Censuses of Population listed 25 black persons born in Nevada before 1870; the earliest recorded birth is that of Benjamin Barber, son of Charlotte Barber of Genoa, born in Nevada in 1854.

First colored baby born in Va. City

Unidentified women. The photograph was taken in Reno. *Courtesy of Nevada State Historical Society.*

Unidentified man, said to have been Mark Twain's janitor. *Courtesy of Nevada State Historical Society.*

117

High school graduating class of 1883, Virginia City. Standing, left to right: Clarence Sands, Principal Van Wagenen, Valedictorian Mark Averill, Harry Lynd. Seated, left to right: Annie Fraser, Mamie Hanning, Jennie Hinch, Katie Ford. *Courtesy of Nevada State Historical Society.* Clarence Sands was one of five children born of David W. and Laura E. Sands; according to the Census of Population of 1880, he was born in Nevada in 1868. His family was one of the leading black families of Virginia City. His father was a trustee of the AME church in 1867, occupied several posts in Ashlar Lodge of Prince Hall Masons and in the Grand Lodge, was a leader in various social activities and was also active in the black community. Two of Clarence Sands' sons are still living in the San Francisco Bay area.

Unidentified black woman with white child, in Carson City or Virginia City. The woman may have worked for H. M. Yerington, Superintendent of the Virginia and Truckee Railroad. *Courtesy of Nevada State Museum* (Graham Hardy Collection.)

Grafton Tyler Brown, black lithographer and artist. *Courtesy of Provincial Archives of British Columbia, Victoria, B.C.*

119

RETURN FROM WASHOE.

Drawing by J. Ross Browne of the Negro who transported him to Woodford's in 1860. From J. Ross Browne, *A Peep at Washoe and Washoe Revisited* (Balboa Island, California: Paisano Press, 1959), p.109.

Lithograph of Fort Churchill, Nevada Territory, by Grafton T. Brown. *Courtesy of Bancroft Library.*

Boston · Railroad · Photo · Car.

PACIFIC COAST ADDRESS,   SACRAMENTO CAL.

Henry Towns, taken about 1893. At that time, Towns was a cowboy at Beowawe, Nevada. He was the son of William E. Towns and brother of Royal E. Towns, Oakland, California. *Courtesy of Royal E. Towns.*

—5—

General Characteristics of Nevada's Black Population, 1870 and 1880

The early 1860s brought a rapid influx of whites into Nevada, leading to the creation of Nevada Territory in 1861 and the admission of the state of Nevada to the Union in 1864. The small number of blacks in Nevada in 1860 increased by several times at the beginning of this decade. Although blacks never constituted a large proportion of Nevada's population in the nineteenth century, from the early 1860s until the late 1880s several hundred could be found in the state at any one time. This number was large enough to permit the creation of a number of institutions within the black community.

TOTAL NUMBERS AND DISTRIBUTION BY COUNTY

The total number of blacks in the state averaged three hundred to four hundred and probably never exceeded five hundred at any one time during the nineteenth century. Table 1 gives the black population of the state according to the United States Census of Population from 1860 to 1970, plus the number of blacks enumerated in a state census in 1875.

Table 1
BLACK POPULATION OF NEVADA, 1860-1970

Year	Number of Blacks in Nevada	Black Proportion of Total Nevada Population	Black Proportion of Total Population of the West[1]	Black Proportion of Total Population of U.S.[2]
1860[3]	44[4]	0.6%	0.9%	14.1%[10]
1870	324	0.8	0.1	12.7
1875	308[5]	0.6[6]	—	—
1880	396[7]	0.6	0.2	13.1
1890[8]	242	0.5	0.4	11.9
1900[9]	134	0.3	0.3	11.6
1910	513	0.6	0.5	10.7
1920	346	0.4	0.8	9.9
1930	516	0.6	1.0	9.7
1940	664	0.6	1.3	9.8
1950	4,302	2.7	4.8	10.8
1960	13,484	4.7	5.8	10.6
1970	27,621	5.7	4.8	11.1

NOTES:

1. Daniel O. Price, *Changing Characteristics of the Negro Population* (Washington, D.C.: U.S. Government Printing Office, 1969), p. 9.

2. Ibid., p. 13.

3. What is now Nevada was part of Utah Territory in 1860; the area that became Nevada was included in this tabulation. American Indians were not counted and therefore are not part of the total population used to compute column two for this year.

4. The published census returns give this figure as forty-five; however, one of the persons listed as mulatto was born in "S. Sea Islands"; I have assumed that he was not an American black.

5. *Census, 1875.*

6. Total state population includes 16,243 Indians. Blacks constituted 0.8 percent of the total population excluding Indians.

7. As explained in the bibliography to this book, ninety Indians at Duckwater were counted as black or mulatto; they have been subtracted from the published state total.

8. Total state population includes 3,599 "civilized Indians." Blacks constituted 0.6 percent of the total population, excluding Indians.

9. Total state population includes 5,216 Indians. From this point on, all Indians were counted and included in the state total.

10. Proportion of *free* black population of country. Charles H. Wesley, *Negro Labor in the United States 1850-1925* (New York: Russell and Russell, 1927), p. 29.

While there were blacks in every county of the state in 1870 and 1880, in both periods they were concentrated in northwestern Nevada, which is also where most whites lived. Tables 2 and 3 give a detailed breakdown of the place of residence of all blacks in the state in both years. In 1870, 95 out of the 324 blacks lived in Storey County; in 1880, 108 of the 396 blacks in Nevada were enumerated in Storey County. Another 31 in 1870 and 61 in 1880 lived in Ormsby County, and Washoe County was the place of residence of 36 in 1870 and 35 in 1880. These three counties together accounted for 45 percent of the total black population of the state in 1870 and 52 percent in 1880. This is not surprising; Virginia City, located on the Comstock lode, was the largest city in Nevada during the nineteenth century, and therefore Storey County was the largest county; Ormsby County was the site of the state capital from territorial days on; and Reno, in Washoe County, was a relatively large city primarily because it was on the transcontinental railroad at the nearest point to Virginia City. The only other relatively large number of blacks in either year was found in White Pine County in 1870, which had a total of 66 blacks. Blacks participated in the "rush to White Pine" in the late 1860s and early 1870s but also left, as did most of the whites, when the Treasure Hill mines stopped producing.

"SEPARATED BY PLAIN LINES OF DISTINCTION"

Within Virginia City, blacks were concentrated at the commercial core of the city, but not by law. Evidently only the Chinese, among the many races living in Virginia City, were legally restricted to a certain part of the city. An unidentified correspondent writing from Virginia City in 1863 remarked that "the Asiatic element [was] confined to its quarter, the white, black and yellow diffusing itself over the balance of the city."[1] He was correct about the Chinese, but other nonwhite groups and white economic classes were concentrated at various places within the city as well.

Virginia City ordinances permitted the forced removal of Chinese and this evidently formed the legal basis for confining the Chinese to a part of the city (although some Chinese lived with white families for whom they were cooks or servants.)[2] In general, though, residents of Virginia City sorted themselves out by both race and economic status. According to Eliot Lord, writing in 1880, "several quarters" of Virginia City "were separated from one another by plain lines of distinction." High on the side of Mt. Davidson lived the wealthiest residents of the city, the "mine super-

Table 2
PLACE OF RESIDENCE OF BLACKS IN NEVADA, 1870

Douglas County			Lyon County	2
Genoa	14			
Elko County			Nye County	
Camp Halleck	1		Belmont	1
Carlin	5			
Elko	18		Ormsby County	
Mineral Hill	2		Carson City	29
Mountain City	1		Empire Township	2
	27			31
Esmeralda County			Storey County	
Pine Grove	1		Gold Hill	5
Silver Peak	1		Virginia City	90
Wellington Station	6			95
	8		Washoe County	
Humboldt County			Franktown	3
Golconda Township	1		Geiger Grade	1
Oreana	1		Truckee Meadows	1
Winnemucca	3		Reno	22
	5		Verdi	1
Lander County			Wadsworth	8
Battle Mountain	2			36
Eureka District	2		White Pine County	
Austin	27		Hamilton	54
	31		Shermantown	1
Lincoln County			Treasure City	11
Pahranaghat	1			66
Panaca	2			
Pioche	6			
Spring Valley	2			
	11			

Table 3
PLACE OF RESIDENCE OF BLACKS IN NEVADA, 1880

Douglas County		Lincoln County	
Carson Valley	12	Bullionville	4
Genoa	9	Eldorado Canon	1
Pine Nut Hills	1	Meadow Valley Wash	2
	22	Panaca	1
Elko County		Pioche	8
Carlin	5		16
Clover Valley	1	Lyon County	
Elko	9	Sutro	1
Halleck	1		
Ruby Valley	2	Nye County	
Simi (?) Creek	1	Belmont	3
Tuscarora	7	Grantsville Precinct	6
Wells q	5	Tybo	4
No area given	2	No area given	1
	33		14
Esmeralda County		Ormsby County	
Aurora	1	Carson City	55
Candelaria	2	Outside Carson City	3
Fish Lake Valley	1	State Prison	3
Table Mountain	1		61
	5	Storey County	
Eureka County		Gold Hill	14
Eureka	46	Virginia City	92
Palisade	2	No area given	2
	48		108
Humboldt County		Washoe County	
Black Rock	1	Below Verdi	1
Lake Township	2	Glendale	1
Lassen Township	5	Reno	31
Paradise Valley	2	Wadsworth	1
Quinn River Valley	3	No area given	1
Spring City	3		35
Winnemucca	9	White Pine County	
	25	Hamilton	1
		Green Springs and Pinto Creek	1
Lander County		Newark Valley	4
Austin	11	Osceola	1
Battle Mountain	7	Spring Valley	1
	18	Ward	2
			10

intendents and leading merchants." Presumably most miners occupied the
area above C and D streets, the chief commercial streets of the city. Just
below C Street was the section inhabited by prostitutes, and just below
them (probably below H Street) were the Chinese.[3] Lord placed the
Indians below the Chinese, at the bottom of Mt. Davidson, while Dan
De Quille (William Wright), a highly respected reporter on the Comstock
for many years, commented that Chinatown was in the "eastern suburbs"
and that the Indians lived on "the slopes of the surrounding mountains."[4]

Although nineteenth-century observers did not report this, the blacks
of Virginia City lived along B and C streets, for the most part, between the
white miners and the prostitutes, in the commercial heart of the city.
Census enumeration forms did not provide addresses in 1870, but enumerators were supposed to go from house to house, and therefore names reported
together probably meant that the persons reported lived close together.
There is one page of forty names among the enumeration forms for
Virginia City in 1870 on which every person listed was black or mulatto;
four more blacks were listed on a page close to this one. Thus, forty-four of
the eighty-seven blacks listed in Virginia City in 1870 evidently lived close
to each other.

In 1880 addresses were provided, and it is clear that the blacks were
concentrated at the center of the city. Of the ninety-two blacks enumerated
in Virginia City in 1880, thirty-eight lived on two blocks of C Street, just
south and north of Union Street, the main east-west street from which the
street-numbering system began. Another fifteen had addresses from 100 to
199 on C Street, eight were listed as living on C Street, but no address was
given, and another lived in the 200 block of South C street. In summary,
fifty-nine blacks lived on C Street, most of them within one block of
Union Street. Most of the other addresses for blacks in Virginia City in
that year were within one block, north or south, of Union Street, although
one man was in the county jail and another was in the county hospital.

Anyone living on C Street at the center of Virginia City in the 1870s
and 1880s must have lived above the businesses that lined this street. From
photographs of the time and the few surviving buildings that can be seen
today, it is apparent that this area contained mainly businesses, with one
or two stories above the street level for apartments. One consequence of
this fact is that blacks lived in the noisiest part of the city; many accounts
report great activity along C Street until late at night. Dan De Quille describes
humorously the "perfect Babel of cries and harangues" that filled the
"principal street" of Virginia City on summer evenings and includes one
of Virginia City's black residents in his description. As part of a confusing

harangue from many people speaking at once, he quotes "Clem Berry
(Scipio Africanus)" advertising a coach ride to Reno for two dollars.[5]
De Quille's account of C Street at night is paralleled by a description
written by Peter Anderson, editor of one of the black weeklies in San
Francisco, when he visited Virginia City in 1876. Anderson noted that
businessmen did not just wait for customers to come to them but began at
about twilight to try to attract customers by sending employees into the
street. He mentioned a band advertising a play at a theater, singers outside
various establishments, and a "nostrum-seller" with "flaming oil-lights."
He remarked, "This excitement goes on until late at night about C street
and other streets in its near vicinity."[6]
While there were only thirty-one blacks in Reno in 1880, and they
were less concentrated than in Virginia City, it is interesting that eight
persons lived on Lake Street, where businesses patronized by blacks exist
today. Another lived at various addresses on Second Street, three were
listed on Commercial Row, and three had addresses on River Front Street.
Probably all of these addresses were close together near the center of
Reno at that time.

AGE AND SEX DISTRIBUTIONS
AND HOUSEHOLD TYPES

Among the black population as well as the white population, the pre-
dominance of adult males continued to be evident in the 1870s and
1880s, although there were more women and children than in the previous
period. From 77 percent in 1860, the male proportion dropped to 67
percent in 1870 and to 63 percent in 1875 and 1880. The age distribution
in 1870 and 1880 of the Nevada black population is shown in Table 4.
In 1870 only 15 percent of the black population was under fifteen, and
this proportion was 17 percent in 1880. In 1870 2 percent and in 1880
7 percent of the black population were sixty or over. In 1870, 45 percent
of the population was thirty to thirty-nine, and this proportion was
virtually the same—46 percent—in 1880. In other words, there were more
families among Nevada's black population during the 1870s and 1880s
but single persons still predominated. In 1870 the census enumerators did
not ask about marital status, but some told them anyway, and enumerators
recorded it; in 1880 the question was asked specifically. In Table 5, it has
been assumed that a man and a woman of roughly the same age and with
the same last name who seemed to be at the same address were married; if
there were children of the same name at the same location, this strengthened

Table 4
AGE DISTRIBUTION OF NEVADA BLACKS, 1870, 1875, 1880

	1870 No.	Percent	1875 No.	1880 No.	Percent
Under 5	21	6	14	20	5
5-14	31	10	36	46	12
15-19	13	4	14	25	6
20-29	59	18	59	67	17
30-39	88	27	58	89	22
40-49	70	21	65	64	16
50-59	35	11	38	55	14
60 and over	7	2	18	28	7
Undetermined	0	0	6	2	0

Table 5
HOUSEHOLD TYPES AMONG NEVADA BLACKS, 1870 AND 1880

Household Types	1870 Families	Individuals	1880 Families	Individuals
Husband-wife (sometimes with other adults)	16	36	17	40
Husband-wife with children	17	73	22	99
Apparent common-law marriage with children	1	3	3	7
Female-headed household with children	9	34	13	38
Single persons living alone	—	45	—	52
Single persons living with others:				
In all-black households	14	50	0	9
In households containing whites	0	72	0	124
Other households	6	11	11	26

the presumption. In both years a few households with children in which the man and the woman had different last names were assumed to be common-law marriages. This table refers to apparent household arrangements at the time of the census; in 1880 some of the single persons were identified as married but listed here as single because they were apparently not living with their spouses. The figures are not precise, but they seem to show a similar pattern in each year. Of the relatively few households that contained children, approximately a third in both years were headed by women.

A few examples of the various household types may indicate something more of the people represented in these figures. A typical young married couple in 1870 was William and Maggie Hughes of Elko. He was born in Michigan and she was born in Connecticut; he was a laborer and she was keeping house. He reported a personal estate of three hundred dollars. A slightly older couple in 1870 was John and Ann Billings of Virginia City; both were fifty-four. A miner from South Carolina, John claimed one hundred fifty dollars in real estate and four hundred dollars in personal estate. Ann was a servant, and both lived in the household of W. E. F. Deal, a thirty-year-old white lawyer from Maryland; the household also contained a seventeen-year-old Chinese boy who was a cook.

The families with children included that of C. H. and Mary Wilson of Elko. Charles Wilson was an important leader of the black community. Both were forty-two in 1870; he was born in Ohio and she was born in Kentucky. He was a barber, with three hundred dollars in real estate and one hundred dollars in personal estate. A son Charles, nineteen, was also a barber and had been born in Ohio; a daughter Mary, six, had been born in California. In 1880 C. H. Wilson had a new wife, Emma D., twenty-six. His daughter Mary was still living at home and attended school during the year but Charles was no longer listed. Hiram and Harriett Lyons of Virginia City headed another family. Hiram was forty in 1870, had been born in New York, and was a porter, with three hundred fifty dollars in real estate and three hundred dollars in personal estate. Harriett was thirty-four in 1870, born in Maryland, and keeping house. Their son George, nine, had been born in California, but their daughter Harriet, five, had been born in Nevada. Their daughter was still living with them in 1880 and had been attending school during the year, but their son was no longer listed at their address. Mr. Lyons was now identified as a "Whitner and Coleman." (Probably this meant that he did whitewashing and delivered coal.)

Among single persons in 1870, there was C. Crowley, a twenty-five-year-old woman from Virginia who was a domestic servant in the home of A. D. and Mrs. King; he was a white cavalry officer at Camp Halleck, in Elko County. H. and Charles Spencer, twenty-two and thirty-one in 1870 and both bootblacks, may have been brothers; they lived in the household of E. C. Cook, justice of the peace at Gold Hill. Samuel Wagner, a bootblack in Virginia City in 1870 who was living with four other black men, was still identified as a bootblack in 1880 but was probably retired; his age was given as seventy-seven. He was still in Virginia City, living in a household with a white widow from Germany and four white males—a saloon keeper, a barber, a waiter, and a printer.

PLACE OF BIRTH

The place of birth of the black population in the three years is given in Table 6.

In both 1870 and 1880 Virginia provided the largest number of people from any one state (forty-eight in 1870 and forty-seven in 1880); in both years the second largest number from a Deep South state were from Louisiana (thirteen in 1870 and fourteen in 1880). Maryland led the border states in both years, with forty-two in 1870 and thirty-nine in 1880. There seems to be no clear-cut pattern among the states outside the South except that the number born in California and Nevada increased during the decade. In 1870, nineteen had been born in California, and this increased to thirty-one in 1880. There were seventeen persons who had been born in Nevada according to the 1870 count and forty-four in 1880. The West Indies provided the largest number of blacks born outside the United States (ten in 1870 and eleven in 1880), followed by Canada, with eight in 1870 and seven in 1880. In 1870 only one person listed Mexico as place of birth, but eight did so in 1880.

Table 6
PLACE OF BIRTH OF NEVADA BLACKS, 1870, 1875, 1880

	1870		1875		1880	
	No.	Percent	No.	Percent	No.	Percent
Deep South	102	32	72	23	106	27
Border	85	26	80	26	105	27
Total South	188		152		211	
U.S. outside South	109	34	117	38	147	37
Outside U.S.	24	7	26	8	35	9
Undetermined	3		13		3	

NOTES

1. Clipping in Bancroft Scraps, vol. 95-1, pp. 242-243, Bancroft Library, University of California, Berkeley. The clipping has a date of September 12, 1863, and was written by an unidentified correspondent from Virginia City.

2. "Ordinances of Virginia City," pp. 235-278, in *The Nevada Directory for 1868-69* (San Francisco: M. D. Carr and Co., 1868); this ordinance is on p. 268. F. M. Huffaker and J. P. Flanningham, comps., *Ordinances of the City of Virginia and Town of Gold Hill, Storey County, Nevada* (Virginia, Nevada: Wm. Sutherland, Printer, 1888); this ordinance is on p. 71. The Gold Hill ordinances do not contain such a provision nor does a compilation of Gold Hill ordinances in 1877. *Revised Ordinances of the Town of Gold Hill* (Gold Hill: Alf. Doten, Town Printer, 1877). These ordinances seem to have been linked to a special concern about Chinese prostitutes. The 1868 ordinance (but not the 1888 one) has a second section forbidding females to act in various ways "for the purpose of inviting prostitution." An unidentified correspondent writing from Austin in 1868 reported that the new board of aldermen was expected to act to enforce an ordinance against Chinese prostitutes. "A city ordinance confines the daughters of the Flowery Kingdom to a certain block on the west side of Pine street; but of late they have been expanding, to the annoyance and disgust of white neighbors who have petitioned to have them removed to their legitimate quarters. Marshal Wheeler will, therefore, drive them back to their corral." Bancroft Scraps, vol. 95:1. The article is dated Austin, May 20, 1868.

3. Eliot Lord, *Comstock Mining and Miners* (Berkeley, California: Howell-North, 1959), pp. 198-199. C. B. Glasscock, perhaps relying on Lord, gives a similar account of the residential patterns of Virginia City; he also does not mention blacks. *The Big Bonanza* (Portland, Oregon: Binfords and Mort, 1931), p. 216.

4. Dan De Quille, *The Big Bonanza* (New York: Alfred A. Knopf, 1947), pp. 214, 291.

5. Ibid., pp. 296-299.

6. *Pacific Appeal*, June 10, 1876.

— 6 —

Economic Status of Nevada Blacks, 1860-1890

Census data on occupations and property ownership can be combined with other information to give a reasonably full picture of the economic status of nineteenth-century Nevada blacks. Several major conclusions about their economic standing emerge from analysis of the available data.

First, most blacks in nineteenth-century Nevada were engaged in low-income and low-status occupations; undoubtedly the average black was an unskilled laborer, if a man, or a domestic servant, if a woman.

Second, a significant number of blacks achieved more economically than the bulk of their group and were doing well even by comparison with the average white person. While there seem to have been only two black professionals in the state in the nineteenth century, there were several black businessmen, ranchers, and miners who were earning significant incomes and acquiring some property.

Third, there apparently was improvement in the economic standing of the black community of Nevada from the 1860s through the 1880s. The black business group apparently increased slowly in numbers and income during this period.

"WE WERE DESTINED TO FILL
THE MENIAL PLACES"

The occupations listed by census enumerators in 1870 and 1880 were classified as carefully as possible into broad categories which are similar to those used by the Bureau of the Census today. Unfortunately this cannot be an exact process since the information provided is not complete enough for accurate placement of each person. The specific listings are also indicated, and some of the problems in interpreting the data are discussed below. Enumerators were supposed to ask about occupation only for those fifteen and older, but where they recorded an occupation for younger persons, it is listed. These listings evidently give usual occupation; when a separate question on employment status was included in 1880, many people who gave occupations were found to have been unemployed for substantial periods of time.

The most obvious thing about the information shown in Table 7 is that most blacks were found in low-status and low-income occupations; most were unskilled laborers or service workers.[1] As a black writer from Virginia City put it in 1862, slavery had left its mark; its "influence has so prejudiced the minds of men against us as a class of people, that they almost believe we were created and destined to fill the menial places and do the drudgery."[2] In 1870 only two of the blacks for whom occupational data were given were identified as unemployed; they are listed below as "undetermined." In 1880 enumerators were asked to determine employment status, and a total of sixty-two persons reported they had been unemployed for at least one month during the preceding year. Of these, the largest number (eighteen) had been unemployed during the entire year. The mean number of months unemployed was 3.9. There was a significant difference by county; eleven of those unemployed for twelve months were in Ormsby County, while only one had been without work for that long in Storey County and six in the rest of the state.

THE LEGACY OF SLAVERY—BLACK
OCCUPATIONAL SKILLS IN 1860

Nevertheless, it should be noted that a significant number of blacks were not unskilled servants but held higher-status and higher-paid occupations; these people provided much of the leadership of the black community and might be called a black middle class. Further, the existence of this group suggests that the black community of Nevada was gradually

Table 7
OCCUPATIONS OF NEVADA BLACKS, 1870 AND 1880

	1870	1880
Professional and technical		
Physician	1	
	1	
Managers, officials, and proprietors		
Boardinghouse		1
Lodging house		1
Restaurant keeper	2	
Saloon keeper	2	3
	4	5
Barbers	33	43
Farm owners or managers	3	6
Farm workers	2	14
Craftsmen, foremen, etc.		
Blacksmith	2	1
Bricklayer	2	1
Butcher		1
Carpenter	2	1
Dressmaker	3	4
Hairdresser	2	
Millinery	2	
Moulder		1
Painter	1	
Paperhanger		1
Seamstress		2
Shoemaker	2	1
Tailor	1	2
	17	15
Private household workers	12	17

Nonhousehold service workers		
Bootblack	13	7
Chambermaid	1	
Cook	35	24
Hotel	1	2
Janitor		3
Laundry worker	1	6
Nurse		2
Porter	17	10
Steward		1
Waiter		5
Washing	7	
	75	60
Miner	6	6
Unskilled labor	46	53
Other		
Barkeeper or bartender	1	2
Calciminer		1
Clerk (hotel, store, liquor store)		4
Expressman	1	
Fishmonger		1
Gardener		1
Hostler	1	
Job Express		1
Messenger	1	1
Midwife	1	
Odd Jobs	4	1
Prostitute	4	6
Teamster	4	5
Whitewasher	3	
Whitner and coleman		1
Woodchopper and wood packer		2
	20	26
Keeping house	45	45
Undetermined	20	32

improving its status during much of the period after the Civil War. For these reasons, a detailed look at the high-status occupations is worthwhile.

In both 1870 and 1880, approximately two-thirds of Nevada's black population had been born in the South; clearly, an understanding of occupational patterns among southern blacks is basic to any understanding of the economic status of Nevada's black community. Basically, there were three major groups of occupations found among southern blacks in the early 1860s, and these three groups were represented among Nevada blacks. The bulk of southern blacks were field hands, but there were also significant numbers of skilled workers and of household workers who were ready to develop as businessmen when allowed to do so.

Agricultural Workers

The image of the slave that comes to mind most readily is the field hand, deliberately kept ignorant of occupational skills not necessary for the menial labor involved in raising cotton or other crops and deliberately deprived of education. When these field hands were freed, their status did not change much, whether or not they left the South. There was no significant effort to make it possible for this group to gain ownership of land or of capital to purchase land or engage in business activities, nor was there a massive educational and training program to overcome the educational deficits of centuries of slavery. It is therefore not surprising that "freedom did not immediately change the relations between the races on the land."[3] Further, when freed field hands journeyed to the West, they found themselves forced to take unskilled jobs at low pay, and they were subjected to varying degrees of white prejudice. Although there are no specific data on this point, probably most of the unskilled and service workers among the blacks in Nevada in the 1870s and 1880s were ex-field hands. If the field hands had been the only occupational category among the slaves, probably there would have been few western blacks who were not laborers or servants. But there were two other categories among the slaves that provided some of the people who occupied higher-status occupations in the nineteenth-century Nevada black population.

Skilled Workers

It was economically advantageous to the slave owners to train some slaves to perform various kinds of skilled labor required on the plantations and later to hire out some of these slaves to whites in the cities. As a result, a major part of the skilled labor of the South was being performed by slaves when emancipation came, and there were also significant numbers of free blacks working at various trades in the North and the South.

Personal Servants

A second major nonagricultural category under slavery consisted of occupations that had developed out of the fact that blacks performed various kinds of personal services for slave owners and, later, other whites. Out of this group there developed various black businessmen, in the South and also in other parts of the country. As one study puts it,

> The hold which the Negro had on domestic service in the antebellum South is of much significance. The owners of slaves could select the most intelligent for service in their homes and get more satisfaction from these than if they had depended upon white hirelings who might not be so obsequious in carrying out the will of their employers. Such Negro servants were trained as barbers, cooks, hairdressers, butlers, coachmen, waiters, stewards, and grooms. The women, in the same manner, became maids, cooks, washerwomen, seamstresses, dressmakers, midwives, and parlor maids.[4]

Most black businessmen of the period after the Civil War had been personal servants. Although "business, of all vocations, was furthest removed from slavery,"[5] there were black businessmen, even before the Civil War, and most of them came out of the servant group. After emancipation, as W.E.B. Du Bois put it, "the master's valet set up his barbershop in town and soon had a lucrative trade; the cook became proprietor of a small eating-stand or restaurant, or, if he was exceptionally efficient and noted for certain dishes, he became a caterer."[6]

In brief, while no slaves were trained as professionals (although there were a few such persons among free blacks), there were by 1860 skilled workmen and house servants with skills that enabled them to develop into businessmen among the slave population of the South. Hence, even among the southern population, which provided the bulk of Nevada's black population, there were occupational categories other than unskilled labor. In addition, the free black population of the country included other occupational categories. Although there are no data on the prior free or slave status of Nevada's nineteenth-century black population, with a few exceptions, it may be noted that a higher proportion of Nevada's black population in 1870 and 1880 came from the North than was the case with the national black population. In Nevada, 34 percent of the black population in 1870 and 38 percent in 1880 was born in nonsouthern states. In 1860, 92.2 percent of the black population of the country lived in the southern states.

Thus, while Nevada blacks obviously developed occupationally in new ways, it seems apparent that major occupational groupings are similar to those of the South.

THE BEGINNINGS OF
BLACK ECONOMIC ADVANCE

A number of Nevada blacks were relatively well off during the 1870s and 1880s. While no income data of any consequence are available, the census and other data on property ownership and some other facts indicate this clearly. In 1870 the census of population reported sixty-nine blacks who owned real estate worth $38,450 and personal estate worth $41,230, for a total of $79,680. The range for total value of individual property was from $50 to $13,000, with a median of $600 and a mean of $1,155. In 1875 only twenty-seven blacks were reported to own property, but the median was the same and the mean—$1,431—was similar to that in 1870. The range in 1875 was from $100 to $17,380. (The 1880 census of population did not report this information.)

In 1873 Mrs. D. D. Carter, a frequent visitor to Carson City, reported that "the colored people in Carson seem to be all doing well, [and] have pleasant homes." The details of a surprise party given for her by the Stoutmeyer family and Miss Mary Young support this judgment: "The table was as fine as ever I saw—set out with silver and glass, it shone like Aladdin's palace, while it fairly groaned beneath the weight of turkeys, chickens, cakes, pies, candies, fruit and nuts, wine in abundance, too." A Thanksgiving dinner provided by several black families in Carson City was similar: "We had turkey, pumpkin pie, mince pie, oysters fresh from Baltimore, champagne and other wines, and much more."

Philip Bell, editor of the *Elevator*, reported earlier that year:

> The colored inhabitants of Carson are very comfortably situated; many of them owning property and residing thereon. Messrs. Grinage and Lane have the most popular barber shop in the city, and Messrs. Hardy and Butler, also barbers, are doing a good business. Mrs. Bailey has a ladies' hairdressing establishment and is doing well. Mrs. Bucknor is, I believe, the only hairworker and wig maker in Carson, and is doing a profitable business.[7]

Specific occupational categories shed more light on the economic status of the black population, and discussion of these categories also permits the introduction of specific individuals.

Professionals

Apparently there were only two black professional persons in Nevada in the nineteenth century, although there were a good many more able and articulate people. The one who lived in Nevada the longest was Dr. W. H. C. Stephenson, who practiced medicine in Virginia City from at least 1863 to at least 1870. Relatively little is known about his early life and medical training. In a letter to a Virginia City newspaper in 1867 he described his qualifications: "I am . . . a practicing physician and have my diploma, and passed a successful examination before entering upon the practice of medicine."[8] Nevada had no licensing law for physicians until 1875,[9] so it is improbable that Dr. Stephenson took an examination administered in Nevada; details of his professional training and competence are not available. One of his advertisements listed him as an "Eclectic Physician," with the further comment: "To the Eclectic system of medicine, all others are subservient. Its basis being experience and reason."[10] This advertisement plus his statement that he had a diploma may mean that he was educated in one of the Eclectic schools, which existed before the Civil War. The American Eclectic school of medicine began in the 1820s; by the time Dr. Stephenson arrived in California, there were several Eclectic medical schools (the most prominent of which were the Eclectic Medical Institute of Cincinnati and two schools in Philadelphia), Eclectic journals, and a National Eclectic Medical Society. Eclectics differed from other medical practitioners in the United States during this period by utilizing medicines and methods of treatment from all schools if they felt that experience proved their efficacy, seeking specific treatments for specific diseases, and disapproving of a wide variety of harsh medicines or methods of treatment—such as purgation, lancing, the promotion of fevers, and the prescription of mercury compounds—which were then not uncommon among physicians.[11]

According to the census enumerator who contacted him in 1870, Dr. Stephenson was forty-five in that year and had been born in Washington, D.C. He was listed as owning real estate worth $1,000 and a personal estate worth $1,000. His wife Jane was thirty and had been born in Virginia. A daughter Carrie, thirteen, had been born in Pennsylvania. If these facts are correct, Dr. Stephenson was born in 1825 and he and his wife had lived in Pennsylvania in 1857.

The date when he arrived in the West is not known, but Dr. Stephenson was living in Sacramento in 1862; in April and May of that year, he wrote four letters to the *Pacific Appeal* from that city. Toward the end of 1862, advertisements and letters in the *Pacific Appeal* indicate that he had moved to Marysville. In December 1863 he took part in a black meeting in Virginia City[12] and apparently lived there at least until some time in 1870. In May 1873 Philip Bell, editor of the *Elevator*, visited Virginia City and attended an evening "entertainment" conducted by "Mrs. James Carter and Mrs. Dr. Stephenson, at their residence on C street."[13] Probably Dr. Stephenson died or left Virginia City some time between 1870 and May 1873.

At least for a substantial period of time, the "office rooms" of Dr. Stephenson were at 150 C Street in Virginia City.[14] This was a location close to the center of the city in the area where most of the blacks lived. Mrs. Stephenson was living on C Street in 1873, possibly at the same address.

In August 1865 the *Elevator*, in reporting the efforts of blacks in Nevada to set up a state executive committee, noted that "Dr. Stephenson is well known in this country as a scholar, a physician, and a divine."[15] While in Virginia City he played prominent roles in black Masonic activities, the Baptist church, and most of the civil rights and political party activities of the blacks of that city in the 1860s.

Grafton Tyler Brown, a noted black lithographer and artist, spent a substantial amount of time in Nevada in the early 1860s, and his lithographs remain among the most important visual representations of Nevada in that period. Charles Collins' 1864-1865 directory of the Comstock contains an advertisement for "Grafton T. Brown, Traveling Artist in Nevada Territory. Views of Mills, Mines, Business Houses, Residences, etc., drawn in the finest style, and with accuracy. Publisher of 'Views of Virginia,' and other towns."[16] From at least 1861, Brown worked as a lithographer for the firm of C. C. Kuchel in San Francisco and was employed by this firm when he did his Nevada work. From 1867 into the 1880s he had his own lithography company in San Francisco and later was an artist and lithographer in other parts of the western United States and Victoria, British Columbia.

Farmers and Cowboys

Given the relationship to the land of most blacks in the South and the fact that agriculture was not very important in Nevada because of its low rainfall in most areas, it is hardly surprising that there were few blacks who were farmers in Nevada during the last century; however, there were a few, and blacks were to be found among both owners of farms and employees of farms and ranches, including cowboys.

In 1867 the *Virginia City Territorial Enterprise* reported that "one of the heaviest taxpayers in Douglas County is a colored man."[17] There were several black farmers around Genoa from the 1860s, and the reference might have been to any of them. The most likely candidate, however, was Ben Palmer. He was reported to have driven fifteen hundred head of cattle, which he had purchased at five dollars per head, from Seattle to Carson Valley in 1875 on a drive that took three months. "Palmer was also a breeder of fine horses and introduced the Bonner Stock to Carson Valley."[18]

According to Grace Dangberg, the historian of Carson Valley, Palmer arrived in the valley in 1853. Some time later he brought his sister, Charlotte Barber, and her children to his ranch. Although they do not seem to have been enumerated by the census in 1860 or 1870, in 1875 the state census of population listed two households side by side. Palmer was identified as a forty-six-year-old farmer born in Illinois and owning real estate worth $6,850 and personal estate worth $10,530. He was living with his sister, whose age was given as fifty and whose state of birth was South Carolina. With them were Betsy Barber, twenty-two and born in Missouri, and Clarissa Church, thirty-two, another of Mrs. Barber's daughters. Next door lived three Barber sons—ages twenty, twenty-four, and twenty-nine—all of whom had been born in Missouri. In 1880 Ben Palmer and Charlotte Barber were enumerated with the two daughters and a twenty-year-old son Benjamin, but the other two sons were not present. A twenty-one-year-old white farm laborer completed the household in that year.

Mrs. Sophia Miller headed a farm household in Genoa next door to the Palmer-Barbers. She had been born in Tennessee and was listed in the census as forty-one in 1870, forty-nine in 1875, and fifty-four in 1880. In 1870 her real estate was listed as worth $4,000 and her personal estate $1,000; in 1875 these figures were $4,150 and $628. In all three censuses she was listed with four children. Three of her children were born in Nevada. Winfield, who was nine in 1870, and Wilson, who was five in 1870, were her sons. Clarina, who was three in 1870, and Henrietta, who was eighteen in 1870, were her daughters; Henrietta had been born in Missouri. In 1870 there were two black laborers (L. Nails [?], forty-seven, and F. Butler, thirty) in the household; in 1875 there was a black male laborer (S. Dunn, fifty-nine) and a white man of forty-three identified as a farmer; and in 1880 there was a white laborer twenty-eight years old and a fifty-five-year-old black man (G. M. Young), whose occupation was not given.

The Robinson household also farmed at Genoa. In 1860 Mrs. Robinson was listed in the census of population as a "Wash Woman" at Genoa; her age was given as forty-eight and it was reported that she had been born in North Carolina. In 1870 Mrs. Tempa (?) Robinson, a fifty-seven-year-old woman born in North Carolina, was listed as farming in Genoa; her real estate was reported as worth $1,000 and her personal estate as worth the same amount. In her household were three other Robinsons, a black laborer, and a white printer. Mrs. Robinson's son G. Robinson, a twenty-seven-year-old laborer, had been born in Tennessee; her daughters L. and Mary Robinson, twenty-four and twenty-six, had been born in Missouri. The black laborer was P. Lethonberg (?), forty, from Texas. In the 1875 census, no occupation was given for Mrs. Robinson, and the value of her real estate was given as $800 and her personal estate as $362. Her two daughters were still with her but her son was not. There were two white male laborers in her household, thirty and twenty-nine, and a white barkeeper. In 1880 Mrs. Robinson, listed as sixty-five, was described as disabled; her two daughters still lived with her, and included in the household was Joseph Killpatrick, a seventy-seven-year-old disabled white physician.

In Lincoln County two brothers, Isaac and Lorenzo Dow Barton, ranched for many years during the nineteenth century. According to a popular account by Georgia Lewis, the brothers had been slaves and had arrived in Nevada in 1864, establishing ranches side by side between Panaca and Caliente.[19] Henry Hudson Lee says that Isaac "Ike" Barton, "with his wife Carrie, had a ranch about 2½ miles east of Caliente which was later acquired by D. J. Cook."[20] Both Isaac and Dow were born in Arkansas; Dow's age was given as thirty-four in the 1870 census and fifty in 1880, while Ike was twenty-five in 1870 and thirty-eight in 1880. In 1870 Dow was listed as owning property worth $800 ($400 each in real and personal estate), and Isaac reportedly owned $900 ($500 in real property and $400 in personal property). They may have retired and left Nevada some time after 1900.[21]

A particularly interesting occupation, because of the recently discovered fact that the myth of the white cowboy in popular literature and movies does not conform to reality, is that of the cowboy. Philip Durham and Everett L. Jones have shown that the cowboys who drove cattle up from Texas in the period from the end of the Civil War to the 1890s included thousands of blacks.[22] According to Kenneth W. Porter, there were 8,000-9,000 such black cowboys in all, which was about a fourth of the total, and there were few trail outfits without blacks or Mexicans.[23] It is interesting to note, then, that there were black cowboys in Nevada in the nineteenth century. The Durham and Jones book contains a photograph of a "noted Negro cowboy," One Horse Charley, taken in Reno in 1886, although they have no further information about him.[24] There were at least two black cowboys in Elko County in the 1890s and one of them became a ranch foreman, which was a rare achievement for a black.[25] John Sparks, governor of Nevada from 1903 to 1908, shared ownership of a large number of ranches in eastern Nevada and southern Idaho in the 1880s and 1890s. According to the historians of northeastern Nevada,

> among the large crew of cowboys employed by the Shoesole outfit [one of the businesses in which Sparks was a part owner], "Nigger Henry" Harris, brought as a cook from Texas, developed so much cattle "savvy" Sparks made him a cowboy foreman. First heading a crew of negro cowboys at the Boar's Nest Ranch, Henry later became cowboy boss of a group of white buckaroos. Henry rode "anything that had hair" and everyone admired and respected him for his skills.[26]

Harris was also mentioned as being a foreman at the Hubbard Ranch.[27] Evidently he had a railroad stop named after him; in a listing of place names in Elko County we find: "Henry—station on the Union Pacific Oregon Shortline R. R. named for Henry Harris, Negro cowboy foreman."[28] In 1896 Harris was foreman at the Middlestack Ranch, another in the chain of ranches owned by Sparks and, at that time, Andrew Harrell. Harris testified at the trial of Diamondfield Jack Davis, a gunman hired by the Sparks-Harrell concern to intimidate sheepmen; Davis was convicted of the murder of two sheepmen and imprisoned for years before another man admitted to the murder.[29]

Harris was said to have supervised a black crew and Boar's Nest Ranch has been described as the "home of colored cowboys who lived at a cave in the hillside."[30] The only other black cowboy in this area at the time whose name is known, however, was Henry's brother Lige. Evidently the two brothers worked at some time for the Utah Construction Co., which owned a number of ranches in northeast Nevada after the turn of the century. Referring to the town of Montello, the historians of northeast Nevada say that "UC employees, Henry and Lige Harris, Negro brothers and native Texans were familiar faces in town for UC cowboying necessitated frequent Montello visits."[31]

Several western blacks expressed a desire to acquire a land base for agriculture in the West. In the 1855 California Colored Convention, a report strongly recommending that blacks take up agriculture was pre-

sented by a committee. In his address at the celebration of the ratification
of the Fifteenth Amendment in Virginia City in 1870, W. H. Hall stated;

> We of these nominal free States, where our characters are so imper-
> fectly understood, and where our condition is so anomalous with that
> of the so-called superior race, must consolidate our resources, and
> imitate the freedmen in the States lately reconstructed, by acquiring
> the broad acres of land, so that our children may not, like us of this
> generation, trudge in the toils of meniality and humble dependence,
> subject to the bias of opposing forces, but may with the proudest of
> the land become producers as well as consumers.[32]

In 1869 Philip Bell of the *Elevator* had stated that blacks needed to
become land owners because "we should make ourselves intelligent
citizens, and also become pecuniarily interested."[33] The 1865 Colored
Convention in California adopted a report of the Committee on Industrial
Pursuits, which strongly endorsed land ownership as well as black involvement in mining and manufacturing.[34]

Mining

In ninetenth-century Nevada mining was the most important economic
activity, and the fortunes of the mines determined the major population
fluctuations and the major patterns of population distribution within the
state. Blacks apparently were not significantly involved as prospectors,
mine owners, or mine workers on the Comstock, which was the largest
and most famous Nevada mining region. Probably this circumstance was
the result of white exclusion of blacks. It is clear that Chinese were excluded from mining activities on the Comstock; although Chinese had
been engaged in placer mining in the Gold Hill area before discovery of
the Comstock lode in 1859, they were excluded by white miners from
either ownership of mining claims or work in the mines after the big
strike,[35] and probably blacks were similarly excluded. The colored
conventions of 1855 and 1865 endorsed mining as well as agriculture
for blacks. In 1864 the *Pacific Appeal* noted that many young men had
recently left San Francisco for the Boise mines, Portland, Arizona,
Colorado, and Nevada to seek their fortunes in mining. The newspaper
remarked that they "seemed animated with the same spirit that had
distinguished the many White adventurers who have sought to obtain
their fortunes by mining and trading operations in the same region."[36]
Given all these indications of black interest in mining, their virtual absence

on the Comstock is probably due to discrimination. In 1860 there were two black miners in that area. In 1870 and 1880 six black miners were recorded in the state, but only one of these (in 1870) was in Virginia City or Gold Hill. Whites probably often assumed that blacks were too ignorant to succeed at prospecting for mineral wealth; Dan De Quille, a long-time respected reporter on the Comstock, told a dialect story based on the assumption that blacks could not distinguish one rock from another.[37]

In 1879 a newspaper article reported that blacks had been excluded from an important miners' union on the Comstock; if this was the case also in the earlier period, it would account for the absence of blacks in Comstock mining. A Lyon County newspaper reported that two blacks were employed in building the Sutro tunnel and that this created a problem because the Silver City Miners' Union was a group into which "no colored men have ever been initiated." Reportedly the union was not opposed to their working there but could not decide whether to accept them into the union or allow them to work as the only non-union members.[38]

One black was reported to have occupied a responsible position in a Comstock mining corporation, and one was a porter for one of the companies. In 1874 the *Elevator* printed this note: "We learn with pleasure that our young friend, James E. Grasses has received the appointment of bookkeeper of the Justice Mine, Gold Hill, Nev., at a liberal salary."[39] In 1868 the same newspaper reported that James Moore, a porter at the Bank of California at Gold Hill, "has doubtless handled more bullion than any white or colored man on the Pacific Coast. Since his residence in Gold Hill he has handled at least $20,000,000 in bullion bars."[40] In 1870 Moore was evidently single; he was living in a household with four white males. His age was given as forty and his birthplace as Montreal. He was not listed in the 1880 census.

Whatever the explanation for their virtual absence on the Comstock, blacks were involved in the relatively short-lived mining boom at Treasure Hill in eastern Nevada. From 1868 to 1870, in "probably the shortest, most intense" mining rush "in the history of the West,"[41] several thousand people flocked to the Treasure Hill area and founded such towns as Treasure City, Hamilton, and Shermantown. The area declined after 1870, and in 1873 and 1874 fires destroyed most of Hamilton and Treasure City.[42]

The chief chronicler of the Treasure Hill mining boom no doubt caught some of the truth about white attitudes toward blacks but failed to note their economic success. W. Turrentine Jackson reported: "as usual, white men shunned and persecuted the Chinese, the Negro, and the Mexican in hopes of destroying their economic and social position" and also that "the few southern Negroes in camp were confined to domestic service and menial tasks, and their antics made the subject for jokes and humorous stories."[43]

Evidently the blacks in Treasure Hill were caught up in the excitement of a mining town in much the same ways as the whites. In January 1869 John C. Mortimer wrote from Austin that "the rush still continues through this place to White Pine" but urged San Franciscans to put off coming until spring.[44] This warning did not deter everyone, however. In February 1869 it was reported that "Robert H. Small of Shingle Springs has gone to White Pine."[45] In January of the same year, a black miner in the White Pine area, whose last name was Harrison, died of wounds suffered some days earlier in a premature explosion, presumably at a mining claim. It was stated that "Harrison was a miner in this district in the early days of 'Reese River,' and was well known in the vicinity of Austin and Yankee Blade."[46] The same edition of this newspaper reported: "A large number of our friends are preparing to emigrate to White Pine as soon as the travelling season opens. Mr. W. H. Hall has already gone, and we learn of others who will soon follow." Isaac Starkey at Shermantown advised others to wait until spring.[47]

In spite of the admonitions to wait until spring, the excitement arising from the fact that rich strikes were being made in eastern Nevada was contagious. In the same issue in which it was reported that Samuel T. Wilcox had left for Treasure Hill, the editor of the *Elevator* commented: "A young friend of ours has shown indications of having the fever in its incipient stage. His case is not altogether hopeless, but we fear he has White Pine on the brain too far for recovery."[48] A letter from William H. Hall from Treasure City asserted that "of the wonderful richness of that country, the half has not been told."[49]

A letter in March from John Gale in Hamilton indicates clearly that some of the young men who ignored advice to wait until spring before going to White Pine regretted it. Gale said that he had walked the 125 miles from Elko to Hamilton in six days. It had snowed every day since his arrival, with two feet on the ground and no sign of a letup in the storm. Prices for lots, houses, water, firewood, and other necessities were extraordinarily high, and there was little prospect of earning anything until spring arrived. Gale reported that W. H. Hall was "paying $200 for six weeks use of a small place 6 x 8, and considers it a favour at that; lumber is so scarce, that the buildings go up very slowly." Gale regretted his early arrival: "In fact, I am sorry that I came so soon, as I could have made some money in Sacramento City; while here it is nothing but spend, and I am running very light."[50]

In April 1869 a group of black miners announced that they had discovered a rich mining ledge near the Eberhardt mine, one of the richest of the Treasure Hill mines:

A valuable mining ledge was recently discovered at White Pine by Messrs. Wm. H. Hall, J. E. Ince and J. C. Mortimer, which in honor to our paper they have named the Elevator. Specimens of the rock have been received in this city, which has been assayed at a high figure. Experts at White Pine pronounce this mine one of the richest on Treasure Hill. Proceedings will immediately be taken to become incorporated when the stock will be thrown in the Market.

A reprint from the *White Pine News* confirmed this news, crediting Hall with the find and stating that he was "ambitious to supply his colored brethren of the low countries, with mines as good as any a white man dare own. He has men hard at work developing the mine, and of its value there can be no doubt."[51]

The next issue of the *Elevator* announced that ore from the mine was assaying at more than $108 a ton and that "the Elevator Mining Company of Treasure Hill, White Pine, was incorporated on Monday last." The company optimistically planned to issue 6,000 shares of stock at $100 each. The newspaper stated proudly that Hall and Mortimer, the discoverers of the mine, were "worthy specimens of the Yankee proclivities of the Afric-American."[52]

By the spring of 1869, there were a number of blacks in the White Pine area, and most were reported doing well in mining and in other occupations. James Banks, William H. Gaines, and Robert Wilson were listed as among those blacks in Hamilton who were "property holders and speculators in real estate." It was reported that "Messrs. Cook and Cary are the principal Hair Dressers of Hamilton, and are doing a large business." Other blacks in that area, also doing well, were John Anderson, William N. Neblot, R. Johns, William H. Gaston, G. G. Meads, R. Woodland, J. Harrison, George Strong, Alexander Puyfebay, S. T. Wilcox, and James Moody.[53]

Hall continued to send optimistic news from Treasure Hill, reporting later in April that "the indications continue as rich as the first assay." The Elevator Silver Mining Company completed its organization, with H. M. Collins as president and P. A. Bell as secretary. An advertisement for the company indicated that, at a meeting on April 21, 1869, "it was agreed to issue 500 Shares at the minimum price of $5 per share, unassessable, in order to raise a working Capital to develop the Mine. A

Public Meeting will be held about 5th proximo, to introduce the enterprise to our friends."[54]

Further news about the Elevator Mine came from a reprinted article from the *Daily Inland Empire* of Hamilton, dated May 1. Samuel Wilcox had shown ore from the mine to the editors of the paper, who reported that "the ore shown us was of a very superior quality, and is entirely free from base metal and will pay handsomely for milling." J. E. Ince, superintendent of the mine, was "pushing the work forward with energy."[55] Ore specimens assaying $250.78 to the ton were noted the next week. Hall wrote that "the validity of title to our claim is undoubted" and gave details about the mine, which was located about fifty feet below the Eberhardt Mine and directly facing it. He said that J. C. Mortimer was the discoverer of the mine. He "is an old miner, and is perfectly familiar with the mining laws of Nevada, and the nature and quality of ores, indications, leads, etc., and he expresses great confidence in the wealth of our mine."[56] Later that month, in commenting on the whereabouts of blacks who had been active in California in the 1850s, the *Elevator* commented that "Hall and Wilson are making fortunes, we hope, in White Pine."[57] Hall, it seems, also ran an "Emporium of Fashion" in the Treasure Hill area.[58]

Mrs. Samuel T. Wilcox reported from Hamilton in May that the Elevator Mine still looked prosperous and that her husband Samuel T. Wilcox and Charles Wilson "have interests in some very flattering Ledges, and if they do not realize something handsome out of them, ere long, it will not be for want of venture; in fact, colored men here are largely represented in mines." Wilcox, meanwhile, was operating a restaurant in Hamilton.[59]

F. G. Grice, a barber from Haiti, left for Elko in the spring of 1869. In June he said, "There is a great excitement in this town, since yesterday, owing to the discovery of a new mine in this district." He reported that there was still a great deal of traffic through Elko to White Pine.[60]

In 1873 the *Elevator* announced the death at Elko of Henry G. Hudson, forty-one. Hudson was said to have been one of the "early pioneers to California" who had "resided for nearly five years at Hamilton, White Pine County, Nevada."[61] He had given a public address at the 1870 celebration of ratification of the Fifteenth Amendment in Treasure City.

Treasure Hill meant economic advance for a number of blacks; five of the blacks who owned a total of $2,000 or more in 1870 were in that area. Daniel W. Cherry, a forty-year-old blacksmith in Hamilton, reported property worth $3,000; Samuel Wilcox, a forty-year-old black "restaurateur" in Hamilton reported property worth $13,000; John Maxwell, a forty-two-year-old laborer from Massachusetts living in Hamilton, reported property worth $2,000; Sanford Venery, a forty-three-year-old saloon keeper from New York also living in Hamilton reported property worth $3,000; and Joseph Anderson, a forty-three-year-old cook born in Maryland and living in Treasure City reported property worth $5,000. The Treasure Hill area declined rapidly after 1870, and by 1880 there was only one black at Hamilton and only eight blacks in all of White Pine County. Three of the five persons listed above apparently were no longer in the state in 1880, and the other two were obviously not well off. Daniel Cherry, now divorced, was a laborer living in Pioche in Lincoln County; he had been unemployed for six months during the previous year and was listed with a disability of a "swelled leg" at the time of the census. Sanford Venery was a gardener in Belmont in Nye County and had been unemployed for two months during the previous year. Details about the fate of the Elevator Mine are not available.

Another black-owned company also called the Elevator Company was involved in mining ventures in Utah in the early 1870s. A letter from F. G. Grice written from Salt Lake City in June 1873 reported that he had arrived in Salt Lake City in June 1871 and since then had helped organize two "colored prospecting companies." One of these, the Elevator Company, sold a mine in 1872 for $15,000 and had financial interests in several other mines. "The 'Elevator' Company has at the present time over 9,000 feet of mining property."[62]

At least one black was present at one of the mining areas in the Aurora area. A letter from Robert J. Perry at Pine Grove, Nevada, noting that several mines were producing, ended with this advice:

> Mr. Editor, I wish you could induce some of our young men to leave the cities, where they have to act as "flunkeys," and fill other menial occupations, and come this way. Tell them to start out and prospect for themselves before the State is filled with eastern men, which it will be when the Railroad is finished, and the iron-horse is running.[63]

Pine Grove, approximately twenty-five miles northwest of Aurora, was developed in 1866.[64]

Business

There were a number of black businessmen in nineteenth-century Nevada, partially because of the skills deriving from the house-servant category of the South and partially because the prospects for black businessmen were improving in the 1870s and 1880s. This situation was

apparent to black observers at the time; for example, on his visit to
Virginia City in 1876, Peter Anderson, publisher of the *Pacific Appeal*,
noted that there were many "industrious" and "representative colored
men and women" in Virginia City and Carson City. He meant by these
terms, he said, "those possessing business qualities, and also those who
are carrying on business in Virginia City."[65]

The census figures for 1870 and 1880 indicate a smaller number of
businessmen than there actually were among the black population. Part
of the reason for this is that some occupational listings obscure the fact
that the person was in business for himself. For example, among the
teamsters in 1870 was Cicero Miner. Born in North Carolina, he was
forty-five in 1870 and owned property worth a thousand dollars. He
owned a wagon and engaged in hauling in Virginia City. He died in the
early 1870s, but his wife Sarah, who had been born in Jamaica, carried
on the business, including hiring an employee. She lost six thousand
dollars in the 1875 fire in Virginia City but remained in business the following year.[66] She was listed as a widow in the 1880 census of population.

The most important group of black businessmen in Nevada, however,
was made up of barbers who were in business for themselves; this group
included a number of businessmen who not only operated shops with a
substantial volume of customers but also sold various products as sidelines.
Clearly the black barbers of nineteenth-century Nevada included a substantial group of businessmen. Those identified as barbers in the censuses
of population have been listed separately from the category of managers
because some of them were employees rather than businessmen; nevertheless, a major, though undetermined, proportion of this group must be
considered businessmen.

The significance of barbering among the black occupations of the last
century has largely been overlooked by both blacks and whites, in the
nineteenth century and today, for several reasons. First, barbering (as
well as several other occupations that developed because of skills blacks
learned under slavery) was widely looked upon as an inferior occupation
because of its connection with slavery and because a high proportion of
barbers during the late nineteenth century were blacks. For example,
Spero and Harris, in discussing black business after the Civil War, comment that "the Negro domestics and those engaged in personal-service
trades, such as barbers, waiters, or porters, continued much as before,
for their work, looked down upon as 'black' jobs, was beneath the aspira-
tion of the whites."[67] The historians of black labor tend to agree. Wesley
speaks of barbering in derogatory terms and quotes Frederick Douglass

as deploring the "malignant arrangements of society" that required a poet to be a barber.[68] (He was specifically referring to the poet James M. Whitfield, who later lived in Nevada.) Greene and Woodson refer to barbering as "menial,"[69] and Du Bois says that "the barbering business has fallen into dislike among Negroes, partly because it had so long the stigma of race attached."[70] This aspect of barbering and similar related businesses is clearly suggested by an editorial comment in the *Elevator* in 1873. Noting that more and more blacks were going into business, the editorial stated:

> Some Negroes remain as servants, others start a bootblack stand, and others open a barber shop, and all do well; now, we do not speak of these avocations in anything like a disparaging tone, . . . but, is this the highest aim and the ultimate position of our people? . . . are they always to grovel in the lowest stratas of business and in servitude?[71]

In spite of these attitudes toward barbering and related businesses growing out of the house-servant group, blacks in these occupations were leaders of their people in the nineteenth century. Du Bois says of these businessmen that they "represented directly after the war, and up until about ten or fifteen years ago, the most prosperous class of Negroes. The caterers, barbers and stewards were leaders in all social movements among Negroes, and held the major part of the accumulated wealth."[72] A study of blacks in California reports that in the nineteenth century barbers played a major role in communicating the news about the activities of the executive committee of the colored convention, "since there was neither a rapid mail service nor telegraphic communication. They transmitted the news by the way of the barber's chair."[73] It is clear that a major part of the leadership for various organizations within the nineteenth-century Nevada black community came from the businessmen, among whom the barbers were especially numerous.

Black barbers served mainly white customers.[74] The forty-three barbers in Nevada in 1880 clearly did not serve solely the black population of 396.

It is difficult to know how lucrative barbering was, but there are some figures from California that give some indication of this. In 1869 there were two advertisements listing barbershops for sale in northern California. One, identified only as being one-and-a-half hours by steamboat from San Francisco, reported that the business averaged $200 a month, for a yearly income of $2,400, and that the barbershop contained "accommodations for a family."[75] Another advertisement for a barbershop in Silveyville, in Solano County, indicated that a two-chair barbershop did a business of $3,000 a year.[76] In 1873 a barber in San Jose advertised for a journeyman barber, whose rate of pay would be $75 a month, or $900 a year.[77] A correspondent from Wadsworth, Nevada, gave information suggesting that barbers in Nevada might earn more than this. Saying, "There are plenty of our people at the bay doing little or nothing, who might find ready employment anywhere up this way, at much better wages than they can command below," he asserted that journeyman barbers earned $125 a month; cooks earned $2.50 to $3.50 a day and waiters $60 a month.[78]

Various data on the property barbers owned indicate less valuable property than that owned by other businessmen, but some owned significant amounts of property. The wife of Thomas Detter was listed in the 1870 census as owning property worth $2,100.

Some barbers began to sell products through their shops. This was true of Detter and of M. Howard, a barber who moved back and forth between San Francisco and Virginia City. Howard also demonstrated the capacity of barbers to move into other kinds of businesses. In February and March 1864 he wrote one of the San Francisco black newspapers from Virginia City.[79] An advertisement that appeared in the other black newspaper in San Francisco in 1865 indicated that Howard was a hairdresser in Virginia City who "intends establishing his business in this city." The same advertisement, which indicated that he sold a hair preparation that "prevents the hair from falling off," appeared in the *Elevator* from April 14, 1865, until June 16, 1865, when his advertisements began to list an address in San Francisco. Similar advertisements, including one indicating that he sold not only a "Hair Restorer" but also a preparation called "Persian Colorific" to restore hair color appeared sporadically in the *Elevator* at least through 1869.

The status of barbers is indicated by the fact that Howard was occasionally referred to as "Professor" Howard and that he was listed as a contributor of $10 to save the *Elevator* from bankruptcy in 1869 and had also pledged quarterly or monthly payments to an *Elevator* fund.[80]

It is not clear when Howard returned to Virginia City, but he was there by October 1875. He reported that he had arrived just after the collapse of the Bank of California when business was poor. "I have been doing very well, and although I have not succeeded as yet in establishing myself exactly to my satisfaction, still I have no cause to complain."[81] He reported extensively on the effects of the 1875 fire in Virginia City on the black community. In 1878 Howard established a saloon in Virginia City, which he described as "a first-class saloon, with two billiard tables, fine cigars, etc., at No. 36 North 'C' Street."[82]

It was also at this time that he served as a juror in Virginia City. He was still in Virginia City in October 1878 when he wrote a letter to the *Pacific Appeal.*[83] A writer from Virginia City in 1878 reported that Howard was "an old and well-known resident of the Pacific Coast, having been here since 1850." In 1863, according to this informant, Howard had joined with Oscar Taylor in attempting to repeal the Nevada laws forbidding the testimony of blacks in court.[84]

Thomas Detter was also a barber. (He was discussed in chapter 1 as one of the leaders of western blacks who arrived in California in the 1850s.) It appears that he became a minister of the African Methodist Episcopal church, probably in California. He probably preached part-time in towns where he lived, but little information concerning this aspect of his life has come to light. The proceedings of the 1863 convention of the AME church in San Francisco list Detter as a minister in Idaho Territory although apparently he did not attend the convention.[85]

Before Detter moved to Nevada in 1869, he lived in a number of mining camps and traveled extensively, yet he also managed to keep in touch with the black community of the West through the pages of the *Elevator* and the *Pacific Appeal* in San Francisco, contributing letters himself from time to time, and also by occasional visits to that city. In April 1863 he was in Lewiston, Idaho Territory. Letters he wrote from there on April 6 and 14, 1863, were published in the *Pacific Appeal,* and a third letter from there was written May 26. A friend of his, J. G. Wilson, wrote from Lewiston on June 22, 1863, that Detter and a number of others had left for the Boise mines: "I never saw so many colored men striking out at gold hunting before, in so short a time." WIlson also noted that he and Detter had ridden to Fort Lapwai to observe three thousand to four thousand Indians who were gathered "to make a treaty."[86] This must have been the main treaty signed between the United States government and the Nez Perce Indians.[87]

Detter arrived in Bannock City, a mining camp in the Boise area, about June 19 and wrote on July 6 that he planned to return to Lewiston in a month or two. He may have done some prospecting himself; he clearly was caught up in the fever and excitement of a booming mining town. Saying, "I entertain a very flattering opinion of this country, for what I have seen since my arrival here," he remarked on the rapid growth of the area. There were several towns within twelve miles of the Boise mines, although Bannock City was the largest. Building lots were expensive, but nevertheless houses were going up very rapidly. Prices were high, though not as high as he had expected. "This is the liveliest camp I have seen since I have been on the coast," he reported. The cause of all of this bustle, of course, was the mines. "I have seen surface diggings that paid $200 per day to the hand; $20 and $30 per day are common." Detter also noted another feature of a mining camp: "Every man is for himself, and cares but little about his fellow."[88]

In his book *Nellie Brown*, Detter described Boise City as a very inhospitable place for blacks, pointing out that "many of its citizens are afflicted with the terrible disease of Negrophobia. . . . A respectable colored man can scarcely get accommodations at any of the hotels or restaurants."[89] Evidently he did not stay long; in January 1864 he wrote from Walla Walla, Washington, that he had made a holiday trip to Portland, Oregon, and requested the editor to send his papers to Walla Walla, "until I order differently."[90] Later that month, Detter wrote again from Walla Walla,[91] and at the end of February another letter from Walla Walla commented on the death of a friend, Issac Myers Connelly.[92]

In 1866 Detter was selling a "hair restorative." An advertisement entitled "Read This, Ye Bald Heads" included testimonials from various satisfied clients, in the manner of the day, including statements from an attorney, two physicians, and a notary public.[93]

In August 1867 Detter was in Idaho City where the mines were not producing well and where a large fire had "caused a suspension of all business." He reported that "the Chinese are the principal miners here" but that probably they would also be gone soon.[94]

In June 1868 the *Elevator* printed an erroneous story reporting the death of Detter's wife and the destruction by fire of his place of business, presumably in Idaho City.[95] In July the newspaper noted that Detter "desires us to contradict our announcement of the death of his wife. . . . We do so with great pleasure."[96]

In May 1868 Detter wrote the *Elevator* from Idaho City describing a harsh winter now succeeded by spring. He averred that "mountain life" was "romantic" because of "the many and sudden changes requiring fortitude and strength." "He who would succeed must not surrender, but fight the battles of life."[97] In August 1868 the *Elevator* reported that Detter was in Silver City, Idaho.[98]

Detter loyally supported both of the black newspapers in San Francisco, even though Peter Anderson and Philip Bell were frequently at odds with each other. For example, in December 1868, he wrote the *Elevator* from Silver City, Idaho, enclosing donations of $32.50 from seven persons.[99]

In February 1869 Detter wrote from Silver City: "This burg is being fast depopulated. Every one seems to have the fever—hence I must follow suit." He indicated that he planned to leave for "White Pine" about February 20.[100] While he seems to have made only a brief visit to Treasure Hill, he did move to Elko, which served the mines of that area.

Detter arrived in Elko at the very beginning of the town. On March 9, 1869, he wrote a long letter describing Elko's beginnings, stating that "it has sprung into existence as if by magic. Six weeks ago there was not half a dozen houses here, now there are nearly three hundred tenements, built mostly of canvas." He reported that the site was level and large enough for a big city. Prices, as usual in such boom towns, were outrageous. "Lots range from two hundred dollars to twelve," flour was eight dollars for a hundred pounds, eggs a dollar a dozen (though potatoes were only ten cents a pound and bacon thirty cents a pound). The "whisky mills and restaurants" were "as thick as fleas on a dog's back" and there were "ten hurdy houses where the disconsolate congregate to while away their leisure hours, and gaze upon the fair but frail daughters of Eve."

Elko came into existence because of the transcontinental railroad but grew chiefly because of the gold and silver discoveries at Treasure Hill; the town was the place where men and materials left the recently completed railroad for the last stage of the journey to Treasure Hill by stage or on foot. "Four daily lines of stages leave on the arrival of the cars; hundreds of footmen are seen daily wending their way to the new El Dorado, seeking their fortunes. . . . If the bottom don't fall out of White Pine, Elko thinks she will be the queen of cities on this line."

Detter made it clear that he was excited by the possibilities for acquiring wealth in the mines but that something kept him from becoming a prospector himself.

> The news from the mines is still encouraging. I see men from there daily, who say it is the place for the boys to make scratch, but I hardly think I'll take any of it in mine at present. I have been struggling long and hard to make it stick; it is up one side side [sic] and down the other with me. I have hung out my shingle here and expect to remain.

Other blacks did join the rush to Treasure Hill, as noted above, and Detter mentioned that Samuel Cuney and "several others" had seen him as they came through Elko.[101] Evidently Detter paid at least one visit to Hamilton, Nevada, for a letter to the *Pacific Appeal* in 1870 was mailed from there.

In 1871, while he lived in Elko, Detter published a book, *Nellie Brown: or the Jealous Wife*.[102] The title page identifies him as "colored," and a few of the pieces in the book deal explicitly with race, but the main part of the work is about a white southern family. Although Nellie Brown and her husband own slaves, race plays little part in the story, which is a not

very convincing account of a happy family nearly broken up by jealousy
and a scheming woman who delights in destroying marriages for no
apparent reason. The point of the story is clearly to make an argument
for marital fidelity; Detter says in his introduction that "the design of
this work is to show the unhappy results of jealousy and misplaced
confidence, and the wicked designs of corrupt parties" and that the work
demonstrates that "malicious persons . . . should be shunned by all lovers
of good society." The slaves who appear are thoroughly subservient,
taking the side of their masters in the marital dispute and speaking a slave
dialect; however, a slave girl named Sue, who is described as a comical
character on the order of Topsy, surprises her mistress by wanting her
freedom. When Mrs. Brown indicates to Sue that she might divorce her
husband and marry another man, this interchange occurs:

Sue: "If you gwine to be married, youd better git me my free papers."

Mrs. Brown: "What in the world has come over you, Sue? What a
strange idea! What do you want to be free for, Sue"

Sue: "Well, Missus; you see you might dies, and dey might send me
down Souf. If I is free dey can't sell me den, Missus."

When Mrs. Brown argues that free Negroes are unable to take care of
themselves, Sue insists that "freedom am very good for eberybody" and
that "I am got two good hands; nebber starve as long as I can work,
Missus."

Another shorter fictional piece, "Octoroon Slave of Cuba," deals
explicitly with the cruelties and stupidities of slavery. The heroine is
a child of a slave who has been raised by a well-to-do white family as
a white person. When she learns that her sister is a slave, she contrives to
free her and start a new life with her far from the plantation in Cuba
where she had been in bondage. The story points up the absurdity of
classifying people as slaves or free on the basis of observable racial
characteristics. When the heroine states that she must never reveal the fact
that she had an African ancestor, she says that to do so "would blast my
hopes forever in this life. It would leave a stain upon me that never could
be wiped out. You know the prejudices that are entertained against
persons in whose veins course the slightest mixture of African blood. I
have moved in the first circles of society and have been the guest of the
wealthiest families of my State."

Nellie Brown contains several quite short fictional and nonfictional items. There are brief descriptions of Elko, Boise, Idaho City, and the Central Pacific Railroad, and several comments on race relations in the United States. The absurdities that can result from classifying as black any person with any discernible black ancestry are explored in "My Trip to Baltimore." In this piece Detter contrasts the various treatments received at different times by a friend of his who was a "white nigger" (without visible black characteristics but with some black ancestry). When he was classified as black, he was forced to eat outside and sleep in a hayloft. When he was classified as white, he was given the hospitality accorded to most white travelers. Detter was forced to conclude that "the whiter the Nigger the better he is, and the nearer he is a man." In this same piece, Detter expressed an opinion that must have grown out of his own experience as a barber when he quoted himself telling a white woman: "Madam, it is difficult for colored men to succeed in business, especially in communities where they have 'Nigger on the brain,' unless he is humble in the extreme, and has a grin for everybody. With many, he must forget that he is a man, to succeed."

In "Uncle Joe" he tells a story in dialect about a slave who pretends to be unable to walk until other slaves frighten him by impersonating a ghost. Two selections give his most general comments about race. "Progress of America" is a glowing tribute to American greatness as measured by wealth and power but also by "the spirit of the heroes of 1776." He lauds Patrick Henry, George Washington, and Crispus Attucks but ends with an endorsement of the "teachings" of Daniel O'Connell, a British subject who "advocated the freedom of all men, regardless of nationality, of creed or color." In "Give the Negro a Chance" he indicates his belief that black people want only equal opportunity. He reported that there was discrimination against blacks even in churches and by boats and stages and remarked that "often the Negro has been hunted down in the broad sunlight of day, assassinated and murdered, and the assassin permitted to go unpunished, because his victim was as powerless as he was innocent." Making a plea to white men to "conquer your prejudices," he asserted: "We love the land that gave us birth, and all we ask of the white man is to give us an even chance in the great race of life. If you need a man to perform labor, and the Negro is competent and trustworthy, give him work. Don't deny him his bread, because he has a dark skin. Give him the same wages that you give the white man."

Detter probably hoped to make some money from the sale of *Nellie Brown*; he placed advertisements in the San Francisco black newspapers when the book was about to be published and shortly afterward. It is likely that the book did not sell very well; its literary qualities were not sufficiently outstanding to compel attention, although the essays and short pieces are well done; there was the prejudice of whites against blacks to overcome, and the black population was small, not very affluent, and with substantial numbers of uneducated people. Nevertheless, his book was one of the earliest written by an American black. It was a serious work, and his writing reveals an intelligent, sensitive person concerned about the cruelties and absurdities of racism. Detter deserves much more recognition than he has received.

Probably Detter had some unpleasant experiences in Elko for he did not stay long. In *Nellie Brown* he made an ambiguous statement about Elko, implying that he had some criticisms he was keeping to himself:

> Of Elko, I shall not say much for or against, as a nobleman once said about America. I use the same language in reference to Elko. "She is a giantess without bones." The time may come when she will be classed among the leading cities of this State. There is a wonderful scope left for improvement. In speaking of her citizens, they are not excelled by any class on this coast.

In August 1871 Detter reported on a trip he had made to Eureka and indicated that he might move there if the road between Elko and Hamilton was not built. He called Elko "the dullest place on record" and Eureka, which reminded him of Idaho City in its boom days, the "leading camp" in the state. About four thousand people lived there, and the mines and businesses were growing rapidly. In general he felt optimistic about the future of Nevada: "I believe the future of this state is destined to be great." Noting that agriculture and stock raising were developing and that there were potentials for industry, he asserted that Nevada's main asset was its mineral wealth: "Her rich storehouses of hidden treasure are yet to be unlocked with the massive key of prosperity."[103]

By December the Detters had moved to Eureka, and he was apparently satisfied with his move. In a long description of the town, he noted that it had a number of mines and four smelters. Although its growth was impeded by the high price of lumber, a railroad to Hamilton and Pioche would greatly aid the town and eastern Nevada. Detter's son Robert would have been five or six at the time, and there is therefore probably a personal note of bitterness in his comment on the fact that black children were not yet being admitted to the schools: "I ask, when will 'man's inhumanity to man' cease?" He evidently was hopeful about the future, however, for he urged continuing efforts to secure equal rights: "Continue to contend for equal advantages of education. . . . The life blood of the negro poured out upon many a gory battle field for those cherished blessings has not yet secured them all."[104] By March 1872 the Nevada Supreme Court had declared the school law that excluded blacks unconstitutional, and Detter reported from Eureka that black children were now being admitted to the schools. "I leave the subject, and honor the Negro who has the courage to attack the enemies of his race and rights. I believe you of California can accomplish the same if the proper remedy is applied" and if everyone was united.[105]

As spring came to Eureka, Detter reported that business was picking up there, especially because of the news of new mining strikes. He was still optimistic about the future of the area: "Miners of great experience say that this portion of the State is not at all prospected."[106]

In September 1873 Mrs. Carolina Detter was listed as an arrival in San Francisco from Eureka.[107] She had gone there for medical treatment and remained for several months until her death on February 10, 1874, at the age of thirty-six. A funeral was conducted in San Francisco by Reverend I. N. Triplett of the Bethel AME Church. The *Pacific Appeal* reported that "Mrs. Detter was one of the most amiable colored ladies that migrated to this State." She was born in Maryland but raised in Philadelphia, the *Appeal* reported. Arriving in San Francisco in 1855, three years after the arrival of Thomas Detter, she married him in 1860.[108]

Detter received another blow on May 19 of the same year when his nine-year-old-son Robert died in Eureka. A poem eulogizing Robert, presumably written by Detter, was printed in the *Pacific Appeal*.[109]

In January 1875 Detter was reported to have arrived in San Francisco, probably for a business visit,[110] since he was soon back in Eureka, and since the San Francisco black papers began carrying advertisements for his cough syrup soon after this visit. "T. Detter's Cough Tonic" sold for $1.25 a bottle and originally was available in San Francisco only from I. N. Triplett. The advertisement for the tonic stated, "This Medicine is made of pure vegetation, and excels any ever introduced for curing deep seated Colds and Consumption." The recommended dosage was "a wine glassful three times a day, before each meal, or a tablespoonful as often as the cough is troublesome."[111] This advertisement was carried in the *Appeal*, with some omissions, through June 1876. The number of places in San Francisco that sold the tonic increased slowly during this period.

In April 1875 Detter was chosen as the orator for a San Francisco celebration of the anniversary of ratification of the Fifteenth Amendment.[112]
In November 1876 Detter married Mrs. Emily Brinson of San Francisco.
The 1880 census listed his new wife as forty. Her birthplace was Virginia;
her father had been born in Ohio and her mother in Louisiana. Although
she was listed as married and "at home," she was enumerated in a household consisting of seven white males and four Chinese males. Probably
she was a servant for a typical household of single men in this period in
Nevada and required to live there. The marriage was held in Eureka with a
Presbyterian ceremony conducted by Reverend Joseph McClain. The
ceremony was at Detter's home and it and the subsequent party were
"attended by nearly all of the colored folk in town, besides some twenty-
five or thirty white people, including some of our most prominent citizens
and their wives," according to a Eureka newspaper. Referring to him as
Dr. Detter, "the wellknown proprietor of the Silver Brick shaving saloon
and bathing establishment," the newspaper concluded that "the affair
was well conducted throughout and the Doctor and his bride have reason
to feel pleased with the auspices under which they commence their
voyage upon the matrimonial sea."[113]
    No news about Detter and his wife after his second marriage has yet
come to light. Since Eureka declined as a mining town in the mid-1880s,
he was probably forced to move once again. A search of the cemeteries
at Eureka did not reveal any markers for himself or his family, although
presumably his son was buried in Eureka. The condition of the cemeteries
is such that many graves remain unidentified, however.
    James M. Whitfield, a major national black poet and leader of his
people in the nineteenth century, lived in Nevada toward the close of his
life and was also a barber. Whitfield was visited in 1850 by Frederick
Douglass, who deplored "the malignant arrangements of society" that
confined a poet to a barbershop and stated: "That talents so commanding,
gifts so rare, poetic powers so distinguished, should be tied to the handle
of a razor and buried in the precincts of a barber's shop . . . is painfully
disheartening."[114] Unfortunately, Whitfield remained a barber for the
rest of his life but nevertheless managed to publish a volume of poetry,
America and Other Poems, in 1853, as well as *A Poem*, printed in San
Francisco in 1867 by the *Elevator*, and numerous shorter poems in various
black papers from 1849 to 1870. From 1854 to 1862 he was a leader in
the effort to found a black emigration movement; he issued the call
for the National Emigration Convention of 1854 and published the *Afric-
American Repository*, a proemigration journal. He may have left Buffalo,

New York, in 1859, and apparently lived in San Francisco from at least 1862 to 1863 and again from 1867 to 1869.[115] From 1863 to 1865 he "barbered in Portland, Oregon, and in Placerville and Centerville, Idaho."[116] From at least May 1869 to July 1870 he lived in Nevada.

Whitfield first visited Nevada in August 1868. He was Grand Master for California of the Prince Hall Masons from 1864 to 1869,[117] and in that capacity traveled to Virginia City to install the Ashlar Lodge at that city.[118] In May 1869 the San Francisco *Elevator* reported that he had left for the Treasure Hill mining area.[119] For whatever reasons, he did not stay long in this booming mining camp; in July 1869 he was in Elko and remained there until at least July 1870.[120] On April 7, 1870, he read a poem at the celebration of ratification of the Fifteenth Amendment held in Virginia City. During his absence from Elko, a poem of his was read at the Fifteenth Amendment celebration in that city.

In July 1870 Whitfield was active in a "literary and political club" called the Elko Republican Club; he debated on women's enfranchisement with W. A. Scott against F. G. Grice and Charles M. Wilson. Also in July 1870 he was one of four black men chosen to sit on a jury in Elko County; reportedly, this was the first time blacks had served on juries in the state.[121]

It is not known where Whitfield lived between July 1870 and his death in San Francisco on April 23, 1871, but it is certain that he spent at least a year in Nevada in 1869 and 1870. Like Thomas Detter, he had lived in various parts of the West after his arrival in California and had also maintained contact with other western black leaders through their newspapers and through a willingness to travel to participate in Masonic or political activities. Unlike Detter, he was a figure of national importance in the black community before he came West, and he has received more attention from scholars since his death. His chief biographer to date says of him: "The barber-poet was clearly a major propagandist for black separatism and racial retributive justice. His sincerity and artistry place his poems among the most robust and convincing of the time. Moreover, no poet so forcefully, with such anger and pathos, described the crippling of a creative soul by race prejudice."[122]

A number of other businesses were conducted by Nevada blacks during the nineteenth century. William Henry Hall, a discoverer of the Elevator Mine at Treasure Hill, was one of the leading blacks on the Pacific Coast and engaged in various businesses at one time or another in California and Nevada. In 1873 Philip Bell reported that he was operating "the most extensive laundry in Virginia."[123]

Another black businessman in Virginia City in the 1860s was George Cottle, proprietor of the Union Hotel. In 1865, advertisements in the *Elevator* announced that Cottle and Theodore Lee had leased the hotel located at the corner of F and Union streets. The advertisement promised "comfortable" rooms, excellent food, and a bar with "the best of Wines, Liquors and Cigars."[124] Cottle died by drowning in 1874.[125]

The census of population of 1870 listed five other black Nevadans who owned property worth $2,000 or more, in addition to the farmers at Genoa and the group at Treasure Hill. These were: Charlotte Detter, wife of Thomas Detter of Elko, property worth $2,100; Moses A. Jackson, a Virginia City saloon keeper, property worth $5,000; Eliza Lawson, a thirty-six-year-old woman from Europe who was living in Virginia City and reported to be keeping house, property worth $11,000; Dr. W. H. C. Stephenson of Virginia City, property worth $2,000; and Samuel Wagner, sixty-four, a bootblack born in Kentucky and living in Virginia City, property worth $2,000.

In 1874 an advertisement for Mrs. J. W. Price's boarding house on E Street in Virginia City indicated that she "is prepared to accommodate Ladies and Gentlemen with Board and Lodging. Her house is pleasantly situated, and every effort will be made to render her friends comfortable."[126]

Several letters from M. Howard about the effects of the 1875 fire tell something about the economic standing of blacks in Virginia City at that time. Howard listed business and/or real estate losses by Virginia City blacks from the great fire in November 1875 as follows (by size of loss): John Davis, $12,000 (no insurance); Joseph Felemente, $10,000 (insured for about $3,000); Hiram Lyon, $6,090; Emanuel Taylor (six houses and a saloon), $6,000 (no insurance); Mrs. Cicero Miner, $6,000; Charles H. Jackson, $4,000 (insured for $2,000); Henry Williams (3 houses), $4,000 (no insurance); Mrs. Taylor, $1,600; John Falls, $1,500; John Martin, $600; M. Howard, $300; and Henry Olney, $250. In addition, Sam Wagner lost three houses at a value not determined. Howard listed eight other people who had sustained losses of $50 to $500 each from the loss of their furniture, clothing, and other possessions.[127]

In a later letter Howard reported that "only one or two of the colored people were insured" but that, nevertheless, Miss Mary Allen, Charles Jackson, Emanuel Taylor, John Falls, M. Howard, Hiram Lyons, and Mrs. Taylor "have all gone to work rebuilding and will soon have their houses completed, weather permitting."[128]

By 1876 evidently a number of black businessmen in Virginia City had recovered from the fire. Peter Anderson, the editor of the *Pacific*

Appeal, visited Nevada in June of that year. In Virginia City, he reported visiting the barbershop run by "Professor" Howard and William Bird. He indicated that Hiram Lyon and Mrs. Sarah Miner had rebuilt their businesses "but on a smaller scale. Mrs. Miner still retains the business of express and furniture wagons" which had been built up by her late husband, Cicero. Anderson reported that Mrs. Anna Graham, who used to have a similar establishment in San Francisco, was operating "a fine hairdressing establishment on C street, Virginia City" next door to the Howard-Bird barbershop.

Emanuel Taylor had just opened his saloon when the fire destroyed it. In October 1875 M. Howard wrote from Virginia City that Taylor, "an old Californian . . . who has a number of acquaintances in San Francisco," had just opened his saloon the previous Saturday night. Howard predicted success for the business. "Although there is quite a number of colored people here, we have been without any place of recreation of our own for the last three or four months, so he has been doing pretty well."[129]

There were a number of black businesses in Carson City in 1876. Anderson listed the following: the barbershop of F. W. Grinage and George H. Rogers; a barbershop run by Mr. Lee; three hairdressing businesses, run by Mrs. Lee, Mrs. Bailey, and Mrs. Gibson; a dressmaking establishment run by an unnamed woman from Stockton; a "fine dining saloon" operated by a Mr. Lawrence, recently of San Jose; and a "fine restaurant on Carson street with high prospects of success" owned by Mr. Woolridge, "recently from Chicago."[130]

In 1876 the Nevada Saloon, at 114 Nevada Street in Carson City, advertised in the *Pacific Appeal*; William Davis was the proprietor. The same newspaper carried advertisements for Mr. Howard's "unrivalled Hair Restorative" and for Miss Anna Graham, a hairdresser with a business at 50½ C Street in Virginia City.[131]

There were also black businessmen in other Nevada towns. In Elko, C. M. Wilson and E. Cuney were barbers in 1877. A visitor to Elko reported that "they have their fine shop in the Depot Hotel, and are apparently doing a good business." The same correspondent reported that a "colored man named Newman has started a restaurant" in Battle Mountain and that a Mr. Poulson from Sacramento had a barbershop in the same town.[132]

Although not a businessman, a black cook had an unusually significant assignment which allowed him to play a role in the building of the transcontinental railroad. According to his son, William E. Towns was a steward at the Occidental Club in San Francisco in the 1860s. The Big

Four, soon to be builders of the Central Pacific railroad, asked him if
he could cook for construction crews building the road. Towns said he
could if he were provided with the right facilities, and was hired. He held
this position until the Central Pacific met the Union Pacific at Promon-
tory Point, Utah, in 1869.[133]

A substantial number of blacks in nineteenth-century Nevada managed
to overcome the handicaps of slavery and white racism to participate in
all phases of the state's economic life. A few earned incomes substantially above the low incomes of the bulk of the black population, and
some acquired property. There were a black physician, a black artist who
spent some time in the state, black ranchers and cowboys, black miners in
the Treasure Hill area (if not on the Comstock), and a variety of black
businessmen. Barbers, especially, often became businessmen and were among
the most well-to-do persons in the black community. Probably the number
of black businessmen and the proportion of the black community owning
property increased during the 1860s and 1870s. In any case, there were
enough black people financially able to support institutions within their
community to allow for the creation of churches, Masonic lodges, charitable organizations, partisan organizations, and what today would be
called civil rights groups.

NOTES

1. The main sources of this table are the published reports of the
Bureau of the Census; however, the numbers of blacks in 1860, 1870,
and 1880 are totals derived from microfilm copies of the original
enumerators' forms and differ somewhat from the published totals.
2. *Pacific Appeal*, December 6, 1862 (letter from W.H.P.).
3. Albert Lawrence DeMond, *Certain Aspects of the Economic
Development of the American Negro, 1865-1900* (Washington, D.C.:
The Catholic University of America Press, 1945), p. 13. The standard
works on black labor in the nineteenth century are W. E. B. Du Bois, ed.,
The Negro Artisan (Atlanta, Georgia: Atlanta University Press, 1902),
Charles H. Wesley, *Negro Labor in the United States, 1850-1925* (New
York: Russell and Russell, 1927), Lorenzo J. Greene and Carter G.
Woodson, *The Negro Wage Earner* (Washington, D.C.: Association for
the Study of Negro Life and History, 1930), and Sterling D. Spero and
Abram L. Harris, *The Black Worker* (Port Washington, New York:
Kennipat Press, 1931).

    4. Greene and Woodson, *Negro Wage Earner*, p. 11.
    5. W. E. B. Du Bois, ed., *The Negro in Business* (Atlanta, Georgia: Atlanta University Press, 1899), p. 5. The standard works on black business, in addition to Du Bois', are: J. G. Harmon, Jr., Arnett G. Lindsay, and Carter G. Woodson, *The Negro as a Business Man* (College Park, Maryland: McGrath Publishing Co., 1929), and Abram L. Harris, *The Negro as Capitalist* (College Park, Maryland: McGrath Publishing Co., 1936).
    6. Du Bois, ed., *The Negro in Business*, p. 9.
    7. *Elevator*, December 13, 1873 (letter from Mrs. Carter dated December 8, 1873), and ibid., May 17, 1873.
    8. *Territorial Enterprise*, February 24, 1867.
    9. See Nevada, *Statutes*, 1875, chap. 4.
    10. *Territorial Enterprise*, May 14, 1867.
    11. See a summary by a leading Eclectic practitioner and professor, Dr. John M. Scudder, "A Brief History of Eclectic Medicine" (n.p., 1888); Harvey Wickes Felter, *History of the Eclectic Medical Institute, Cincinnati, Ohio, 1845-1902* (Cincinnati, Ohio: Alumnal Association of the Eclectic Medical Institute, 1902); Harold J. Abrahams, *Extinct Medical Schools of Nineteenth Century Philadelphia* (Philadelphia: University of Pennsylvania Press, 1966), pp. 177-184, 232-254, 334-417, 435-455.
    Apparently Dr. Stephenson was not an alumnus of the Cincinnati or Philadelphia schools. There is an entry for him in Silas E. Ross, *A Directory of Nevada Medical Practitioners, Past and Present* (n.p., 1957), p. 139, but the only information in this entry is that derived from the 1870 census.
    12. *Pacific Appeal*, December 19, 1863.
    13. *Elevator*, May 10, 1873. A Dr. Stephenson was reported to have given a patient too large a dose of nux vomica in December 1873; it is not known whether this is the same person. See Walter Van Tilburg Clark, ed., *The Journals of Alfred Doten, 1849-1903* (Reno: University of Nevada Press, 1973), p. 1213.
    14. See *Territorial Enterprise*, May 14, 1867.
    15. *Elevator*, August 4, 1865.
    16. See Charles Collins, comp., *Mercantile Guide and Directory for Virginia City, Gold Hill, Silver City and American City* (San Francisco: Agnew and Deffebach, 1864-1865), p. 237. Material on Brown was secured from "Grafton Tyler Brown: Black Artist in the West," docent notes for the Oakland Museum exhibition, kindly provided by Susan E. Burns, research associate of the museum, and Phillip T. Drotning, *A Guide to Negro History in America* (Garden City, New York: Doubleday, 1968), p. 21. At least four lithographs by Brown of Nevada scenes and four of his lithographs showing Comstock mining claims are to be found in the library of the Nevada Historical Society or the Special Collections room of

Getchell Library at the University of Nevada, Reno. In the Special Collections reading room, three of the five lithographs of Virginia City displayed on the west wall are by Brown. An exhibit of his work at the Oakland Museum from February 11 through April 22, 1972 contained at least eight of his lithographs with Nevada topics.

17. *Territorial Enterprise*, March 3, 1867.

18. Grace Dangberg, *Carson Valley—Historical Sketches of Nevada's First Settlement* (Reno, Nevada: A. Carlisle and Co., 1972), p. 59. This book contains a photograph of Clarissa Church (p. 60).

19. Georgia Lewis, "The Black Ranchers of Lincoln County," *The Nevadan*, July 18, 1971, pp. 28-29. This article contains two photographs of the brothers.

20. "My Memoirs," n.d., Nevada Historical Society, Reno, Nevada.

21. Lewis, "Black Ranchers," p. 29.

22. Philip Durham and Everett L. Jones, *The Negro Cowboys* (New York: Dodd, Mead and Co., 1965).

23. Kenneth W. Porter, "Negro Labor in the Western Cattle Industry, 1866-1900," in Milton Cantor, ed., *Black Labor in America* (Westport, Connecticut: Negro Universities Press, 1969), pp. 24-52. The estimate of the number is on p. 25.

24. Durham and Jones, *The Negro Cowboys*, pp. 86-87.

25. Durham and Jones, p. 24, note that few blacks in the cattle companies became foremen, and Porter, "Negro Labor," says that "they were almost never, except in the highly infrequent case of an all-Negro outfit, to be found as ranch or trail boss," ("Negro Labor in the Western Cattle Industry," p. 26).

26. Edna B. Patterson, Louise A. Ulph, and Victor Goodwin, *Nevada's Northeast Frontier* (Sparks, Nevada: Western Printing and Publishing Co., 1969), p. 386.

27. Ibid., p. 323.

28. Ibid., p. 384.

29. See David H. Grover, *Diamondfield Jack* (Reno, Nevada: University of Nevada Press, 1968). The reference to Harris as foreman is on pp. 31-32; his testimony at the trial and his involvement in other legal proceedings are noted on pp. 54, 107-108, and 137.

30. Patterson et al., *Nevada's Northeast Frontier*, p. 383.

31. Ibid., p. 638.

32. *Elevator*, May 6, 1870.

33. Ibid., May 7, 1869.

34. *Proceedings of the California State Convention of Colored Citizens, 1865* (San Francisco: R and E Research Associates, 1969), p. 92.

35. In 1859 the Gold Hill miners adopted a regulation denying Chinese the right to file claims; while other mining regulations of this era did not copy this provision, evidently exclusion of Chinese was common in mining areas of the state. Further, the miners' unions on the

Comstock excluded Chinese from their organizations and therefore from employment in the mines. See Eliot Lord, *Comstock Mining and Miners* (Berkeley, California: Howell-North, 1959), pp. 44, 355-359. The constitutions and bylaws of the Gold Hill and Virginia City miners' unions, the two most important labor organizations on the Comstock, did not exclude nonwhites explicitly. Candidates for membership in the union had to be miners of good moral character who were proposed by a member of the union at a meeting, seconded by another member, and elected by acclamation. The surviving minutes of the Gold Hill Miners' Union from December 1866 through August 1868 and November 1872 through May 1875 were examined for evidence of attitudes toward blacks, but they contain no mention of race except for a single reference to Chinese. The materials on these unions were examined at Special Collections of Getchell Library, University of Nevada, Reno, or the library of the Nevada Historical Society, Reno.

36. *Pacific Appeal*, March 5, 1864.

37. De Quille's story speaks for itself: "Even the colored population, who seldom trouble themselves about mines, caught the infection and went out prospecting and locating mines—became experts on ore. One of these coming into town with a big chunk of rock in his hand met a friend whose eyes began to dilate at what he thought might be a lump of solid silver. Said the—

"FIRST EXPERT: 'Wha—what yer got thar?'

"SECOND EXPERT: 'Look at dat, sah! Dat's out'en de Day of Jubilee mine. Boy, I tell yer dat's gwine to be a mine. What—what you say, now, dat's gwine to pay at de present prices of deduction, hey?'

"FIRST EXPERT: 'Fore de Lord, I doesn't know! Gwine to pay, think?'

"SECOND EXPERT: 'Gwine to pay? *Gwine to pay?* Now you makes me laugh. Jes' look at dat rock, Edward Arthur—look at dat side of it! See de pure chloroform dat's percolated all ober it! Now ax me ef dat rock's gwine to pay! Look at de formation and de stratification! Ax me ef dat rock's gwine to pay! Why, you see you doesn't know de fust principles 'bout dem oldah prefatory periods when dis here yearf was a multitudinous mass, floatin' roun' in a chaotic hemisphere; time o' de propylites and jewrasic periods. Your ignorance perfectly afflixes me." Dan De Quille, *The Big Bonanza* (New York: Alfred A. Knopf, 1947), pp. 312-313.

38. *Lyon County Times*, May 3, 1879.

39. *Elevator*, November 14, 1874.

40. Ibid., January 31, 1868.

41. Russell R. Elliott, "The Early History of White Pine County, Nevada, 1865-1887," *Pacific Northwest Quarterly* (April 1939): 150.

42. Ibid., p. 156.

43. W. Turrentine Jackson, *Treasure Hill* (Tucson: University of Arizona Press, 1963), pp. 86, 91-92.

44. *Elevator,* January 1, 1869.
45. Ibid., February 5, 1869.
46. Ibid., February 12, 1869. Probably this is the man referred to by Jackson, *Treasure Hill,* p. 63.
47. *Elevator,* February 12, 1869.
48. Ibid., March 12, 1869.
49. Ibid.
50. Ibid., April 2, 1869.
51. Ibid., April 9, 1869.
52. Ibid., April 16, 1869.
53. Ibid.
54. Ibid., April 23, 1869.
The incorporation papers of the Elevator Silver Mining Company, at the California State Archives, Sacramento, list the incorporators as Henry M. Collins, John C. Mortimer, H. H. Pearson, John E. Ince, and C. E. Pearson. Files of James Abajian, San Francisco.
55. *Elevator,* May 7, 1869.
56. Ibid., May 14, 1869.
57. Ibid., May 28, 1869.
58. Ibid., June 25, 1869, reprinting an advertisement in the *White Pine News,* n.d.
59. Ibid., June 4, 1869.
60. Ibid., June 11, 1869.
61. Ibid., November 15, 1873.
62. Ibid., June 28, 1873. W. Sherman Savage quotes from an earlier letter from Grice. "The Negro on the Mining Frontier," *The Journal of Negro History* 30 (January 1945): 43.
63. *Elevator,* February 12, 1869.
64. See Earl W. Kersten, Jr., "The Early Settlement of Aurora, Nevada, and Nearby Mining Camps," *Annals of the Association of American Geographers* 54 (December 1964): 503.
65. *Pacific Appeal,* June 10, 1876.
66. Ibid., November 13, 1875, June 10, 1876.
67. Spero and Harris, *The Black Worker,* p. 14.
68. Wesley, *Negro Labor,* pp. 76, 232-233.
69. Greene and Woodson, *Negro Wage Earner,* pp. 3, 244.
70. Du Bois, *The Negro in Business,* p. 10.
71. *Elevator,* March 8, 1873.
72. Du Bois, *The Negro in Business,* p. 10.
73. Delilah Beasley, *The Negro Trail Blazers of California* (Los Angeles: Times-Mirror Printing and Binding House, 1919), p. 81. See also p. 188.
74. In fact, there were even complaints in the nineteenth-century West that black barbers were discriminating against customers of their own race. In 1873 an anonymous letter to the *Pacific Appeal* from Sacra-

mento asserted that there was only one Negro barber in that city who would cut a Negro's hair. *Pacific Appeal,* August 9, 1873.

75. *Elevator,* May 7, 1869.

76. Ibid., August 13, 1869.

77. Ibid., February 8, 1873.

78. Ibid., April 2, 1869 (letter from "Up Country").

79. *Pacific Appeal,* February 27, March 19, 1864.

80. *Elevator,* January 22, August 20, November 26, 1869.

81. *Pacific Appeal,* October 16, 1875.

82. Ibid., April 6, 1878.

83. Ibid., April 12, 1878.

84. Ibid., April 20, 1878.

85. *Journal of Proceedings of the Third Annual Convention of the Ministers and Lay Delegates of the African Methodist Episcopal Church* (San Francisco: B. F. Sterett, Printer, 1863), pp. 4, 20.

86. *Pacific Appeal,* April 25, June 13, 1863.

87. In 1855 a treaty guaranteeing the Nez Perce Indians most of their aboriginal lands was signed. After miners had encroached substantially on these lands, the government negotiated a new treaty, which drastically reduced the territory belonging to members of the tribe. Partly because only some of the tribal leaders signed the 1863 treaty, warfare broke out in subsequent years. See Alvin M. Josephy, Jr., *The Nez Perce Indians and the Opening of the Northwest* (New Haven: Yale University Press, 1965), esp. pp. 388-431.

88. *Pacific Appeal,* July 18, August 1, 1863.

89. Thomas Detter, *Nellie Brown* (San Francisco: Cuddy and Hughes, 1871), p. 155.

90. *Pacific Appeal,* January 30, 1864.

91. Ibid., February 13, 1864.

92. Ibid., May 19, 1864.

93. *Elevator,* May 26, 1866.

94. *Pacific Appeal,* August 17, 1867.

95. *Elevator,* June 26, 1868.

96. Ibid., July 17, 1868.

97. Ibid., May 22, 1868.

98. Ibid., August 7, 1868.

99. Ibid., December 4, 1868.

100. Ibid., February 26, 1869.

101. Ibid., March 19, 1869.

102. Detter's book, which was published in San Francisco, was preceded by only six other published novels by American blacks. See Maxwell Whitman, *A Century of Fiction by American Negroes, 1853-1952* (Philadelphia: Maurice Jacobs, 1955), pp. 17-18.

103. *Pacific Appeal,* August 12, 1871.

104. Ibid., December 16, 1871.
105. Ibid., March 30, 1872.
106. Ibid., April 13, 1872.
107. Ibid., September 27, 1873.
108. Ibid., February 14, 1874. The 1870 census reported her as thirty-two and having been born in Maryland. She was listed by that census as "keeping house."
109. Ibid., May 30, 1874.
110. Ibid., January 2, 1875.
111. Ibid., January 9, 1875.
112. Ibid., April 3, 10, 1875.
113. Ibid., November 18, 1876, reprinting article from *Eureka Sentinel.*
114. *Anti-Slavery Bugle,* August 24, 1850, quoted in Joan R. Sherman, "James Monroe Whitfield, Poet and Emigrationist: A Voice of Protest and Despair," *The Journal of Negro History* 57 (April 1972): 169.
115. Ibid., pp. 169-170, 173-175.
116. Ibid., p. 175.
117. Ibid., p. 176.
118. *Elevator,* August 21, 1868.
119. Ibid., May 14, 1869. The entire story reads: "White Pine— Mr. James M. Whitfield departed for Silverland last week."
120. From July until December the *Elevator* occasionally thanked Whitfield and various readers (including Thomas Detter) for financial contributions to the newspaper. During this time Whitfield was identified as a resident of Elko. See ibid., July 30, August 20, September 3, December 31, 1869.
121. Ibid., July 8, 1870.
122. Sherman, "James Monroe Whitfield," p. 176.
    For further details on Hall's life, see Francis N. Lortie, Jr., *San Francisco's Black Community, 1870-1890* (San Francisco: R and E Research Associates, 1973), p. 9, and Elizabeth L. Parker and James Abajian, *A Walking Tour of the Black Presence in San Francisco During the Nineteenth Century* (San Francisco: San Francisco African American Historical and Cultural Society, 1974), p. 4.
123. *Elevator,* May 10, 1873.
124. Ibid., April 4, May 12, 1865.
125. *Pacific Appeal,* August 8, 1874.
126. Ibid., February 28, 1874.
127. Ibid., November 13, 20, 1875.
128. Ibid., November 27, 1865.
129. Ibid., October 16, 1875.
130. Ibid., June 10, 1876.
131. Ibid.
132. Ibid., September 15, 1877 (correspondent unidentified).
133. Interview with Royal E. Towns, Oakland, California, January 11, 1975, and letter from Mr. Towns, December 26, 1974.

—7—

Organizations of the Black Community

Even the incomplete evidence that has survived to this point indicates a substantial degree of organized group activity, in spite of the small size of Nevada's nineteenth-century black population. Especially in Virginia City and Carson City, where the black population was larger than in other places, the black residents of early Nevada initiated a number of different kinds of organizations and sustained some of them for several decades. Some of these organizations developed within the black community to deal with the internal needs of that community, and some were brought into being to cope with the white world surrounding it.

A number of groups within the black community performed essentially the same functions for that community as similar groups among whites. Undoubtedly such groups developed for several reasons, although the relative importance of each is impossible to reconstruct with precision now. Especially in the early and mid-1860s, there were few white institutions open to blacks. Also, black churches and the Masonic order were in existence in other places before the black settlers came to Nevada, and they simply brought with them the institutions with which they were familiar. Finally, many of the blacks probably preferred separate institutions to joining the existing white institutions.

173

"TO WORSHIP IN THEIR OWN
PECULIAR WAY"

Black churches were well developed in the North, and to a lesser degree in the South, by 1860, and undoubtedly the black immigrants brought their churches with them to Nevada as a matter of course.[1] But the factor of white discrimination was probably also present. One of the founders of the first black Baptist church in Nevada, Samuel T. Wagner, stated explicitly that "well knowing the feeling of prejudice existing against their race by their white brethren," the blacks wanted their own church so that "they might worship God according to the dictates of their own conscience and in their own peculiar way, without interfering with or coming in contact with their white brethren."[2]

The black church whose founding Wagner described was the first Baptist church in Nevada. In September 1863 the *Virginia Evening Bulletin* reported that "the colored people of Virginia have a very neat meeting house on B street, nearly opposite the 'dump' of the Gould & Curry claim, at which quite a large congregation attend."[3] Evidently some white Baptists, lacking a church of their own, attended the black church. Myron Angel says that "with the exception of one person all the members were colored people," and Hubert Howe Bancroft says that "the baptists first organized at Virginia in 1863 with a membership chiefly of colored people."[4] Reverend Charles Satchell, who had been a minister in Cincinnati before coming West and the first minister of the Third Baptist Church of San Francisco, was the first pastor of Virginia City's First Baptist Church.[5] He was in Virginia City in June 1863 when he wrote a letter to the *Pacific Appeal* urging blacks to volunteer to fight for the Union cause, and was present in January 1864 when the Ladies' Benevolent Association of San Francisco, also known as the Daughters of Naomi, made a gift to the church of "a magnificent bound pulpit Bible, and one dozen splendid bound hymn books."[6] Reverend Satchell reportedly left after about one year and was replaced by Dr. W. H. C. Stephenson, who had been clerk of the church.[7] Some time during 1866, because the church was in debt, the building was sold at auction. When Dr. Stephenson bought the church at the auction and subsequently sold it, he evidently kept the proceeds from the sale and thus earned the enmity of some members of his former congregation. In 1867 Samuel Wagner, one of the black businessmen of Virginia City and a leader of the black community for several years, purchased two advertisements in the *Territorial Enterprise* in which he attacked Dr. Stephenson on two grounds. Wagner claimed that Stephenson, assisted by his wife and another woman, had collected money for the church but had "rendered no account of the manner of its disbursement, doubtless appropriating the greater part to his own use." He also asserted that Dr. Stephenson had caused the church to be sold so that he could purchase it and appropriate "the proceeds to his own use."[8]

The truth of these charges is impossible to determine. The *Enterprise* did not comment on them, although it printed an advertisement by Justice of the Peace D. O. Adkison and Constable Augustus Ash correcting minor factual errors by Wagner and continuing with the statement, "We would further say that the conduct of Dr. Stephenson in the whole matter was perfectly honorable and correct, so far as we know."[9] Dr. Stephenson refused to debate the charges in the newspapers, asserting that discussing them with Wagner was impossible "without forfeiting my own dignity and self-respect and the same entertained for me by the intelligent, respectable and honorable citizens in this community." While this remark was not really explained, evidently Dr. Stephenson referred to Mr. Wagner's illiteracy—his advertisements were signed with an X. Dr. Stephenson noted that Wagner "signs his name X" and asserted that "his cross mark, and what his amanuensis wrote for him at his dictation, are sufficient evidence which should bespeak for him the charitable consideration of an enlightened public in his declining years. In his dotage he is an object who deserves pity."[10] Whatever the facts of this particular dispute, it seems highly likely that the small size of the congregation made it impossible to pay even a part-time minister what he would consider adequate compensation.

Although the history of the African Methodist Episcopal church in nineteenth-century Nevada is still incomplete, it is clear that the small size of the black population created continuing difficulties for their churches. Nevertheless, there were early, valiant, and persistent efforts to establish and maintain such churches. At the first annual convention in 1863 of the AME church of California (which included California, Oregon, Nevada, Idaho, and British Columbia), Elder Jacob Mitchell reported on a visit to Virginia City during the previous year. He said that

on his arrival there he was cordially received. Preparations for meetings had been made by the brethren, who had been apprised of his intended visit. The Court House of that city was opened for him to preach to the people in. On the first Sabbath our meeting was numerously attended; the audience appeared deeply interested, and a collection of $100 was taken up. Our brethren there have organized a building committee, and bought a lot for the erection of a house

of worship. The original size of their lot was 100 x 100 feet. Of this
the brethren had been induced to sell two lots, each 100 x 25 feet.
They deem their lot sufficiently large, and it has finally cost them
$100. They have now in their fund, towards a building, $390.

Elder Mitchell also reported that the white Methodist Episcopal church,
which had just constructed a new building, "freely loaned us the use of
their former meeting-house. Here we met and worshipped. Here, in the
name of Jesus, I had the happiness of taking twenty-three of my brethren
and sisters by the hand, and organizing a branch of the Church militant,
under the A. M. E. Discipline."[11] He specifically thanked Reverend
Anthony of the Virginia City ME Church for his "kindness."[12] Elsewhere,
the cash collected at Virginia City was reported to be forty dollars and
the number of members of the church there twenty-two (out of a total
in the conference of 267).[13] Evidently, then, an AME church was established at Virginia City at some time during the year preceding the annual
convention in September 1863.

By the time of the convention, apparently two ministers had served in
Virginia City; the proceedings listed James Brown and John E. Waters
as ministers there. Peter Green was assigned as a minister to the city for
the succeeding year. Elder Mitchell was to supervise the church there, as
well as the churches at Placerville, Coloma, Grass Valley, and Nevada
City, California, while Elder T. M. D. Ward was to supervise the remaining churches. Finally, the convention "instructed" the ministers at
Sacramento, Placerville, and Virginia City "to commence the building
of new churches." The structure at Virginia City was to be built of stone
while the other two were to be of brick.[14] An 1864-1865 directory lists
Reverend Green as the pastor and states that "a neat and substantial
church has lately been built on F street, and religious services are held
every Sunday."[15]

John E. Waters apparently remained in Virginia City for some time
after the annual convention; in December 1863 he was listed in a newspaper article as one of the people scheduled to participate in the Emancipation Proclamation celebration at the beginning of 1864.[16] The next
AME minister we hear of in Virginia City is John T. Jenifer, whose first
assignment as an AME minister had been in Sacramento during the year
before the 1863 convention.[17] In August 1865 the *Elevator* commented
editorially on some of the members of the Nevada executive committee
and said of Reverend Jenifer that he was "a young man of bright promise
and judgment beyong [*sic*] his years."[18] The same month a letter from
Jenifer in Virginia City reported that a fund-raising festival by the

Virginia City AME congregation had netted $147.55.[19] In October the *Elevator* reported that Reverend Jenifer had preached his last sermon in San Francisco and had left for the East.[20]

Reverend Jenifer's brief stay in Virginia City may have been due to a decision by the church hierarchy to appoint another man to the position. AME churches were typically organized by bishops or persons appointed by them. It is not clear what happened to Elder Mitchell, who had been given the duty of supervising Virginia City in 1863, but by 1865 Elder Ward had become a bishop and was responsible for Virginia City. In mid-1865, a letter from a Bishop Campbell of Philadelphia announced the appointment of Reverend William Offer to be a "co-laborer" in the West with Bishop Ward. Reverend Offer was to have "pastoral charge of Virginia City, and to take the oversight of Grass Valley and Placerville circuits," thus relieving Bishop Ward of responsibility for serving these places.[21] This suggests that Reverend Jenifer was locally recruited. Reverend Offer, described as "a young man but recently ordained to ministry," arrived in San Francisco and preached his first sermon there in July 1865.[22]

Evidently his congregation made substantial efforts to provide him adequate pay. A reporter from the *Territorial Enterprise* attended a fruit festival organized by the ladies of the church in June 1866 to raise money. He reported that "the Festival was well attended, not only by colored people, but also by numerous ladies and gentlemen of the white race." The "good things exposed for sale" at the festival included ice cream, "luscious fruits, cakes sandwiches, meats, tea [and] coffee," which were displayed "bountifully and temptingly." In addition, entertainment was provided. "A piano and violin discoursed excellent music, and later in the evening dancing commenced."[23]

It is not clear how long Reverend Offer stayed in Virginia City, but evidently he became dissatisfied with the income he received from his congregation. In September 1867 he arrived in San Francisco from Virginia City, and two weeks later the following advertisement was placed in the San Francisco *Elevator* by D. W. Sands, Cicero Miner, John Martin, and Joseph W. Price, trustees of the AME church in Virginia City:

We have been informed that Rev. Wm. H. Offer has stated in California that he has only received twenty-five dollars from his congregation in this city, which is incorrect. He has been paid, from September, 1865, to June, 1866, the sum of $524.25, and other collections, making in all $551.25, and during that time he was twice in California attending his Quarterly Meetings. These are facts, as our books will show.[24]

It is not clear whether Virginia City had an AME minister for several years after mid-1867, but there seems to have been a church building. In 1870 Bishop Ward published a notice that "the Church at Virginia City will be dedicated October 1."[25] In February 1872 J. B. Handy signed an advertisement appealing for funds for the retirement of Bishop Ward,[26] and in March 1872 Reverend Handy attended the annual AME conference in California as a delegate from Virginia City. At the end of 1873 and the beginning of 1874, Reverend Beard was minister of the AME church in Virginia City.[27] In December 1873 a visitor to western Nevada reported that Reverend Beard "supplies Virginia City and Carson, preaching for the A. M. E. Church. . . . I heard him once. He is an earnest speaker."[28]

In May 1874 the minister was Wilson Bean, the number of members was reported as thirteen, and the amount of cash received during the year by the annual conference from Virginia City was twenty dollars.[29] In May 1875 the eighth annual AME conference appointed Reverend Samuel Johnson minister for the Virginia City church.[30]

The great fire that destroyed much of Virginia City in the fall of 1875 also destroyed the building housing the AME church although probably the structure was rebuilt.[31] It also seems possible that the church gave up attempts to provide a minister for a time; the official announcements of church appointments for 1877 and 1878 list no minister for Virginia City.[32] However, Myron Angel reported that in 1879 "the Rev. Mr. Wier was appointed Pastor, and remained less than a year. Because of lack of financial support no pastor was subsequently appointed."[33]

Carson City was able to maintain a small AME church, sometimes sharing ministers with Virginia City, at least in the 1870s. As noted above, Reverend Beard preached in both cities in 1873. Also in 1873, the conference of the AME Zion church, a smaller group, appointed Reverend John Warren to serve a fourth district comprising Sacramento, Sonora, Stockton, and Carson City.[34] In 1876 the women of the Carson church held a festival to raise funds for their church; the *Carson Daily Appeal* ran two notices of the event, thanked the ladies for complimentary tickets to the festival, and stated: "We bespeak a full attendance and liberal patronage."[35] In 1877 the AME Zion church charged Elder J. F. Anderson with responsibility for a general mission comprising Sacramento, Nevada City, Forbestown, Mariposa, and Carson City.[36] In 1890 Reverend R. C. O. Benjamin was elected presiding elder of a conference district comprising California, Oregon, Washington, and Nevada.[37]

Evidence on the degree to which black and white churches were closed to members of the other race is scant. At least while there was no white Baptist church, the black First Baptist Church had some white members. At least in the late 1860s and early 1870s, some white churches were occasionally open to blacks, though whether they had black members is not known. On a visit to Nevada in 1869, Bishop T. M. D. Ward spoke on Sunday in Virginia City at the "M. E. Church, and in the evening at A.M.E. Church."[38] Mrs. D. D. Carter, a black visitor to western Nevada from Placerville, reported in 1873 that she had heard Methodist minister Reverend A. N. Fisher preach in Carson City. Calling Fisher the "Beecher of the Pacific Coast," Mrs. Carter said that "he has enlarged Christian Views, a cultivated mind, ready delivery united to great zeal."[39] (Reverend Fisher, who was also state superintendent of public instruction, had earlier spoken out against the exclusion of blacks from the public schools.) Philip A. Bell, editor of the *San Francisco Elevator*, also "listened to an able sermon delivered by Rev. A. N. Fisher" on his trip to Nevada in May 1873 and attended services at the Episcopal church in Virginia City on the same visit, hearing a sermon by Reverend Whittaker.[40] Bishop Whittaker performed the marriage ceremony for a black couple in Virginia City in December 1873. Methodist minister Reverend A. H. Tevis married another black couple in Carson City in 1874. The groom was Frederick W. B. Grinage, a barber and leader of the black community.[41]

To summarize, there was a black Baptist church in Virginia City for three or four years in the 1860s; an AME church existed at least intermittently in Virginia City from 1863 through at least 1879; there was an AME Zion church in Carson City for a few years in the 1870s, if not longer; and at least one AME minister in Virginia City also served the congregation in Carson City for a time. It seems fair to say that Nevada's small black population made extensive and persistent efforts to maintain its churches throughout this period in the face of great difficulties in finding adequate financial support for these institutions.[42]

PRINCE HALL MASONS

The oldest and largest secret fraternal organization among blacks, Prince Hall Masonry, was represented in nineteenth-century Nevada by two lodges. Although one of these lodges was probably active for twenty years and the other for ten years, the historian of white Masonry in Nevada ignored them entirely (although he reported the activities of white lodges with much shorter histories), and the best nineteenth-century Nevada history notes the existence of the Carson City lodge but says nothing of the Virginia City group.[43] Prince Hall Masonic lodges trace their ancestry to the eighteenth century. In 1775 several blacks, including Prince Hall, were initiated as Masons by a military Masonic

lodge in Massachusetts, which had received its charter from the Grand
Lodge of England. Prince Hall and his followers subsequently formed
a lodge, which was also granted a warrant by the Grand Lodge of
England in 1784 although the warrant was not brought to the United
States until 1787. All Prince Hall Masons in the United States trace
their origin to this charter from England; white Masons in the United
States also trace their origin to the English Grand Lodge.[44]

Prince Hall Masonry arrived in California in 1849, when the Olive
Branch, Wethington, and Mosaic lodges were founded; in 1871 these
three lodges formed the Conventional Independent Grand Lodge of
California. Three other lodges—Hannibal, Philomathean, and Victoria—
formed the Grand Lodge of Free and Accepted Ancient York Masons
for the State of California in 1855 and 1856. In 1874 these two Grand
Lodges for California merged to form the Sovereign Grand Lodge of
Free and Accepted Masons for the State of California, the ancestor of
the present California Grand Lodge.[45] A warrant was issued to Ashlar
Lodge No. 9 of Virginia City in August 1867, presumably by the York
Grand Lodge of California.[46] This was five years after the first white
Masonic lodge in Nevada was founded.[47]

Ashlar Lodge apparently had a lodge building before it was issued
its warrant. A newspaper article in February 1867 reported that a meeting
to raise money for legal action had been held in the "ante room" of Ashlar
Lodge.[48] The lodge was probably in existence for some time before its
warrant was issued, since this is the practice of Masonry.

A Masonic Festival at Ashlar Lodge in November 1867 was attended
by 65 to 80 black men and women and "30 or 40 white spectators." A
meal featuring roast pig and turkey was described by a white reporter
as the "finest spread I have seen for many a day." After the meal, music
for dancing was provided by two violins, a cornet, and a piano.[49]

In April 1868 the officers of Ashlar Lodge thanked a festival committee
of women for raising $240 to benefit the lodge.[50] In May 1868 an adver-
tisement in a San Francisco black newspaper indicated that the lodge
met regularly on the first Monday of each month.[51] Ashlar Lodge was
dedicated on June 12, 1868, by Grand Master J. M. Whitfield of the
California Grand Lodge. After the ceremonies, which included the installation of the current officers, a banquet was served, at which the lodge
members were joined by their wives and other women of Virginia City's
black community.[52]

In May and November 1875 two devastating fires destroyed much of
Virginia City; the Ashlar lodge building was burned in the November
fire. Shortly after the fire, an estimate was made that the building had

been worth $900.[53] In 1877 the report of the annual communication of the California Grand Lodge noted that "Ashlar Lodge No. 8—Virginia City, Nevada—Has no Lodge room, but as they are true Masonic brethren, they meet, collect dues, take care of their sick and bury their dead, which speaks well for them."[54] A new hall was dedicated in September 1877 but evidently it was not very large; the festival, a fund-raising event attended by "quite a number of white persons," was held later in the same evening at the Miners' Union hall. As with earlier festivals, there was a substantial meal and dancing to the music of a black band with a white leader.[55] The *Proceedings* of the Grand Lodge indicate that Ashlar Lodge was still active after 1877. Presumably in 1881, the Grand Master of the California Grand Lodge reported that "Ashlar, of Virginia City, I find still in debt, but peace, harmony, and good feeling prevails. Their membership is small, but much energy is exhibited in consequence of having lost all they had in the great fire, from which they have not recovered."[56] In 1880 a meeting to decide whether to found a Garfield and Arthur club was held in the Masonic lodge.[57]

The fate of Ashlar Lodge after 1880 is unclear. From the partial records provided in 1968 by Frank E. Boone, historian of the California Grand Lodge, it seems that Ashlar Lodge was not represented at the 1885 and 1886 annual communications of the Grand Lodge but that it still had fourteen members in 1886. The Bancroft history of Nevada, which reports events through 1888, lists the Ashlar Lodge.[58] Boone states that the warrant of Ashlar Lodge was withdrawn for nonpayment of dues, presumably after 1888. The historian of nineteenth-century Prince Hall Masonry, William H. Grimshaw, was unaware of the existence of Ashlar Lodge from 1867 to 1885 since he dates the beginning of Masonry in Nevada at 1885.[59] The discrepancy between these reports still has to be clarified.

The second Prince Hall lodge in Nevada was established in Carson City in 1875. In March 1875 there was a newspaper announcement of a "ball . . . for the benefit of the general fund of St. John Lodge," which was to be attended by Grand Master Fletcher of California.[60] The ceremony formally establishing St. John's Lodge No. 13 was held at the state capitol, and about forty white residents of Carson City, including Sheriff Swift and his wife, D. G. Corbett and his wife, W. H. Corbett, and W. S. Hobart, attended the banquet and dance in the evening at Corbett Hall. The *Carson Tribune* reported that "there did not seem to be any jealousy between the ebony, brown and white attendance" and that "the whole affair was well conducted, and reflected great credit on our colored fellow citizens, of whom Carson City has a very respectable

representation."[61] Grand Master Robert J. Fletcher of the California
Grand Lodge attended to establish St. John's Lodge under dispensation,
and assistance was also rendered by officers and members of Ashlar
Lodge, notably David W. Sands, then Deputy Grand Master.[62] Fletcher
reported that the lodge "has erected a hall of her own, and has it fully
furnished." The lodge was granted a warrant later that year.[63]

In June 1875 a ball was held at Turn Verein Hall to raise money for
the charity fund of the lodge. The *Carson Daily Appeal*, in reporting
this event, stated that the price of tickets, which had been set at one
dollar, was "too little by a dollar and a half, at least." It suggested also
that an attempt should be made to sell tickets to persons who could
not attend the ball and ended with the assertion that the "charity fund
can be replenished right handsomely if these colored Masons will act
on this hint of ours."[64] Possibly the members of St. John's Lodge took
the hint; in December 1875 another ball was announced, to be held at
Moore and Parker's Hall on December 27, "the Anniversary of St. John
the Evangelist." Tickets for this ball were $2.50.[65] Judge Thomas Wells
gave an oration, followed by supper and dancing. From reports it received
about the ball, the *Appeal* concluded that it had been "a decorous and
intelligent assemblage" and that "the celebration was a thorough success."[66] At the 1876-1877 annual communication, the Grand Master
noted, "In July, Secretary of this Lodge informed me that the Lodge
was $200 in debt, and in a demoralized condition." Evidently St. John's
overcame this difficulty because it continued to be listed as an active
lodge in proceedings of the annual communication in the late 1870s and
early 1880s. Myron Angel wrote of it that "the lodge furniture and regalia
is estimated to be worth $600. The lodge has disbursed in benefits,
charities, etc., $1,500; is out of debt and is in a healthy and flourishing
condition."[67] Probably temporary fluctuations in the zeal of the small
group of members accounted for these variations. In December 1876 a
fund-raising festival was held at Turn Verein Hall in Carson City. Tickets
sold for two dollars each and included supper for two and admission to a
dance.[68] Grand Master John A. Barber of the California Grand Lodge
attended, and there was an installation of local officers. In addition, "an
elaborate address was delivered by C. S. Mott of Carson on the antiquity
and universality of Masonry."[69] Mott was evidently a white Mason; he
was listed as one of the "visiting brethren" who attended a Masonic
service on the top of Mt. Davidson following the 1875 fire.[70]

At an annual communication in the 1880s, probably in 1881, the
Grand Master recommended that "this Lodge, being weak, I advised

them to surrender and annex themselves to Ashlar Lodge, of Virginia City." By 1886 the proceedings of the Grand Lodge indicated a membership of only five for St. John's Lodge, and Boone indicated that its warrant was withdrawn at some later time.

During their active life, these lodges managed to participate in the life of the Grand Lodge. Reports of the proceedings of the annual communications that have survived indicate that one or more officers of Ashlar Lodge attended the annual meetings of one or more of the Grand Lodges in 1872, 1873, 1874, 1877, and 1880. In 1881 and 1882, Ashlar Lodge was represented by proxy but in 1885 and.1886 was not represented at all. In 1869, 1872, 1873, 1874, 1875, 1877, and 1879, at least one of the officers of the Grand Lodge was from one of the Nevada lodges.

OTHER GROUPS

Undoubtedly churches and the Masonic order were of primary importance within the black community of nineteenth-century Nevada, but there were also other groups with educational, cultural, or social aims.

In 1864 a letter from a correspondent in Carson City to the *Pacific Appeal* reported the formation in that city of the United Sons of Freedom, an organization described as a "benevolent association of colored persons." Specific information about the purpose of the organization was not given, but a full slate of officers was reported, and there were plans to meet monthly at the Eureka Exchange.[71]

A "Colored People's Ball" was held in Virginia City in January 1864 at Selfridge's Hall. Reportedly about sixty persons attended, and it was a dress affair. "Most of the gentlemen wore white kids, and patent leather boots, and several 'long tail blues' with gorgeous buttons, were observed in the assemblage." Evidently the reporter who covered the event thought that blacks dressed up were ludicrous. After commenting that most of those present "were gotten up for the . . . occasion, as Jenkins would say 'regardless of taste or cost,'" he remarked: "Although there were present quite a large number of the chiefs of the tonsorial art, there was but little variety in the coiffures of the ladies, and a great sameness of style among the gentlemen." The dance "ended in a general row," with "crockery . . . scattered about at a fearful rate."[72]

In early 1865 the journalist Alfred Doten, with two other white men, one a state assemblyman, stayed two hours at a "darkey ball" in Carson City and were "well treated."[73]

In 1866 black residents of Gold Hill established an organization to assist freedmen. The first meeting took place at the home of Israel Grayson, "for the purpose of organizing a society for the relief of the freedmen of the United States." Grayson was elected secretary and Gus York treasurer, and the group decided to meet again in a week. While it was not clear what this group intended to do, it seems likely that the black residents of Gold Hill were thinking of the freedmen of the South.[74]

The Dumas Social and Literary Club was organized in Virginia City in 1874-1875. By March 1875 six meetings had been held, at least some of them in the AME church, and the membership was said to number twenty-two "ladies and gentlemen, a good representation of the eclat [sic] of our society." A speech to the club on February 8 by James Parker indicated that the club was dedicated to self-improvement of its members. "We are united . . . upon reform—Lend us your hands, your hearts, and we will go forward slowly but steadily."[75] A more explicit commitment to advancement through education was stated at another meeting by Andrew Hall, who said that education "was the only boon that brought other great nations to position and honor, and would fit us for positions where caste would be obliterated forever by the brilliancy of our intellectual attainments." The seriousness of the members is suggested by the fact that, on March 5, 1875 they listened to a two-hour address by George H. Rogers on Josephine, wife of Napoleon.[76]

The Dumas Club may also have had white speakers; Secretary George H. Rogers reported that a Mr. Cromwell was invited to speak, was made an honorary member after his address, and attended a social function after the meeting. These facts seem to suggest that Cromwell was white.[77] A barber named Theodore Cromwell was listed as having rooms at 30 South B Street in Virginia City in 1875 but his race is not given.[78]

At least one party after a meeting of the Dumas Club lasted until early morning and ended when the women who had been at the party were "serenaded . . . at their residences."[79]

Black residents of western Nevada joined to hold a Grand Calico Ball at the Miners' Union Hall in Virginia City on October 27, 1874. Supper and dancing to the music of the Francis String Band were planned, and tickets sold for three dollars. Persons planning the ball included prominent black residents of Virginia City (notably D. W. Sands, Theodore A. Lee, and J. H. Price), Gold Hill (Charles Brooks), Carson City (Frederick Grinage and a Mr. Lane), and Carson Valley (John Butler).[80]

Blacks in Carson City organized a "social and literary club" in 1877. The president was George H. Rogers, who had been secretary of the Dumas Club.[81]

POSSIBLE CONFLICTS WITHIN
THE BLACK COMMUNITY

This study has demonstrated that, even though we lack full information about the black population of nineteenth-century Nevada, the small number of blacks in the state included a significant number of intelligent, articulate men (and, to a lesser extent, women) who provided leadership for a number of groups within the black community and who spoke ably and aggressively for the community in dealing with whites. Much less is known about the less articulate members of the black community, and some of the clues we have about these people and their relationship with the leaders are contradictory.

The leaders whose activities have been reported here spoke and wrote standard English for the most part. (In a few cases, such as that of Sam Wagner who could not write, it seems likely that the exact language attributed to him was actually that of whoever it was who wrote out his statements.) Probably most of the black population of the country spoke either Negro pidgin English or plantation Creole, nonstandard English dialects undoubtedly regarded by almost all whites of the time as simply an inferior brand of English.[82] Does this mean that a higher proportion of Nevada blacks spoke standard English than was true of the race as a whole? If so, why? And what was the relationship between the blacks who spoke standard English, whether they may also have known one or more of the other languages, with those who spoke only Creole or pidgin English? Given the strength of white racist attitudes about language use, which held the two most common dialects among blacks amusing and inferior (as various comments by white writers quoted in this study indicate clearly), it is not implausible that at least some of the standard-English-speaking blacks also looked down on members of their race who did not speak their language.

Whites in nineteenth-century Nevada occasionally saw conflict between some of the people who clearly spoke standard English and other blacks and were usually inclined to attribute the conflict to racial differences between the two groups. That such conflict, if it existed to any appreciable extent, was more likely to be related to language differences seems more plausible, especially in light of the facts that overt white racism was strong and that such evidence as there is does not suggest a significant difference in racial characteristics between the two groups.

Dr. Stephenson's conflict with some other members of the First Baptist Church has been noted. In addition, a newspaper article may refer to him in describing an altercation with a black woman. In 1864 a newspaper reported:

We heard a young lady of the colored persuasion making a complaint
before judge Atwell, this morning, against a "cullered gemmin," who
styles himself "Doctor," for striking her on the head with a cane. We
did not learn the result of the complaint, but trust that Mr. Doctor
was mulct [sic] heavily for daring to strike one of the fair sex.[83]

Whites of the time often interpreted conflicts of this sort as due to
jealousy between mulattoes and darker blacks. In reporting a fight that
developed at a "Colored People's Ball" in Virginia City in 1864, a
reporter for the *Virginia Evening Bulletin* theorized over the cause of
the fight: "There appeared to be a lurking jealousy and mistrust on the
part of the pure unalloyed Africans towards the adulterated article which
culminated shortly after midnight in a general row." The reporter added,
"We overheard one of the gentlemen who was polishing our boots tell
another who was preparing to whitewash a neighbor's kitchen, that some
'yaller fellow that put put [sic] on airs over him last night should apolo-
gize, or he would make him give him that satisfaction that one gemman
has a right to demand from another."[84]

Another incident allegedly involving a similar conflict also suggests the
difficulty of ascertaining the truth of some kinds of historical incidents. In
August 1862 a black barber named Joseph J. Underwood, who had a barbershop in Carson City, was killed by Charles Butler. There are three accounts
of this murder that agree on these facts, but from that point on little else.

In the first account:

In the bad days of 1861-62, there was a high-toned mulatto barber
at Carson named Underwood. He was partially educated, and affected
to regard full-blooded negroes with unbounded contempt, and seldom
lost an opportunity to express himself on the subject. "Doc," a black
man, entered his shop one evening, and a conversation between them
soon drifted into a row.

"You niggers ain't got the sand!" Underwood explained. "Doc"
drew an immense knife; Underwood fled out of the shop and across
the street, but "Doc" overtook him on the plaza.

"Ain't got the sand, eh?" exclaimed "Doc" repeatedly, each time
plunging the long blade into the shrieking mulatto, who soon fell dead.[85]

The *Silver Age*, which reported the incident at the time it occurred,
gives this second version: Butler, who had a bootblack stand in front
of Underwood's shop, was a "simon-pure negro" and Underwood a

mulatto. Further, Underwood was "rather airish on account of the white blood reputed to course through his veins, and an education received at Oberlin College," and he "took every occasion, it is said, to annoy the Doctor by referring to the kinks in his hair, and the heavy shade of his color." However, the article asserts that the "altercation" that led to Underwood's death began when Underwood caused Butler's bootblacking stand to be moved from in front of his barber shop. The rest of the incident is reported by the *Silver Age* as follows:

> The removal of the stand capped the climax, in the Doctor's estimation, and he determined to have satisfaction. . . . Accordingly, yesterday morning . . . the Doctor encountered Underwood on Second street . . . and demanded to be satisfied concerning the treatment he had received. Upon this demand Underwood turned partially around and put his hand in his pocket, and the Doctor, supposing that he was in search of a Derringer which he usually carried with him, anticipated the movement by drawing a revolver upon him. This last act of the Doctor startled Underwood, who hastened away as fast as his legs would carry him, and the Doctor tells us that, by way of frightening him, he fired three shots at him, one of which unfortunately took effect.[86]

A letter to the *Silver Age* from Isaac Morton—the third version—corrected several biographical statements about Underwood and then commented about the statement that he had been "airish on account of . . . white blood":

> I, who have been personally acquainted with him for the last seven years, who have worked with him and been on intimate terms, do assert that he was not proud of the white blood that did course through his veins, and not reputed, for he was a gentleman of too much good sense and culture. The account goes on to say that he took every occasion to annoy the Doctor by referring to the kinks in his hair and the heavy shade of his color; but, sir, I do assure your informant that I am just as black a man as the Doctor is, and I must say that Underwood did not do anything of the kind, and Butler has talked with me himself about the same matter, and expressed his astonishment that Underwood was so circumspect on the subject.[87]

I have arranged the three accounts in order of increasing accuracy: Myron Angel's version has Butler stabbing Underwood, while the other two agree that Underwood was shot. Angel's version does not refer to the dispute over the bootblacking stand, and Morton clearly was more accurate in reporting biographical details about both Underwood and Butler than either of the other writers. It is therefore not unlikely that the versions attributing racial prejudice to Underwood are in error on this point, but there seems no way to establish the truth of the incident at this remove.

Various writers have noted economic differences between light- and dark-skinned blacks based on conditions under slavery and white prejudice. Charles H. Wesley reported that the occupational achievements of mulattoes were greater than those of darker blacks: "This fact was occasioned not necessarily by a difference of ability but by the conditions which made the mulatto more acceptable than the black among Americans in general. . . . The favored class among the slaves was more often the mulattoes. . . . They were also more acceptable in personal associations with the whites and in general they were relatively less offensive to them."[88] A study by Edward Byron Reuter published in 1918 showed that a higher proportion of American blacks who had done well in white society were mulatto than was the case for the entire black population. It is not necessary to accept racist explanations for this phenomenon, as Reuter did at that time, to explain this finding.[89] The blacks who became house servants were more likely both to have children by whites and to have advantages not available to field hands, and in addition whites often made the assumption that lighter skin was associated with ability and/or virtue; the cumulative effect of these factors could easily explain differentials in achievement between mulattoes and darker blacks. In turn, these differentials could easily explain some hostility between the two groups, to the extent that the blacks involved saw a difference based on skin color.

It does not seem, however, that there was any difference in skin color between the most and least successful members of Nevada's nineteeth-century black population, at least if census reports are accurate. The census returns that identified individuals as either black or mulatto could, of course, have been inaccurate. A suggestion that this is so comes from the fact that Dr. Stephenson was identified by an 1870 census enumerator as black, while he himself said, at another time: "I am as much Anglo-Saxon as African, which is no fault of mine."[90] However, the errors enumerators made may be irrelevant for a comparison of groups within the black population, if they are random. In any case the proportions of the most successful blacks who were listed as mulatto were not higher than the mulatto proportions of the total black population in either 1870 or 1880. Table 8 gives data for the entire population and for a group chosen because they had occupations that have been treated above as higher-status and better-paid than the occupations of most blacks or because the 1870 census listed them with total property of five hundred dollars or more.

Table 8

BLACK AND MULATTO PROPORTIONS OF TOTAL BLACK
POPULATION OF NEVADA AND OF MOST ECONOMICALLY
SUCCESSFUL GROUP,[a] 1870 AND 1880

| | Number and Proportion of Population | | |
	Black	Mulatto	Other
1870: Total population	274 (84%)	42 (13%)	8 (2%)
Successful group	66 (85%)	10 (13%)	2 (2%)
1880: Total population	260 (66%)	129 (34%)	7 (2%)
Successful group	43 (70%)	20 (31%)	0 —

[a]*Specifically, persons listed as professionals, managers or businessmen, barbers or hairdressers, farm owners or managers, or skilled workers, or owning property worth five hundred dollars or more.*

Among the most outstanding black leaders, the census data do not suggest lighter skins. In 1870 Thomas Detter, J. M. Whitfield, and F. G. Grice, in addition to Dr. Stephenson, were identified by census enumerators as black; Charles H. Wilson was listed as mulatto, and William H. Hall was not enumerated at all. In 1880 only Detter was still in the state, and he was still listed as black.

Table 8 suggests that the percentage of mulattoes increased from 1870 to 1880 in Nevada. It is not certain that this is so since the accuracy of enumerators' judgments is unknown, but if so, this result must have been due to developments outside the state; there is very little evidence of intermarriage between blacks and whites in Nevada. Among the very small number of blacks in Nevada in 1860, few were married, but those who were evidently were married to blacks. In 1870 there was only one apparent marriage between a black and a white, and this may be a result of enumerator error. In Hamilton, Louis L. Shingtin (?), a thirty-six-year-old black miner, was reported living with Pheba Shingtin(?), forty, a dressmaker who was identified as white. This may be correct, but Pheba (or Phibbi or Phoebe) is a "day name" often used as a first name by slaves; it seems more likely that the enumerator mistakenly wrote W instead of M.[91]

There were several households in 1870 that suggest common-law marriages; three were between blacks and whites and one between a black and an Indian. In Winnemucca a thirty-two-year-old black "washerwoman"

was listed in the same household with a thirty-year-old white laborer born
in South America, and in Reno a forty-one-year-old black "jobber" was
living with a thirty-one-year-old white woman; both were foreign-born. In
Elko a forty-four-year-old black male cook was living with a thirty-five-
year-old white woman who was "keeping" a restaurant and owned three
thousand dollars in property. In Reno a thirty-three-year-old mulatto
male cook was living with an eighteen-year-old Indian woman with no
last name who was "keeping house." A puzzling household was one in
Virginia City; it contained a thirty-six-year-old black woman keeping
house, a sixteen-year-old white boy with the same last name as the woman,
and two white miners from Ireland with different last names.

In 1880 enumerators asked about marriage relationships, and three
interracial marriages involving blacks were reported, but only one of
these was a black-white marriage. At a location "on Steamboat Ditch below
Verdi" lived a sixty-year-old white farmer, Hiram Roberts, whose wife
Johanna, fifty-seven, was identified as mulatto. In Reno the cook living
with an Indian woman in 1870, William Jackson, was now reported married to an Indian woman with a different first name from the woman who
had been living with him in 1870; they had four children, all identified
as mulatto. A third interracial couple consisted of Evans Coats, a thirty-
eight-year-old laborer from Kentucky, and Fanny Evans Coats, twenty-
eight, identified as Chinese.

Other households that may have been interracial common-law marriages were: a fifty-seven-year-old black man "keeping house" at the
same address as a thirty-five-year-old white woman, also keeping house;
a fifty-year-old black female hairdresser in the same household as a
thirty-seven-year-old white saloon keeper; a forty-seven-year-old black
female cook in a household with a fifty-four-year-old white boarding-
house keeper, and a thirty-nine-year old black female housekeeper in a
household with a fifty-year-old white male boarder identified as a "sport."

Also in 1880, there was an instance of a black child identified living
in a white family; this may have been an enumerator's error. In Spring
City in Humboldt County, a white male tollroad keeper named W. H. Cox
was married to a thirty-five-year-old woman named Pheba, identified as
white. They had four children identified as white plus a fifth child identified as mulatto; he was six and had been born in Nevada. It is possible
that Mrs. Cox had such slight black ancestry that the enumerator classified her as white but that one of her children was slightly darker and
was thus listed as mulatto. In Austin, a nine-year-old mulatto girl, Eliza
Wixom, was identified as the adopted daughter of Isaac and Mary E.
Wixom, both white, who also had two white children.

In brief, there is little evidence from census data of miscegenation of any kind involving blacks; some of these interracial marriages involved blacks and other nonwhites.

The few hundred blacks in nineteenth-century Nevada, scattered among a number of locations although with concentrations in Virginia City and Carson City, managed to found and maintain a number of institutions to serve the needs of their community. At least four churches representing the three major black denominations existed during the nineteenth century, two lodges of the Prince Hall Masons were in existence for at least one or two decades, and there were literary and social groups and organized balls at various times during the forty years from 1860 to the end of the century. Probably there were also some other organizations that existed but have not yet been discovered. When it is realized that the same community was vigorously asserting its rights and engaging in electoral politics, the impression of competence and pride becomes stronger.

NOTES

1. See Carter G. Woodson, 2d ed., *The History of the Negro Church* (Washington, D.C.: Associated Publishers, 1921).

2. *Territorial Enterprise*, June 29, 1867. Samuel Wagner was illiterate, and therefore this statement was undoubtedly written for him by someone, but there is no reason to doubt that the thoughts expressed were his own.

3. *Virginia Evening Bulletin*, September 10, 1863.

4. Myron Angel, *History of Nevada, 1881* (Berkeley, California: Howell-North, 1958), p. 217; Hubert Howe Bancroft, *History of Nevada, Colorado and Wyoming, 1540-1888* (San Francisco: The History Company, 1890), p. 300.

5. Phil M. Montesano, "The Black Churches of San Francisco in the Early 1860's: Their Political Activities," ms., 1971, in Library of the California Historical Society, San Francisco, p. 2.

6. *Pacific Appeal*, June 20, 1863, January 23, 1864.

7. Angel, *History of Nevada*, p. 217. In 1869 Reverend Satchell had a church in New Orleans, and in the 1880s he was referred to as one of the five "leading clergymen in the Colored Baptist churches" in Ohio. *Elevator*, June 25, 1869, and George W. Williams, *History of the Negro Race in America from 1619 to 1880* vol. 2 (New York: G. P. Putnam's Sons, 1883), p. 476.

8. *Territorial Enterprise,* June 29, 1867. In a second advertisement, Wagner repeated these charges, adding some details. Ibid., July 4, 1867.

9. Ibid., June 30, 1867.

10. Ibid.

11. *Journal of Proceedings of the Third Annual Convention of the Ministers and Lay Delegates of the African Methodist Episcopal Church* (San Francisco: B. F. Sterett, 1863), p. 7.

See Phillip M. Montesano, "Some Aspects of the Free Negro Question in San Francisco, 1849-1870," MA thesis, University of San Francisco, 1967, pp. 73-75.

12. Reverend Anthony was one of the earliest Methodist ministers in Virginia City. He arrived in the winter of 1862; the church building referred to was completed in 1863 and reportedly cost $45,000. A visitor to Virginia City in March 1863 wrote that, under the leadership of Reverend Anthony, "there is not a better or more important station on this coast, out of San Francisco, if any there must be excepted." See Angel, *History of Nevada,* p. 208, and *Christian Advocate,* March 5, 1863.

13. *Journal of Proceedings,* pp. 14, 19.

14. Ibid., pp. 4, 34.

15. Charles Collins, comp., *Mercantile Guide and Directory for Virginia City, Gold Hill, Silver City and American City* (San Francisco: Agnew and Deffebach, 1865), p. 28.

16. *Pacific Appeal,* December 19, 1863.

17. *Journal of Proceedings,* p. 4.

18. *Elevator,* August 4, 1865.

19. Ibid., August 11, 1865.

20. Ibid., October 13, 1865.

21. Ibid., Bishop Campbell to Bishop Ward, August 11, 1865. Bishop Ward had a long and distinguished career as the leading minister of the AME church on the West Coast. See Montesano, "The Free Negro Question in San Francisco," pp. 71-77, where he is referred to as "the Negro Thomas Starr King."

22. Ibid., August 4, 1865.

23. *Territorial Enterprise,* June 22, 1866.

24. Ibid., September 27, 1867. In 1872 Reverend Offer was in Oakland (*Pacific Appeal,* February 3, 1872) and in June 1873 he was presiding elder of the California annual conference of the AME church (*ibid.,* June 7, 1873). He died in Wheeling, West Virginia, on May 26, 1886 (*Elevator,* July 3, 1886).

25. *Pacific Appeal,* October 1, 1870.

26. Ibid., February 3, March 30, 1872.

27. Ibid., December 6, 1873, February 14, 1874.

28. *Elevator,* December 13, 1873 (letter from Mrs. D. D. Carter).

29. *Pacific Appeal,* May 23, 1874 (proceedings of AME annual state conference for 1874).

30. Ibid., May 29, 1875.

31. Ibid., November 27, 1875 (letter from M. Howard). Historian Hubert Howe Bancroft says that the building was completed in June 1875, a few months before the fire. *History of Nevada, Colorado and Wyoming*, p. 284.

32. *Pacific Appeal*, August 11, 1877, August 10, 1878.

33. Angel, *History of Nevada*, p. 209.

34. *Elevator*, July 26, 1873. *Pacific Appeal*, July 26, 1873.

35. *Carson Daily Appeal*, October 25, 26, 1876.

36. *Elevator*, April 7, 1877. The historian of the AME Zion church evidently was unaware of the existence of these churches in nineteenth-century Nevada. While he mentions briefly AME Zion churches in California dating from the 1850s, he does not mention Nevada churches at all. See David Henry Bradley, Sr., *A History of the A.M.E. Zion Church*, Part I, *1796-1872* (Nashville, Tennessee: Parthenon Press, 1956), pp. 121, 146, 162, 167, and Part II, *1872-1968* (Nashville, Tennessee: Parthenon Press, 1970), pp. 31, 38, 51, 54, 57, 60.

37. *San Francisco Sentinel*, September 20, 1890.

38. *Elevator*, December 17, 1869 (letter from AEV—probably Anne E. Vincent—Virginia City).

39. Ibid., December 13, 1873.

40. Ibid., May 17, 1873.

41. Ibid., December 27, 1873, December 5, 1874.

42. Myron Angel was apparently unaware that the AME church had a longer history in Virginia City; he states that it was organized in 1873, and that its building was constructed in 1875. Thomas Wren evidently follows Angel on this point. *A History of the State of Nevada* (New York: Lewis Publishing Co., 1904), p. 190.

43. White Masons even today usually refuse to recognize the legitimacy of Prince Hall Masonry; this question is discussed more fully in chapter 3. See C. W. Torrence, *History of Masonry in Nevada* (Reno: A. Carlisle and Co., 1944), and Angel, *History of Nevada*, p. 242.

44. See William H. Grimshaw, *Official History of Freemasonry Among the Colored People in North America* (1903; reprint ed., New York: Negro Universities Press, 1969), pp. 71-78, William J. Whalen, *Handbook of Secret Organizations* (Milwaukee: Bruce Publishing Co., 1966), pp. 113-116, Arthur Preuss, comp., *A Dictionary of Secret and Other Societies* (St. Louis, Missouri: B. Herder Book Co., 1924), pp. 324-326, Albert C. Stevens, comp., *The Cyclopedia of Fraternities* (New York: E. B. Treat and Co., 1907), pp. 72-78.

45. Arthur Evans, ed., *Centennial Year Book of the Most Worshipful Prince Hall Grand Lodge* (Oakland, California, 1955), pp. 9-13, *Elevator*, June 27, July 4, 11, 1874, and *Pacific Appeal*, June 27, 1874.

46. Present-day dictionaries give both "ashlar" and "ashler" as alternative spellings of this word. The sources used in this study vary

somewhat between these two terms, but most of the Masonic sources seem to favor "ashlar"; for the sake of consistency, this spelling will be used throughout this section.

47. Frank E. Boone, "Negro Freemasonry in California," ms., n.d., University of Nevada, Reno Library, and Torrence, *History of Masonry*, p. 1.

48. *Elevator*, February 28, 1867.

49. Walter Van Tilburg Clark, ed., *The Journals of Alfred Doten, 1849-1903* (Reno: University of Nevada Press, 1973), p. 960.

50. *Elevator*, May 15, 1868.

51. Ibid.

52. Ibid., August 21, 1868 (letter from Orion).

53. *Pacific Appeal*, November 13, 1875 (letter from M. Howard).

54. In April 1968 Frank E. Boone, Grand Historian of the California Grand Lodge, visited the University of Nevada, Reno, and provided some information about nineteenth-century Prince Hall lodges in Nevada. He supplied parts of a manuscript history of "Negro Freemasonry in California," n.d., and pages of various *Proceedings* of the Grand Lodge during the nineteenth century. Unfortunately, the full *Proceedings* are not available, and it is not always possible to date some of the pages he supplied copies of.

55. *Territorial Enterprise*, September 19, 1877.

56. Records supplied to the University of Nevada, Reno, library by Frank E. Boone.

57. *Territorial Enterprise*, August 17, 1880.

58. Bancroft, *History of Nevada, Colorado and Wyoming*, p. 303.

59. Grimshaw, *Official History of Freemasonry*, p. 299.

60. *Carson Daily Appeal*, March 26, 1875.

61. *Pacific Appeal*, May 1, 1875. Probably the ceremony was held on April 6.

62. *Proceedings of 1875-1876 Grand Communication of California Grand Lodge*, p. 24.

63. *Proceedings of 1874-1875 Grand Communication of California Grand Lodge*, p. 31.

64. *Carson Daily Appeal*, June 20, 1875.

65. Ibid., December 11, 1875.

66. Ibid., December 28, 1875.

67. Angel, *History of Nevada*, p. 238.

68. *Carson Daily Appeal*, December 19, 20, 1876.

69. Ibid., December 28, 1876.

70. Angel, *History of Nevada*, p. 238.

71. *Pacific Appeal*, March 19, 1864 (letter from Peter William Livingston, secretary of the organization).

72. *Virginia Evening Bulletin*, January 2, 1864.

73. Walter Van Tilburg Clark, *Journals of Alfred Doten*, p. 818.

74. *Territorial Enterprise*, June 21, 1866. The *Enterprise* added its endorsement of the aims of the organization, wishing "success to our colored friends in their endeavors for the amelioration of the condition of their race."

75. *Pacific Appeal*, March 6, 1875 (letter from Andrew Hall).

76. Ibid., March 20, 1875.

77. Ibid.

78. John D. Bethel and Co., *A General Business and Mining Directory of Storey, Lyon, Ormsby, and Washoe Counties, Nevada* (Virginia City: John D. Bethel & Co., 1875), p. 32.

79. *Pacific Appeal*, March 20, 1875.

80. Ibid., October 24, 1874.

81. *Carson Daily Appeal*, January 24, 1877.

82. See J. L. Dillard, *Black English* (New York: Random House, 1972), pp. 98-99.

83. *Virginia Evening Bulletin*, January 5, 1864.

84. Ibid., January 2, 1864.

85. Angel, *History of Nevada*, p. 558.

86. *Silver Age*, July 22, 1862, reprinted in *Pacific Appeal*, July 24, 1862.

87. *Pacific Appeal*, July 24, 1862.

88. Charles H. Wesley, *Negro Labor in the United States, 1850-1925* (New York: Russell and Russell, 1927), p. 41.

89. Edward Byron Reuter, *The Mulatto in the United States* (1918; reprint ed., New York: Negro Universities Press, 1969).

90. *Territorial Enterprise*, Feb. 24, 1867.

91. Dillard, *Black English*, pp. 124-125.

—8—

From "No Proscription" to the "Mississippi of the West": The Return of White Racism

White Nevada's racist beginning, the partial erosion of that racism, the role black Nevadans played in this improvement, and the economic progress that Nevada's black community made in the late 1860s and 1870s have been noted above. A number of black Nevadans felt that the progress would continue and that there was a "good time coming." Instead, all the available evidence points to a reversal of the trends at the end of the nineteenth century and the beginning of the twentieth century, the result of a revival of white racism. Not until the late 1950s would a new wave of opposition to racism develop; when it did, some black people described Nevada as "the Mississippi of the West" and demanded laws to end private discrimination. While precise measures of these matters are lacking, it appears that the status of black Nevadans vis-à-vis white Nevadans was lower in the 1950s than it had been in the 1870s, particularly in an economic sense.

SEGREGATION AND DISCRIMINATION, 1860-1890

Evidence of the way whites treated blacks in this period is scarce, but it seems probable that discrimination against blacks declined through the 1860s and 1870s. It is difficult to believe that a society whose leaders enacted the racist legislation of the early 1860s would treat blacks with equality in aspects not covered by law, but by the late 1870s we have the testimony of even some blacks that they were fairly treated; it is probable that a gradual reduction of legal discriminations against blacks was accompanied by a reduction of discrimination in other areas.

The situation is complicated by the fact that such evidence as there is suggests that, to a substantial extent, blacks had separate organizations for most of this period. It is difficult to know the extent to which this social pluralism was the result of joint decisions by whites and blacks or the result of white discrimination. Probably most blacks preferred their own organizations but were more willing to accept white members than whites were to accept them. For example, although the first black church in Nevada was established partly because of white discrimination against blacks, apparently it had white members. Similarly a Virginia City saloon frequented by blacks was at least open to whites in the mid-1860s. In 1866 there was a report of an accidental shooting in the Boston Saloon at the corner of D and Union streets, which was described as "the popular resort for many of the colored population." An accidental discharge of a derringer wounded a white man, identified only as "Frenchy," who was said to be the only white man in the saloon although "it appears [he] was one of the party" playing poker around a table when the accident happened.[1]

The extent to which white businesses discriminated against blacks is not clear, but an article in a Virginia City newspaper in 1868 may indicate that most businesses did not exclude blacks:

> Sir, I am informed by several responsible persons that it is customary now in a certain saloon and also in a restaurant in this city, for the colored man on entering said places to uncover his head in due respect—I suppose to the proprietors and frequenters thereof. Now, Mr. Editor, would it not be well, such being the case, for our business houses and other places to adopt the same rule? I make this suggestion so as to make all the same, and also to assist in tramping down us poor uneducated colored people.[2]

However, it is not clear whether the blacks referred to in the letter were customers or employees making deliveries; the *Enterprise* stated that blacks were often sent to saloons or restaurants as waiters and found it difficult to remove their hats while carrying things. In any case, the newspaper joined the writer, "Colored Man," in objecting to the practice.

It asked rhetorically whether the rule was consistent with the golden
rule and whether

> the poor colored people among us [are] to be oppressed because of
> the wrongs inflicted on their race elsewhere? We make these inquiries
> in behalf of a people polite and respectful in their manners, faithful
> to their trusts, honest in all their dealings, and who are entitled to all
> the privileges of citizens of the United States.

In 1864 an announcement of the opening of the Eureka Exchange in
Carson City was carried in the advertising columns of a black newspaper
in San Francisco. The proprietors, Mr. and Mrs. Chester, may have been
black. If not, they must have been soliciting black customers. The Eureka
Exchange, at the corner of Fourth and Ormsby, advertised that it was

> now open for the accommodation of gentlemen and ladies travelling
> to this city. The house has been thoroughly renovated, . . . also
> furnished with good beds and a well-stocked larder. Our table shall
> consist of the best the market can afford. There shall be no pains
> spared to make all comfortable who may favor us with their
> patronage.[3]

It is clear from the information presented previously on the economic
status of nineteenth-century blacks that many whites patronized their
businesses. Dr. Stephenson stated that he had white patients, and it is
also clear that the Virginia City black community was too small to support
a black physician who did not have patients outside his own community.
If the economic status of Nevada blacks was improving in the 1870s and
1880s, probably this was partly because of decreasing white prejudice.
    Apparently blacks were accepted in state-run institutions in the 1870s.
Although it is not certain that all blacks admitted to these institutions
were identified, often the race of such persons was given in state reports.
The presence of at least one black child in the Nevada Orphans' Home has
been noted above. There was at least one black treated for insanity by the
state from 1865 to 1894 when state reports stopped listing patients by name;
at no time did state law discriminate on a racial basis in dealing with
insane persons. Before 1882, when the Nevada Insane Asylum was opened
in Reno, indigent patients from Nevada who had to be treated for mental
illness were sent to California institutions at state expense. From 1871
to 1882 indigent insane patients were sent to the Pacific Asylum operated

by Dr. Samuel Langdon and Dr. Asa Clark. In 1881 Dr. A. Dawson and G. W. Huffaker made an official inspection trip to this asylum. Among other things, their report recommended the discharge of three patients on the ground that they were not insane. One of these was Hannah Times, identified as "colored."[4] In addition, a C. Minor (or Miner) committed to the Langdon-Clark Asylum on October 3, 1874, from Storey County may have been Cicero Miner, a black teamster who lived in Virginia City. In any case, the patient died in the hospital on October 17, 1874.[5]

Sam Wagner, a bootblack by occupation, was also the "bell-ringer and town-crier of Virginia City," and it seems that he had a semi-official status. Apparently, he performed his role for pay but also out of a sense of civic duty; in any case, his role was widely recognized. A doggerel poem recalling well-known Comstock personages speaks of him as

> Old Sam Wagner the bell man - sure.
> He paraded the streets at little cost
> Announcing auctions or "Child lost! Child lost!"

John Taylor Waldorf, whose reminiscences of nineteenth-century life in Virginia City were published in 1968, recalled that Wagner announced the arrival of aid from Reno and Carson City after the disastrous fire of 1875.[6] Although a bootblack, Wagner was not poor; in the 1870 census he is listed as owning property worth $2,000, and he lost three houses in the 1875 fire.

CRIME AND BLACKS

Apparently blacks did not experience substantial discrimination in the application of criminal laws in the nineteenth century in Nevada. Although there may have been a tendency to apply criminal laws more harshly against blacks than against whites in some cases, there is no evidence of an unusually high number of convictions of blacks. Neither is there evidence of a white fear of black criminality or of black protests against the application of the criminal laws to them; their efforts to change discriminatory laws were persistent, however. While protection against violence was not well established for whites in nineteenth-century Nevada, especially in the early 1860s, it does not seem that blacks had to go without protection from law enforcement officers or were mistreated by such officers, as a general rule. (This is in contrast with the experience of Indians and Chinese, who often suffered violence from whites in early

Nevada and who often found law enforcement officers participating in
the violence.) In 1864, it was reported that a "colored" woman from Gold
Hill who was walking into Virginia City to attend a prayer meeting was
"grossly insulted by a drunken fellow named Kelly." The woman "took
refuge" in a shoemaker's store on C Street, and the shoemaker, Mr.
Kline, "sent for a policeman and gave the fellow into custody for being
drunk and disturbing the peace."[7]

As the 1870 parade, which accompanied observance by Virginia City
blacks of the ratification of the Fifteenth Amendment, was forming, it
was reported:

> There was some disposition manifested on the part of a few during
> the forming of the procession who attempted to annoy the colored
> people by passing back and forth through their line. This, however,
> was promptly checked and to prevent any further trouble which low
> bred persons might seek, Chief Downey, in company with several
> policemen, went out to the Divide in order to suppress any attempted
> annoyance to the procession.[8]

In 1868 the *Territorial Enterprise* burlesqued the Ku Klux Klan in an
article reporting that many people had wondered about the meaning of
"mysterious signals and answers" and "glimpses of gliding forms [which]
have been seen moving stealthily about in the shadows." The newspaper
had an answer: "The mystery is now explained; the cats of the city have
formed a Ku Klux Klan."[9] The light tone of the article implies that the
KKK was remote enough from Virginia City to be laughed at.

Several inmates of the state prison were identified as "colored" during
the nineteenth century. (Substantially more Indians and Chinese were in-
carcerated in the state institution during this time.) Those who can be
identified are:

1865: Frank Ratty, convicted of "unlawful exhibition of a deadly
weapon in the presence of two or more persons, not in necessary self-
defense" in Orsmby County, and Edward Hall, convicted of grand larceny
in Storey County.

1869: F. H. Hazelwood, convicted of grand larceny in Storey County,
and G. Atchison, convicted of assault with intent to rob in Nye County.

1872: H. Hickman, convicted of assault to commit rape in Storey
County.

1873: Jefferson Howard, convicted of manslaughter in Lincoln County.

1874: Nathaniel Armstrong, convicted of assault with intent to kill in Washoe County.

1875: William Smith, convicted of burglary in Storey County.

1876: James Johnson and George Washington, convicted of grand larceny in Elko County.

1898: Luke Stythe, not identified as black although he was listed as born in Africa, convicted of burglary in Washoe County.[10]

For a period of time during the 1870s, a black man named Pruitt or Pruett was a state prisoner. In September 1871 there was a massive prison break in which twenty-nine prisoners escaped. One of these was reported to be "M. Pruitt (colored)." Three days after the escape, a newspaper reported: "The negro Pruitt went into Genoa Monday night and obtained provisions."[11] Governor L. R. Bradley offered rewards for information leading to the return of the prisoners but a number were not recaptured; in his report to the 1873 legislative session, the warden reported that seventeen prisoners had been recaptured but twelve were still at large. Pruitt was evidently among those recaptured. In 1875 the *Carson City Appeal* noted that "Pruett, the colored man who was sent to the State Prison from Douglas county for the doing of some sort of cussedness, we forget what, was pardoned out yesterday." The newspaper wrote that Pruett had had four more years to serve and that it did not know why he had been released early; however, the writer of the story did not seem to regard Pruett as dangerous. After commenting, "The boy—he is hardly anything else—is as smart as a trap and an excellent hand at horses," the writer hoped that prison had done him some good and that he would stay out of trouble.[12]

It seems neither that the number of blacks in the state prison was large in relation to their proportion of Nevada's population nor that blacks were convicted of the most serious crimes. Only one black was convicted of an offense involving rape in Nevada in the nineteenth century.

In Elko County in 1877 a black man named Samuel Mills was convicted of killing a James Finnerty at Halleck Station. Evidently Mills had been drinking, had had a previous quarrel with a man named Webb during which Webb had struck him several times, and then had secured a shotgun and fired into the saloon, killing Finnerty. Mills appealed his conviction to the state supreme court, asserting that there had not been premeditation, which was necessary for a first-degree murder conviction. The supreme court turned down his appeal,[13] and he was hanged in Elko on December 21, 1877. While on the scaffold, Mills made this short speech:

Well, gents, to you all I have to say that I am a poor colored man with
no friends nor money. If I had had money and a good lawyer, such as
lawyer Wines, I could have got clear; but the fact that I had no money
nor friends has brought me to this. But I tell you all at this last moment
of my life, I had no intention to kill Finerty. Mr. Seitz [the sheriff]
and all the officers have been very kind to me. They have not been
prejudiced against me on account of my color. I have no doubt that
there are a great many negro lovers in this country, but I have not
had a fair show; I only fought for my rights, but if you all think it is
Justice, I am not afraid to die, but will die like a man.

After thanking the sheriff again and saying goodbye to several "colored
friends" who were present, Mills was hanged.[14] It is difficult to draw
any conclusions from what is known of this incident. Reportedly, Mills
was the first person hanged legally in Elko County; this may mean that
a black was more likely to be punished for a crime than a white person,
for murders were not uncommon in that area, which had been settled
by whites for only a few years. On the other hand, there is no doubt that
Mills killed Finnerty; he admitted this himself. Finally, Mills in his gallows
speech seemed to be ambivalent about whether he had been treated fairly.
He probably believed that he had not committed first-degree murder
and therefore should not have been punished by hanging, but whether
racial prejudice had anything to do with the specific charge against him
for his act is unclear.

Evidently there were a few black prostitutes on the Comstock in
1863 although they must have been rare. The census of population listed
four in 1870 and six in 1880. In December 1863 a Virginia City newspaper reported a "row" late at night "between two colored prostitutes."
It also reported that "a thing that appeared like a white man, whom one
of the pair supports" was also involved in the argument.[15] Apparently
blacks were not more inclined to become prostitutes than whites.

White newspapers in Nevada in the nineteenth century reported various
instances of violence involving blacks. While reports of these incidents
were sometimes accompanied by racist remarks, there is no indication
that race prejudice entered into them. For example, in 1863 the *Virginia
Evening Bulletin* reported two violent incidents. William Shad was fatally
shot by Frank Ballecto. Both were black and the incident seemed to
involve a woman. A black steward, Richard Pringle, was stabbed by a
black woman, Mary Ann Richardson. The facts of these incidents were
given in a straightforward manner, but then the reporter went on:

Our local, who went to obtain the particulars of these affairs was informed by one "culled gemmen," who stretched himself to his fullest hight [sic] and placed his arms akimbo: "Sah, you white folks will soon see dat we culled pussons can use de weapons of gemmen as well as you. Dat lub warms our bussoms and makes us fight like white gemmen when our feelings are hurted!"[16]

In reporting the arrest of a black man charged with assault and battery upon another black man, a newspaper in 1863 described the accused as "Mr. Chander, a gentleman with a skin of rather an inky appearance— otherwise, a 'colored citizen.'" Also in 1863, a black man was charged with assault and battery upon another black man "at the Hotel de Africque."[17]

An article reprinted from an unnamed Virginia City newspaper in 1875 reported a fight between two black bootblacks, Mat Stevenson and Charley Morris, which resulted in Stevenson's having his nose bitten off and then sewed back on. Both men were arrested, and Morris was charged with mayhem for biting off Stevenson's nose.[18]

In 1875 a black man named James Bass, the owner of a "job wagon," was shot and killed in Pioche by the constable when Bass became violent as the result of an argument with the constable over the speed with which he was driving his wagon through the streets. The newspaper article attached no racial significance to this incident.[19] Bass was forty in 1870. He was identified by the census enumerator as a teamster with a personal estate of $1,200 and was married, with two children, eleven and seven in 1870, both of whom had been born in Missouri.

"THERE IS NO PROSCRIPTION"

In the 1860s blacks quite actively protested the legal discriminations against them. But by the 1870s, there were reports by blacks and others that indicated that they were no longer being discriminated against. M. Howard reported after the great fire of 1875 in Virginia City that the relief committee, which was providing aid for the victims, did not discriminate against blacks: "All that is necessary for any one to do; who is in want, is to apply to the Relief Committee, prove themselves worthy and their wants are at once attended to, whether in the shape of provisions, bedding, clothing or fuel."[20] When Peter Anderson visited Virginia City in 1876, he went to the state house and was welcomed by "nearly all the State officers" as well as the superintendent of the United States Mint.[21]

One of the most optimistic reports on the treatment of blacks in the
1870s in Nevada was contained in a long letter from "Whiskiyou," a
correspondent of the *San Francisco Elevator*, written in 1874 from Elko.
After a long description of the physical setting of Elko, its climate, which
he found unpleasant, and several other features of the town, Whiskiyou
described its "social relations" as nearly perfect from the standpoint of
blacks, although he did say, "I have reference to social intercourse independent of social equality in the common acceptation of that term."
After reporting that Elko had accepted black students in its public schools
without the necessity of legal action and that a black had recently served
on a criminal jury there, he asserted that there was no necessity for
"any additional Civil Rights Bill" because blacks already had all the rights
they wanted:

> There is no proscription in any hotel or restaurant; there is no dis-
> crimination in any billiard or drinking saloon. In truth, we worship
> at the same shrine, imbibe from the same fount of knowledge, eat
> at the same board, drink at the same bar, and stake on the same card.
> There may be climes more genial; there may be surroundings better
> adapted to subserve the happiness and comfort of man; but for freedom
> from ostracism on account of caste, and for willingness to concede to
> every man every right that belongs to him, Elko will compare favorably
> with any community in the world.[22]

"Whiskiyou" was undoubtedly Charles H. Wilson; he had used this pen
name when he lived in Siskiyou County in California in the 1850s, and
he lived in Elko when this letter was written.[23] Wilson's report of an
absence of discrimination is highly significant for he had been one of the
most active participants in the convention movement in California in the
1850s; it is extremely unlikely that he had forgotten the goals for which
he had worked so bravely twenty years earlier or had lost his capacity to
observe correctly current conditions.

An incident that occurred on a train passing through Nevada in 1876
may indicate the changed climate, although most of the people involved
may not have been Nevadans. On a train traveling from Ogden, Utah,
across Nevada, one of the passengers was "an invalid colored girl, the
daughter of poor parents." When the girl died on the train, the conductor
wired ahead to Battle Mountain to have a coffin prepared for her burial.

Because the unidentified friends with whom she was traveling were poor, the conductor and two passengers collected money from the passengers to pay for the expenses of the funeral; reportedly all contributed. When the train reached Battle Mountain, the girl's body was placed in the coffin "and borne from the cars by pall bearers who had been selected from among the passengers, all of whom marched towards the graveyard, the friends of the deceased leading, and then all of the passengers, two by two." At the grave a hymn was sung and the girl was buried, after which the passengers returned to the train. The correspondent who reported the incident said that "the inhabitants [of Battle Mountain] expressed their surprise at the marked feeling of these strangers for an unknown colored child, and were loud in praise of the noble humanity manifested by these travelers." The *Carson City Appeal*, which reprinted the story from the *Sacramento Record-Union*, commented, "It is humanizing and softening and reassuring to one's faith in the better impulses of humanity, after reading the current stories of atrocities committed upon the timid blacks of the South, to read such an account."[24]

Thus, while the available evidence is spotty and incomplete, it seems that discrimination against blacks declined in the late 1860s and 1870s in tandem with the elimination of most racist laws. Particularly, it seems that there was black economic advance; although only some of the black community engaged in business that could attract white trade, those who did found that whites would frequent them. Barbers were typical of this development. There were far more of them than would have been possible if they had been confined to serving the black community alone, and a number of them obviously were prosperous. For this reason leaders of the black community, such as Thomas Detter, often came from the ranks of the barbers. At the end of the 1870s, it must have seemed to many black Nevadans that, although the average black man or woman was engaged in unskilled labor which did not pay well or have high status, there were paths to a different and better economic life open to them. By the turn of the century, both the absence of discrimination and the economic development had apparently come to an end; black Nevadans were once more in the depressed status they had known in the 1850s and early 1860s in the West, although this time the laws were not overtly racist. If what happened in Nevada also occurred elsewhere in the West and North, the implications for understanding the current status of black Americans are substantial. It is well known that the last part of the nineteenth century brought a checking of previous progress for the bulk

of the black population of the country—those who lived in the South. If
this also happened in the rest of the country, the negative effects on
black people must have been overwhelming. Nathan Glazer and Daniel
Patrick Moynihan have asked (in *Beyond the Melting Pot*), why black
Americans have not followed the paths of some other nonwhite non-Anglo-
Saxon Protestant groups in overcoming initial discrimination, economic
and otherwise.[25] In addition to the obvious fact that slavery has no
counterpart in the history of any other group in America, if it is true
that blacks everywhere in the country found the advances of the 1860s
and 1870s not just halted but reversed, another difference from other
non-WASP groups with substantial import will have been discovered. A
study of one state in which blacks were never very numerous cannot
establish whether this pattern of advance and then decline was general
but at least it is suggestive.

One thing that happened to black Nevadans after about the middle of
the 1880s was that the economic decline that caused a drop in white
population was evidently felt even more severely among the black population. Between 1880 and 1890, chiefly as a result of the failure of
mining in several areas, notably what had been the state's most prosperous
area, the Comstock, the total population of the state declined by 23.9
percent, and there was another decline of 10.6 percent between 1890
and 1900. The black population also dropped during this period, from
396 people in 1880 to 242 in 1890 and 134 in 1900, declines of 38.9
and 44.6 percent. The black populations in Virginia City and Carson
City, which had been large enough to sustain various community organizations, dropped to quite low levels. In 1890 there were 37 blacks in
Storey County and 56 in Ormsby County; in 1900 the totals were:
Storey, 9; Ormsby, 12. As a result, there must have been extensive
changes in the community, and there can have been little continuity
between the black population of nineteenth-century Nevada and that
of the twentieth century. After 1900 the black population increased
again, although it did not exceed 700 until the 1940s, but the new
people must have had few personal ties with their predecessors of the
previous century.

Although a complete picture is impossible at this time, there are a
number of clear indications that the status of blacks in early twentieth-
century Nevada was inferior to their status during the 1870s and 1880s.
There was more hostility toward them from the white community than
had been the case earlier, and their economic status declined.

"THE TOWN WILL SOON BE
CLEARED OF THE BLACK ELEMENT"

Rising white hostility to blacks can be inferred from several sorts of facts. There appears to have been an increase in derogatory terms applied to blacks when newspapers reported news about them. The use of such terms appears to have been routine for several decades in contrast with the situation in the nineteenth century. Then, Republican-oriented news-papers, the most influential segment of the press in early Nevada, had avoided derogatory terms for the most part although Democratic-oriented papers were more inclined to refer to "niggers." After 1900, routine news about blacks often involved the use of terms denoting their inferior status. For example, in 1901 a newspaper reported the birth of a child to a black couple with this headline: "Dar's a New Coon in Town."[26] In 1906, the Eagles of Tonopah staged a "Coon Ball" on Washington's birthday, with participants expected to prepare themselves for the ball with burnt cork. In Tonopah also, a newspaper reporting the arrest of a mulatto on a charge of vagrancy stated that "the coon promptly plead guilty" and was allowed to leave town.[27] A newspaper in Rawhide said of several blacks who had just arrived there: "There are no blacker coons on earth than these."[28]

Blacks were excluded from some Nevada communities at various times during the twentieth century and were forced out of other communities. Evidently this development, for which there is no known nineteenth-century precedent (although there was similar treatment of the Chinese), reflected a rising white Anglo-Saxon Protestant ethnocentrism directed against various non-WASP groups. For example, the Rawhide paper quoted above claimed in 1908 that

Rawhide is preeminently a "white man's camp." There are none of the swarthy representatives here from Southern European countries classified with the general term of "Dagoes." Several adventurous spirits of these races have come to this scene of feverish activity, and have gone— left on the cordial invitation of a committee of determined citizens. . . . On more than one occasion, too, American citizens of color, the southern white man's burden, have been kindly but friendly [sic] informed to move on, and they too, sought a more hospitable environment.[29]

The newspaper reported that three or four blacks had recently come into the camp and had been allowed to stay "up to this writing."

Rawhide was apparently not unique. In Fallon for some years there was a "big sign that was right at the depot. It said, 'No Niggers or Japs allowed.'"[30] The identity of the excluded groups evidently varied from place to place. In early Goldfield, there were a number of black residents but "they never let a Chinese or a Jap get off the train. If they came, they were told to go right back."[31]

Blacks were driven out of some Nevada communities in the early 1900s. In Reno in 1904 Police Chief R. C. Leeper openly carried out a policy of arresting all unemployed blacks and forcing them to leave the city, and the policy was endorsed firmly by both daily newspapers. On November 16, 1904, the *Reno Evening Gazette* reported that the police were conducting a "general round up of the idle and vagrant negroes of the city" and that these persons were "being expelled from the city."

"There are too many worthless negroes in the city," said Chief Leeper this morning. "In the last few weeks there has been a big influx to Reno and few of them have any visible means of support. Their presence is a menace to the order of the town and we mean to get rid of them. All who have employment will not be disturbed, but the others must go."[32]

Blacks who resisted the order to leave were sentenced to serve on a county road gang. A black man named J. Hamphill was ordered to leave and put on a train by Officer Cadle of the Reno police; however, "another Negro was standing near . . . and told Hamphill to get off the train and stay in Reno if he wanted to." When Hamphill did get off the train, he was promptly arrested by Officer Cadle and taken to jail. The next day Hamphill appeared before Justice of the Peace O'Connor who found him guilty of vagrancy and sentenced him to a fine of sixty dollars or thirty days in jail.[33] When Hamphill agreed to pay the fine, O'Connor said, "with a broad grin, 'You will have to work the sixty dollar fine out at the rate of $2 a day in the county chain gang.'" Hamphill protested this treatment but apparently had no choice in the matter. Asking "Do dey hab slaves in dis here State?" he reportedly also said: "I didn't think old Abe Linkum's emancipation proclamation would be disobeyed by white men even in Reno."[34]

At the beginning of the process of deporting unemployed blacks one of the daily newspapers commented editorially:

Chief Leeper's determination to rid Reno of at least a portion of the worthless, dissolute and criminal element that has been harboring itself here will meet with the approval of every good citizen in the city. The presence of the class against whom the movement is directed is a constant menace to the safety and fair name of any city, and proper means should be taken to see that the order to "move on" be obeyed.[35]

The other daily newspaper also approved:

Chief Leeper has decided to drive every vagrant negro from the city and those who do not obey the comands [sic] of his officers are immediately arrested and placed in the cells. This may be a little different from the regular proceedings of the law, but it is working good in Reno and the town will soon be cleared of the black element.[36]

The extreme nature of the racial antagonism displayed in Reno at this time is well illustrated by the fact that a black man was forced to leave Reno for knocking at the door of a "leading business man of the city" around midnight. When the businessman opened his door he found a "big black negro" there who was surprised to see him and immediately became frightened. "'Don't shoot, Mister, I never done anything; I only made a mistake in the house, that's all,' said the burly brute." The businessman kicked the man, chased him off his porch, and then called the police. The black man was "caught by the police but after a fair warning never to be caught in the city again he was allowed to go. He was badly frightened and it is thought that he will heed the notice he has received and will never again enter the city."[37]

It is not known how widespread the policy of forcing blacks out of Nevada cities was, but in 1914 a newspaper in eastern Nevada reported that "all along the Southern Pacific railroad the Nevada towns are making war upon unemployed negroes. The attacks are directed principally against unemployed blacks in the restricted districts."[38]

Some kind of conflict between black soldiers and a white bartender in Winnemucca in 1899 led to the killing of the bartender by one or more of the soldiers. Although the incident seems to have caused little stir at the time, perhaps partly because the soldiers were merely passing through and partly because of the strong patriotism aroused by the Spanish-American War, it suggests a level of black-white hostility not apparently found earlier in the state. The incident began when a special train bearing two companies of the Twenty-first Infantry and one company of the Twenty-fourth Infantry stopped in Winnemucca. These were all-black infantry regiments, and they were passing through Winnemucca on their way to Manila. Some of the soldiers from the train "raided a nearby saloon, demolishing bottles and furniture and after an altercation with Charles Deiss, the protesting bartender, shot him down in cold blood."[39] After the murder, the sheriff and district attorney delayed the train for several hours while an attempt was made to find the person or persons who had committed the murder. Although all the soldiers were called off the train several times for inspections, the citizens of Winnemucca could not identify any individuals who had been involved in the incident and the train finally left. A newspaper reported, "All Winnemucca is in a fever of rage at the dastardly crime, and if the murderer could have been identified, without doubt he would have been hung to the nearest telegraph pole."[40] Nevertheless, apparently nothing further happened after the departure of the train. Each Reno newspaper ran only one story on the incident, and neither commented editorially.

In the 1920s, there were Ku Klux Klan groups in several Nevada towns, and two organizations were chartered in the state. In December 1922 the newspapers began to note rumors of Klan organization in Elko.[41] In November 1924 the Klan held a march in "full regalia" through the streets of Elko and presented an envelope "said to contain a considerable sum of money for the church" to the minister of the Presbyterian church.[42] In January 1925 the Klan held a public meeting in Elko.[43] In Winnemucca at about the same time, a fiery cross was burnt on Winnemucca Mountain.[44] In 1925 two rival Klan groups incorporated in the state and engaged in litigation over the use of the name "Ku Klux Klan."[45]

The discrimination against not just nonwhites but non-Anglo-Saxon Protestant whites that developed in twentieth-century Nevada was more extreme than anything recorded for the nineteenth century. A particularly interesting example of this is the residential and occupational segregation rigidly established by company policy in the copper-mining towns of Ruth, McGill, and Kimberly in the Robinson district of eastern Nevada after about 1905. Employees of English, Irish, German, or Scandinavian ancestry were considered "whites" and were assigned the better jobs and better housing in these communities; all others were considered "foreigners" and relegated to an inferior status. Although the "foreigners" included some Japanese, the Austrians, Greeks, Italians, Serbians, and other white but non-WASP groups were lumped together as nonwhite.[46] One of the residents of early McGill remembered that while there were "very few colored people there," each of the ethnic groups represented "had a place where they lived, like the Austrians and Italians."[47] Another resident of McGill also reported that there were "not many colored" people but described the discrimination in the assignment of housing and jobs between "whites" and "foreigners" at some length. This informant recalled that "white" boys would throw rocks at Austrian men passing through the "white" residential area on their way home from work.[48]

The 1915-1916 *Biennial Report* of the superintendent of the state orphans' home recommended that the legislature find a way to exclude Chinese, black, and Indian children from the home. Probably the superintendent practiced what he preached; five girls named Straughter were identified as "Negro children committed to the Home, but cared for by private family at the expense of the Home and Elko County."[49]

In Reno in the 1930s and 1940s Mrs. Alice Smith, a black founder of the Reno-Sparks branch of the NAACP, remembered that "in the windows of restaurants you would see a little sign that stated 'No Negroes allowed,' 'No Colored Trade Solicited' and the most attractive and impressive and aggravating one also, to me was a sign that was on east Fourth Street on a restaurant and it read like this: 'No Indians, dogs or Negroes allowed.'"[50] When the civil rights movement began in Nevada in the late 1950s, the state had been dubbed the "Mississippi of the West" and it was clear that there was widespread discrimination against blacks in public accommodations, employment, and housing.[51]

ECONOMIC DECLINE—THE END OF THE BLACK MIDDLE CLASS

It seems also that blacks in twentieth-century Nevada occupied an inferior economic status to that achieved in the 1870s and 1880s. The main reason for this was the decline of the group referred to earlier as the black middle class of the nineteenth century; this decline, in turn, must have been due chiefly to the loss of white customers for black professionals and businessmen.

While census data are not very adequate for Nevada blacks in 1890, they show that there were no professionals in the state and that fifty-six percent of black persons ten years of age or older engaged in gainful occupations were in domestic and personal service.

There is a substantial literature that documents the decline in economic standing of blacks in the South in the 1890s; partly because the overwhelming majority of blacks in the country were still in the South

at that time, little attention has been paid to what must have been a
similar process in the North (including the West). There is also ample
documentation of the exclusion of blacks from the craft unions at the
end of the nineteenth century, but again the implications for northern
blacks have been given less attention than the implications for southern
blacks. Northern politicians had little difficulty, for the most part, in
accepting the reimposition of white rule in the South in the 1890s; this
ready acceptance of an obvious retreat from the antiracist actions of
the 1860s and 1870s must have been associated with a rise in white
racism in the North as well.

Nevada's chief national representatives clearly accepted southern
white "redemption" during the 1870s. In his *Reminiscences*, published
in 1908, Senator William M. Stewart, who had served for more than
twenty-seven years as one of Nevada's senators, endorsed the white
supremacist view of Reconstruction and its effects. As he expressed it:
"The Northern men, generally of a speculative quality, gathered in the
several Southern States, and by cooperation with an ignorant colored
population, secured control of the Legislatures in some of the Southern
States, and a powerful influence in all of them. Corruption and mis-
government were the inevitable consequence."[52]

In 1877 after President Hayes had withdrawn federal troops from the
South and thus formally abandoned any attempt to enforce the Civil
War amendments and civil rights acts, Nevada's Congressman Thomas
Wren endorsed Hayes's "southern policy," asserting that it could not be
"undone," that most people approved it, and that it would "perfect
a more harmonious feeling between the two sections of our country."[53]

Francis G. Newlands, congressman from Nevada from 1893 through
1902 and senator from 1903 until his death in 1917, supported Chinese
and Japanese exclusion on the general ground that the United States ought
to have "a policy . . . which would preserve this country for the white
race" and that "history teaches us that it is impossible to make a homo-
geneous people by the juxtaposition of races differing in color upon
the same soil."[54]

Although the process cannot yet be described fully, there must have
been rising white prejudice against black professionals and businessmen,
beginning in the 1890s. Dr. Stephenson, as we have seen, had white
patients in Virginia City in the 1860s and 1870s. Evidently the only
black doctor in the state from the 1870s to the 1950s had more difficulty
in getting white patients. Dr. Samuel M. Barnes, who received his M.D.
degree from Howard University in 1891, attempted to practice in Elko

County. As the author of a study of physicians in northeastern Nevada puts it, "Doctor Barnes, a negro, sought opportunity and felt Nevada to be an unprejudiced state, but found little business at his office and left Elko after a brief period." Apparently he was practicing in Jarbidge in 1927.[55] When the next black physician, Dr. Charles I. West, came into the state in the mid-1950s, he established his practice in the Westside of Las Vegas, which had become a sizable black ghetto by that time. Apparently before the 1970s there had never been a black physician (or other professional) in Washoe County, which had had for some time a much larger black population than the entire black population of the state at any time during the nineteenth century.

The decline among black businessmen also seems evident; there are probably fewer black businessmen in present-day Washoe County than there were in Virginia City in the 1870s, although the black population of the county is several times as large as the corresponding population of Virginia City at that time. It seems clear that most black businessmen serve mainly the black community in present-day Nevada, but this was not the case during the earlier period. The decline of black barbers is particularly striking; obviously there are far fewer black barbers in Nevada today because such barbers are chiefly serving black customers. A particularly poignant example of the change is the story of a long-time black resident of Orsmby County's facility for indigents, popularly known as the poor farm. W. Wallace White, who lived in Carson City for many years as an employee of the state department of health, reported that he had heard the story of "old Mose," an "old Negro gentleman who had spent almost all of his adult life as a charge of Ormsby County" at the poor farm. White says of this man:

> He told me that he came to Carson City as a young man, he was a barber, but no one in Carson would give him a meal, nor a place to sleep, nor a place to eat, nor could he get a job. I believe he told me he worked for a little while shining shoes and lived in the back room of a barber shop. He eventually ended up taking care of the garden and whatever other chores had to be done at the poor farm.

White remarks that "as far as I know, he was rather an able person, he had some skills. And in a time in the future, this man could just as well have at least worked enough to provide his own creature comforts and exist. But in the past this was not possible in Nevada."[56]

There was a time in the past when black people like Mose had been able to earn their living and even hope for improved conditions. The losses forced upon the black community of Nevada at the close of the nineteenth century and the beginning of the twentieth must surely rank among the most important events in the history of black-white relations in the state.

NOTES

1. *Territorial Enterprise,* August 7, 1866.
2. Ibid., March 28, 1868.
3. *Pacific Appeal,* March 19, 1864.
4. *Report of the Commissioners for the Care of the Indigent Insane for 1881-1882,* p. 8.
5. *Pacific Appeal,* October 31, 1874.
6. Wells Drury, *An Editor on the Comstock Lode* (New York: Farrar and Rinehart, 1936), p. 37. Jerome J. Quinlan, "As I Remember Them," in photograph collection of the California Historical Society, San Francisco. John Taylor Waldorf, *A Kid on the Comstock* (Berkeley, California: Friends of the Bancroft Library, 1968), pp. 42, 84-85.
7. *Virginia Evening Bulletin,* January 23, 1864.
8. *Territorial Enterprise,* April 8, 1870.
9. Ibid., May 14, 1868.
10. *Reports* of the warden published during the nineteenth century listed each prisoner by name, with various supplementary information, until the 1890s.
11. *San Francisco Alta,* September 19, 22, 1871.
12. *Carson City Appeal,* November 13, 1875.
13. State of Nevada v. Sam. Mills, 12 Nevada 403 (1877).
14. *Daily Elko Independent,* December 21, 1877.
15. *Virginia Evening Bulletin,* December 5, 1863.
16. Ibid., August 31, 1863. The latter incident was also noted, without comment, by the *Sacramento Daily Union,* September 3, 1863.
17. *Virginia Evening Bulletin,* July 31, 1863.
18. *Pacific Appeal,* October 16, 1875.
19. *Pioche Record,* June 27, 1875, reprinted in *Pacific Appeal,* July 10, 1875.
20. *Pacific Appeal,* November 20, 1875.
21. Ibid., June 10, 1876.
22. *Elevator,* February 25, 1874.
23. *Mirror of the Times,* August 22, December 12, 1857.
24. *Carson City Appeal,* December 2, 1876.

25. Nathan Glazer and Daniel Patrick Moynihan, *Beyond the Melting Pot* (Cambridge: The MIT Press, 1963).

26. *Walker Lake Bulletin,* September 4, 1901.

27. *Tonopah Bonanza,* February 17, October 20, 1906.

28. *Rawhide Press-Times,* March 12, 1908.

29. Ibid.

30. Lester J. Hilp, "Reminiscences of a White Pine County Native, Reno Pharmacy Owner, and Civic Leader" (Reno, Nevada: Oral History Project, University of Nevada, 1968), p. 11.

31. Minnie P. Blair, "Days Remembered of Folsom and Placerville, California, Banking and Farming in Goldfield, Tonopah, and Fallon, Nevada" (Reno, Nevada: Oral History Project, University of Nevada, 1968), p. 45.

32. *Reno Evening Gazette,* November 16, 1904.

33. *Nevada State Journal,* November 22, 1904.

34. Ibid., November 23, 1904.

35. *Reno Evening Gazette,* November 17, 1904.

36. *Nevada State Journal,* November 22, 1904. In the middle of the deportation process, a black man wanted by the police in connection with a crime engaged in a shootout with a Reno police officer at night near the William Tell House on Sierra Street. Although several shots were fired by both men, fortunately no one was hurt, and the man surrendered to the police the next day. Ibid., November 16, 17, 1904.

37. Ibid., November 18, 1904.

38. *Pioche Record,* February 21, 1914.

39. *Nevada State Journal,* July 1, 1899.

40. Ibid., See also *Reno Evening Gazette,* June 30, 1899. Arlen L. Fowler, *The Black Infantry in the West, 1869-1891* (Westport, Connecticut: Greenwood Publishing Corporation, 1971), gives a history of these two regiments.

41. *Sparks Tribune,* December 4, 1922, reprinting an article from *Elko Independent.*

42. *Silver State,* November 11, 1924.

43. *Battle Mountain Scout,* January 3, 1925.

44. *Silver State,* October 21, 1924.

45. See *Reno Evening Gazette,* January 12, 23, 1925.

46. See Russell R. Elliott, *Nevada's Twentieth-Century Mining Boom* (Reno, Nevada: University of Nevada Press, 1966), pp. 228-231.

47. Hilp, "Reminiscences," pp. 10-11.

48. W. Wallace White, "Caring for the Environment: My Work with Public Health and Reclamation in Nevada" (Reno, Nevada: Oral History Project, University of Nevada, 1970), pp. 27-29.

49. *Biennial Report of the Orphans' Home Directors and Report of the Superintendent, 1915-1916,* pp. 7, 16, 18.

50. *Voices of Black Nevada* (Reno, Nevada: Bureau of Governmental Research, University of Nevada, 1971), p. 88.

51. See Joseph N. Crowley, "Race and Residence: The Politics of Open Housing in Nevada," pp. 55-73 in Eleanore Bushnell, ed., *Sagebrush and Neon* (Reno, Nevada: Bureau of Governmental Research, University of Nevada, 1973), for a discussion of one aspect of the current scene and *Voices of Black Nevada* for other aspects.

52. George Rothwell Brown, ed., *Reminiscences of Senator William M. Stewart of Nevada* (New York: Neale Publishing Co., 1908), p. 230.

53. *Territorial Enterprise,* September 19, 1877.

54. Arthur B. Darling, ed., *The Public Papers of Francis G. Newlands* (Washington, D.C.: W. F. Roberts Co., 1937), I: 216-217, 286-300. See also William D. Rowley, "Francis G. Newlands: A Westerner's Search for a Progressive and White America," *Nevada Historical Society Quarterly* 17 (Summer 1974): 69-79.

55. See Silas E. Ross, *A Directory of Nevada Medical Practitioners Past and Present* (n.p., 1957), p. 6, letter from Marion Mann, dean, Howard University College of Medicine, June 17, 1971, and Edna B. Patterson, *Sagebrush Doctors* (Springville, Utah: Art City Publishing Co., 1972), p. 119.

56. White, "Caring for the Environment," p. 104.

Bibliography

The works used in this study are cited in typical fashion following this note; however, some comments about some of the more important sources may be helpful to readers, especially to persons wishing to do similar research.

For 1860, 1870, and 1880 I used data on microfilm of the original enumerators' returns for the census of population for Nevada; copies are available in Getchell Library, University of Nevada, Reno. Returns for 1890 have been destroyed by fire, except for a census of military veterans, which contained no individuals in Nevada identified as black. By law, individual returns after 1890 could not be examined at the time research was being done for this book; a subsequent change in the law now allows access to the returns of the 1900 census.

While the census returns provided much information not available elsewhere, there are limitations to such data. First, they are handwritten; some enumerators had very poor handwriting, and some could not spell well. Second, the enumerators obviously made some errors of judgment. One of the most interesting from the standpoint of this study was that an enumerator in 1880 erroneously identified ninety

Indians at Duckwater as black, and this error was not caught by the tabulators. A careful examination makes it obvious that an error has been made. Most of the ninety "blacks" at Duckwater had only first names, and where they had two names these were usually of the sort whites often gave to Indians at the time, e.g., Duckwater Sallie. Further these ninety "blacks" were all reported as having been born in Nevada, with both parents also born in Nevada, and none of them was able to read or write. The occupations given for them include farm laborer, farm hand, servant, or housework, and one is identified as a medicine man. A third category consisted of arithmetic errors in tabulating returns. Fourth, there was both over- and under-counting because all the enumerating was not done on the same day or because there were persons the enumerators could not locate. Fifth, the categories specified for recording racial groups were always inadequate in several respects, and they varied from one year to another. The sum total of these sources of error is not inconsiderable, but the census returns nevertheless provide a valuable source of information about individuals and also group characteristics which is not available anywhere else.

Another major source was the files of black newspapers published in San Francisco during the nineteenth century. There are microfilm copies of most of the surviving issues of the most important of these, the *Pacific Appeal* and the *Elevator*, at Bancroft Library, University of California, Berkeley. Bancroft also has a few copies of the *Vindicator*, the *Sentinel*, and the *Western Outlook*. Photographs of the few remaining copies of the *Mirror of the Times* were examined at the Library of the California Historical Society, San Francisco. I was not able to check the surviving number of the *Lunar Visitor*. A brief description of these newspapers can be found in Philip M. Montesano, "Some Aspects of the Free Negro Question in San Francisco, 1849-1870," MA thesis, University of San Francisco, 1967, and Francis N. Lortie, Jr., *San Francisco's Black Community, 1870-1890: Dilemmas in the Struggle for Equality* (San Francisco: R and E Research Associates, 1973).

The microfilm collections of Nevada newspapers at the Special Collections room of Getchell Library, University of Nevada, Reno, were used extensively. Unfortunately, there were no indexes for these newspapers and the volume was too great to examine every issue (which is possible with the black newspapers used for this study). Undoubtedly many items relevant to black history in the state were overlooked in spite of the assistance given me by other students who would tell me about items they found while using the newspapers for other purposes.

The reports of various Nevada state agencies issued during the nineteenth century were valuable. I have made no attempt to list all these reports in the bibliography, because the nature and location of such reports is so irregular; some no longer survive except in newspaper files, some were never published, and there is much variation in the identification of published items. Many of the reports of state agencies can be found in the appendices to the legislative journals. For a list of the contents of these appendices for the nineteenth century plus an index, see Robert D. Armstrong, "Appendix to Journals of Senate and Assembly: Contents and Index," *Nevada Libraries* 7 (1970): 107-112, 135-140; 8 (1971): 87-91, 117-120.

My biggest disappointment in working on this book was that I discovered no diaries, journals, or other personal documents by black residents of nineteenth-century Nevada. Perhaps such materials exist and will be discovered some day.

BOOKS

Abajian, James. *Blacks and their Contribution to the American West.* Boston: G. K. Hall, 1974.

Address of the State Executive Committee, to the Colored People of the State of California. Sacramento: Printed for the Committee, 1859.

Angel, Myron, ed. *History of Nevada, 1881.* Berkeley, California: Howell-North, 1958.

Bancroft, Hubert Howe. *History of California.* Vol. 5, *1846-1848.* San Francisco: The History Company, 1886.

————. *History of Nevada, Colorado, and Wyoming, 1540-1888.* Vol. 25, *The Works of Hubert Howe Bancroft.* San Francisco: The History Company, 1890.

Beasley, Delilah L. *The Negro Trail Blazers of California.* Los Angeles: Times-Mirror Printing and Binding House, 1919.

Bell, Howard Holman. *A Survey of the Negro Convention Movement, 1830-1861.* New York: Arno Press, 1969.

Bethel, John D., comp. *A General Business and Mining Directory of Storey, Lyon, Ormsby, and Washoe Counties, Nevada.* Virginia City: John D. Bethel and Co., 1875.

Bonner, T. D., ed. *The Life and Adventures of James P. Beckwourth.* New York: Alfred A. Knopf, 1931.

Bradley, David Henry, Sr. *A History of the A.M.E. Zion Church, Parts I and II.* Nashville, Tennessee: Parthenon Press, 1956, 1970.

Brown, George Rothwell, ed. *Reminiscences of Senator William M. Stewart.* New York: Neale Publishing Co., 1908.

Browne, J. Ross. *A Peep at Washoe and Washoe Revisited.* Balboa Island, California: Paisano Press, 1959.

Carr, Robert K. *Federal Protection of Civil Rights.* Ithaca, New York: Cornell University Press, 1947.

The Celebration of the Eighty-eighth Anniversary of the Declaration of Independence, July 4th, 1865, at Virginia and Gold Hill, Nevada. San Francisco: Commercial Steam Presses, 1865.

Clark, Walter Van Tilburg, ed. *The Journals of Alfred Doten, 1849-1903.* Reno: University of Nevada Press, 1973. 3 vols.

Collins, Charles, comp., *Mercantile Guide and Directory for Virginia City, Gold Hill, Silver City and American City.* San Francisco: Agnew and Deffebach, 1865.

Dale, Harrison C. *The Ashley-Smith Explorations and the Discovery of a Central Route to the Pacific, 1822-1829.* Glendale, California: The Arthur H. Clarke Co., 1941.

Darling, Arthur B., ed. *The Public Papers of Francis G. Newlands.* Washington, D.C.: W. F. Roberts Co., 1937.

DeMond, Albert Lawrence. *Certain Aspects of the Economic Development of the American Negro, 1865-1900.* Washington, D.C.: The Catholic University of America Press, 1945.

De Quille, Dan.*The Big Bonanza.* New York: Alfred A. Knopf, 1947.

Detter, Thomas. *Nellie Brown.* San Francisco: Cuddy and Hughes, 1871.

Dillard, J. L. *Black English.* New York: Random House, 1972.

Drotning, Phillip T. *A Guide to Negro History in America.* Garden City: Doubleday, 1968.

Du Bois, W. E. B., ed. *The Negro in Business.* Atlanta, Georgia: Atlanta University Press, 1899.

————— · *The Negro Artisan.* Atlanta, Georgia: Atlanta University Press, 1902.

Durham, Philip, and Jones, Everett L. *The Negro Cowboys.* New York: Dodd, Mead and Co., 1965.

Elliott, Russell R. *History of Nevada.* Lincoln, Nebraska: University of Nebraska Press, 1973.

————— . *Nevada's Twentieth-Century Mining Boom.* Reno, Nevada: University of Nevada Press, 1966.

————, and Poulton, Helen J. *Writings on Nevada*. Reno: University of Nevada Press, 1963.

Evans, Arthur, ed. *Centennial Year Book of the Most Worshipful Prince Hall Grand Lodge*. Oakland, California, 1955.

Fatout, Paul. *Mark Twain in Virginia City*. Bloomington, Indiana: Indiana University Press, 1964.

Folkes, John Gregg. *Nevada's Newspapers: A Bibliography*. Reno: University of Nevada Press, 1964.

Fox, Theron, ed. *Mother Lode Race Incident*. San Jose, California: Harlan-Young Press, 1966.

Fredrickson, George M. *The Black Image in the White Mind*. New York: Harper and Row, 1971.

Frémont, John Charles. *Memoirs of My Life*. Chicago and New York: Belford, Clarke and Co., 1887.

————. *Report of the Exploring Expedition to the Rocky Mountains*. Ann Arbor: University Microfilms, 1966.

Gillette, William. *The Right to Vote: Politics and the Passage of the Fifteenth Amendment*. Baltimore, Maryland: Johns Hopkins Press, 1965.

Gillis, William R., comp. *The Nevada Directory, for 1868-9*. San Francisco: M. D. Carr and Co., 1868.

Glasscock, C. B. *The Big Bonanza*. Portland, Oregon: Binfords and Mort, 1931.

Glazer, Nathan, and Moynihan, Daniel Patrick. *Beyond the Melting Pot: The Negroes, Puerto Ricans, Jews, Italians, and Irish of New York City*. Cambridge, Massachusetts: The MIT Press, 1963.

Goode, Kenneth G. *California's Black Pioneers: a Brief Historical Survey*. Santa Barbara: McNally and Loftin, 1974.

Greene, Lorenzo J., and Woodson, Carter G. *The Negro Wage Earner*. Washington, D.C.: Association for the Study of Negro Life and History, 1930.

Grimshaw, William H., *Official History of Freemasonry Among the Colored People in North America*, 1903. Reprint. New York: Negro Universities Press, 1969.

Grover, David H. *Diamondfield Jack*. Reno, Nevada: University of Nevada Press, 1968.

Harmon, J. G., Jr.; Lindsay, Arnett G.; and Woodson, Carter G. *The Negro as a Business Man*. College Park, Maryland: McGrath Publishing Co., 1929.

Harris, Abram L. *The Negro as Capitalist.* College Park, Maryland: McGrath
  Publishing Co., 1936.
Heizer, Robert F., and Almquist, Alan F. *The Other Californians.* Berkeley:
  University of California Press, 1971.
Hopkins, Sarah Winnemucca. *Life Among the Piutes.* Bishop, California:
  Chalfant Press, Inc., 1969.
Huffaker, F. M., and Flanningham, J. P., comps. *Ordinances of the City
  of Virginia and Town of Gold Hill, Storey County, Nevada.* Virginia,
  Nevada: Wm. Sutherland, Printer, 1888.
Jackson, W. Turrentine. *Treasure Hill.* Tucson: University of Arizona
  Press, 1963.
Jordan, Winthrop. *White over Black.* Baltimore, Maryland: Penguin
  Books, 1969.
*Journal of Proceedings of the Third Annual Convention of the Ministers
  and Lay Delegates of the African Methodist Episcopal Church.* San
  Francisco: B. F. Sterett, Printer, 1863.
Katz, William L. *The Black West.* Garden City, New York: Doubleday and
  Co., 1971.
Koontz, John, and Palmer, Arthur J. *Political History of Nevada.* 6th
  ed. Carson City: State Printing Office, 1973.
Lapp, Rudolph M. *Archy Lee.* San Francisco: Book Club of California, 1969.
Life and Adventures of James Williams, A Fugitive Slave. 3d ed. San
  Francisco: Women's Union Print, 1874.
Lingenfelter, Richard E. *The Newspapers of Nevada, 1858-1958.* San
  Francisco: John Howell Books, 1964.
Litwack, Leon L. *North of Slavery.* Chicago: University of Chicago
  Press, 1961.
Lonn, Ella. *Reconstruction in Louisiana after 1868.* New York: G. P.
  Putnam's Sons, 1918.
Lord, Eliot. *Comstock Mining and Miners.* Berkeley, California: Howell-
  North, 1959.
Lortie, Francis N., Jr. *San Francisco's Black Community, 1870-1890:
  Dilemmas in the Struggle for Equality.* San Francisco: R and E
  Research Associates, 1973.
Mack, Effie Mona. *Mark Twain in Nevada.* New York: Charles Scribner's
  Sons, 1947.
Marsh, Andrew J. *Letters from Nevada Territory, 1861-1862.* Carson
  City, Nevada: Legislative Counsel Bureau, 1972.
———. *Nevada Constitutional Debates and Proceedings.* San Francisco:
  Frank Eastman, 1866.

————. *Reports of the 1863 Constitutional Convention.* Carson City, Nevada: Legislative Counsel Bureau, 1972.

Miller, Loren. *The Petitioners.* New York: Random House, 1960.

Morgan, Dale L. *Jedediah Smith and the Opening of the West.* Lincoln, Nebraska: University of Nebraska Press, 1953.

Mumey, Nolie. *James Pierson Beckwourth, 1856-1866.* Denver, Colorado: Old West Publishing Co., 1957.

Neihardt, John G. *The Splendid Wayfaring.* New York: The Macmillan Company, 1920.

Nevins, Allan. *Frémont, Pathmarker of the West.* New York: Frederick Ungar, 1961.

Parker, Elizabeth L., and Abajian, James. *A Walking Tour of the Black Presence in San Francisco During the Nineteenth Century.* San Francisco: San Francisco African American Historical and Cultural Society, 1974.

Patterson, Edna B. *Sagebrush Doctors.* Springville, Utah: Art City Publishing Co., 1972.

Patterson, Edna B.; Ulph, Louise A.; and Goodwin, Victor. *Nevada's Northeast Frontier.* Sparks, Nevada: Western Printing and Publishing Co., 1969.

Porter, Kenneth W. *The Negro on the American Frontier.* New York: Arno Press and the New York Times, 1971.

Price, Daniel O. *Changing Characteristics of the Negro Population.* Washington, D.C.: U. S. Government Printing Office, 1969.

Preuss, Arthur, comp. *A Dictionary of Secret and Other Societies.* St. Louis, Missouri: B. Herder Book Co., 1924.

Proceedings of the First State Convention of the Colored Citizens of the State of California, 1855, 1856, 1865. San Francisco: R and E Associates, 1969.

Reuter, Edward Byron. *The Mulatto in the United States,* 1918. Reprint. New York: Negro Universities Press, 1969.

Revised Ordinances of the Town of Gold Hill. Gold Hill: Alf Doten, Town Printer, 1877.

Ross, John Stewart. *Compilation of Approved Decisions and Regulations of Free and Accepted Masons of California.* San Francisco: Published by Order of Grand Lodge, 1932.

Sherman, Joan R. *Invisible Poets: Afro-Americans of the Nineteenth Century.* Urbana: University of Illinois Press, 1974.

Smith, Henry Nash, ed. *Mark Twain of the Enterprise.* Berkeley: University of California Press, 1957.

Spero, Sterling D., and Harris, Abram L. *The Black Worker*. Port Washington, New York: Kennipat Press, 1931.

Stampp, Kenneth M. *The Peculiar Institution*. New York: Random House,
1956.

Stevens, Albert C., comp. *The Cyclopedia of Fraternities*. New York:
E. B. Treat and Co., 1907.

Stonehouse, Merlin. *John Wesley North and the Reform Frontier*.
Minneapolis: University of Minnesota Press, 1965.

Sullivan, Maurice S. *Jedediah Smith, Trader and Trail Breaker*. New York:
Press of the Pioneers, 1936.

———. *The Travels of Jedediah Smith*. Santa Ana, California: The Fine
Arts Press, 1934.

Thornbrough, Emma Lou. *The Negro in Indiana: a Study of a Minority*.
Indiana Historical Bureau, 1957.

Thurman, A. Odell. *The Negro in California before 1890*. San Francisco:
R and E Research Associates, 1973.

Thurman, Sue Bailey. *Pioneers of Negro Origin in California*. San Francisco:
Acme Publishing Co., 1952.

Torrence, C. W. *History of Masonry in Nevada*. Reno: A. Carlisle and
Co., 1944.

U. S. Congress. House. *Memorial of Leonard Dugged, George A. Bailey
et al*. Misc. Doc. 31. 37th Cong., 2d sess., 1862.

Voices of Black Nevada. Reno, Nevada: Bureau of Governmental Research,
University of Nevada, 1971.

Wesley, Charles H. *Negro Labor in the United States, 1850-1925*. New
York: Russell and Russell, 1927.

Whalen, William J. *Handbook of Secret Organizations*. Milwaukee: Bruce
Publishing Co., 1966.

Whitman, Maxwell. *A Century of Fiction by American Negroes, 1853-1952*.
Philadelphia: Maurice Jacobs, 1955.

Williams, George W. *History of the Negro Race in America from 1619 to
1880*. New York: G. P. Putnam's Sons, 1883.

Wilson, Elinor. *Jim Beckwourth*. Norman, Oklahoma: University of
Oklahoma Press, 1972.

Woodson, Carter G. *Free Negro Heads of Families in the United States
in 1830*. Washington, D.C.: Association for the Study of Negro Life
and History, 1925.

———. *The History of the Negro Church*. 2d ed. Washington, D.C.:
Associated Publishers, 1921.

Wren, Thomas. *A History of the State of Nevada*. New York: Lewis
Publishing Co., 1904

ARTICLES

Bell, Howard. "Negroes in California, 1849-1859." *Phylon* 28 (Summer 1967): 151-160.

Beller, Jack. "Negro Slaves in Utah." *Utah Historical Quarterly* 2 (October 1929): 122-126.

Crowley, Joseph N. "Race and Residence: The Politics of Open Housing in Nevada." In Eleanore Bushnell, ed. *Sagebrush and Neon*. Reno, Nevada: Bureau of Governmental Research, University of Nevada, 1973.

de Graaf, Lawrence B. "Recognition, Racism, and Reflections on the Writing of Western Black History." *Pacific Historical Review* 44 (February 1975): 22-51.

Elliott, Russell R. "The Early History of White Pine County, Nevada, 1865-1887." *Pacific Northwest Quarterly* (April 1939): 145-168.

Fisher, James A. "The Political Development of the Black Community in California, 1850-1950." *California Historical Quarterly* 50 (September 1971): 256-266.

Hanchett, William. "Yankee Law and the Negro in Nevada, 1861-1869." *Western Humanities Review* 10 (Summer 1956): 241-249.

Kersten, Earl W., Jr. "The Early Settlement of Aurora, Nevada, and Nearby Mining Camps." *Annals of the Association of American Geographers* 54 (December 1964): 490-507.

Lapp, Rudolph M. "Jeremiah Sanderson: Early California Negro." *Journal of Negro History* 53 (October 1968): 321-332.

————. "The Negro in Gold Rush California." *The Journal of Negro History* 49 (April 1964): 81-98.

Lewis, Georgia. "The Black Ranchers of Lincoln County." *The Nevadan* (July 18, 1971): 28-29.

Lythgoe, Dennis L. "Negro Slavery in Utah." *Utah Historical Quarterly* 39 (Winter 1971): 40-54.

Pettit, Arthur G. "Mark Twain's Attitude Toward the Negro in the West, 1861-1867." *Western Historical Quarterly* 1 (January 1970): 51-62.

Porter, Kenneth W. "Negro Labor in the Western Cattle Industry, 1866-1900." In Milton Cantor, ed. *Black Labor in America*. Westport, Connecticut: Negro Universities Press, 1969.

Rowley, William D. "Francis G. Newlands: A Westerner's Search for a Progressive and White America." *Nevada Historical Society Quarterly* 17 (Summer 1974): 69-79.

Savage, W. Sherman. "The Negro on the Mining Frontier." *The Journal of Negro History* 30 (January 1945): 30-46.

Sherman, Joan R. "James Monroe Whitfield, Poet and Emigrationist: A Voice of Protest and Despair." *The Journal of Negro History* 57 (April 1972):126-143.

UNPUBLISHED MATERIALS

Blair, Minnie P. "Days Remembered of Folsom and Placerville, California, Banking and Farming in Goldfield, Tonopah, and Fallon, Nevada." Reno, Nevada: Oral History Project, University of Nevada, 1968.

Boone, Frank E. "Negro Freemasonry in California," ms., no date. University of Nevada, Reno Library.

Brown, Harold N. "A History of the Public Elementary School System of Nevada, 1861-1934." Ph.D. dissertation, University of California, Berkeley, 1935.

Cahlan, John F. "Reminiscences of a Reno and Las Vegas, Nevada Newspaperman, University Regent, and Public-spirited Citizen." Reno, Nevada: Oral History Project, University of Nevada, 1970.

Hilp, Lester J. "Reminiscences of a White Pine County Native, Reno Pharmacy Owner, and Civic Leader." Reno, Nevada: Oral History Project, University of Nevada, 1968.

Montesano, Phil M. "The Black Churches of San Francisco in the Early 1860's: Their Political Activities," ms., 1971, in Library of the California Historical Society, San Francisco.

Montesano, Philip M. "Some Aspects of the Free Negro Question in San Francisco, 1849-1870." Masters thesis, University of San Francisco, 1967.

Ross, Silas E. "A Directory of Nevada Medical Practitioners, Past and Present." Nevada State Medical Association, 1957.

White, W. Wallace. "Caring for the Environment: My Work with Public Health and Reclamation in Nevada. Reno, Nevada: Oral History Project, University of Nevada, 1970.

Index

ABOUT THE AUTHOR

Elmer R. Rusco is associate professor of political science and director of the Bureau of Governmental Research at the University of Nevada, Reno. His special interests are American political theory and ethnic relations. Dr. Rusco has published numerous studies of poverty, race relations, and voting behavior.